MAGNUM!
THE WILD WEASELS
IN
DESERT STORM

MAGNUM!
THE WILD WEASELS
IN
DESERT STORM

Braxton 'Brick' Eisel
and
Jim 'Boomer' Schreiner

Pen & Sword
AVIATION

First published in Great Britain in 2009 by
Pen & Sword Aviation
an imprint of
Pen & Sword Books Ltd
47 Church Street
Barnsley
South Yorkshire
S70 2AS

ISBN 978 1 84415 907 9

Typeset in Palatino by
Phoenix Typesetting, Auldgirth, Dumfriesshire

Printed and bound in Thailand by
Kyodo Nation Printing Services Co., Ltd

Pen & Sword Books Ltd incorporates the imprints of Pen & Sword Aviation, Pen &
Sword Maritime, Pen & Sword Military, Wharncliffe Local History,
Pen & Sword Select, Pen & Sword Military Classics and Leo Cooper.

For a complete list of Pen & Sword titles please contact
PEN & SWORD BOOKS LIMITED
47 Church Street, Barnsley, South Yorkshire, S70 2AS, England
E-mail: enquiries@pen-and-sword.co.uk
Website: www.pen-and-sword.co.uk

Contents

Dedication   vi
Acknowledgements   vii
Introduction   ix

Chapter One   1
Chapter Two   12
Chapter Three   24
Chapter Four   29
Chapter Five   36
Chapter Six   46
Chapter Seven   59
Chapter Eight   70
Chapter Nine   85
Chapter Ten   96
Chapter Eleven   124
Chapter Twelve   142
Chapter Thirteen   156
Chapter Fourteen   167
Chapter Fifteen   175
Chapter Sixteen   191
Chapter Seventeen   199

Appendix I – Operational Wild Weasel Platforms   212
Appendix II – Iraqi Integrated Air Defence Order of Battle   219
Appendix III – CENTAF Weasel HARM 'Shot Log'   230

Bibliography   268
Index   271

Dedication

Eisel: For Dad, a SAC tanker 'toad' for all those years, and Mom, a teacher for even more.

Schreiner: To those Americans who took the time to show how much they cared for all of the deployed servicemen and women by writing letters and sending care packages. You'll never know how much we all truly appreciated your thoughtful words and actions.

Acknowledgements

This book is based upon a journal Jim Schreiner kept during his deployment to the Persian Gulf region for Operations *Desert Shield* and *Desert Storm*. Building upon that record and the recollections of other F-4G Wild Weasel aircrew, the authors hope to show a slice of what life and war was like during that time.

The United States Navy and Marine Corps, and Britain's Royal Air Force contributed heavily to suppressing and defeating the Iraqi air defences along with many other aircrews and other Coalition air forces. This book, however, deals with primarily with the United States Air Force's F-4G Wild Weasel mission. This in no way detracts from the efforts and success of the other services.

In that same vein, the recollections presented here are of those Wild Weasel pilots and EWOs interviewed and are not meant to be all-encompassing for the many other F-4G crewmembers who flew missions in *Desert Storm*. Some of those experiences will be similar, some will be quite different. Indeed, crews in the same flight on the same mission will recall events differently at times.

The authors would like to

thank the Wild Weasels who contributed their time and memories to this project, as well as thanking them for serving their country.

Although facts are presented and official accounts and scholarly references used, the opinions expressed are strictly those of the authors. Likewise, any errors in the work are also solely due to the authors.

Introduction

When Iraqi President Saddam Hussein sent his military forces to invade and occupy the tiny neighbouring country of Kuwait in August 1990, his actions and the actions of the subsequent American-led coalition that stood against him made for a global chess game. The pieces on the board were controlled by those with the 'big picture'.

The pawns in that game, the ones that had to actually do the fighting and dying, were the hundreds of thousands of men and women who left their homes and families to live for seemingly endless months in the vast, trackless desert while the world stage-play unfolded. To them, the war was deeply personal.

At times, the war was scary; at other times, it was funny as hell. Usually, if you survive the former, it turns into the latter.

Jim Schreiner:

17 JANUARY 1991 D + 156

Operation *Desert Storm* is now in full swing. At about 0245L (local – Baghdad time), the first bombs impacted in Iraq. At 0400L the first of two AGM-88A HARMs erupted off of my aircraft on its way to some hapless SA-8 driver. Whether it actually hit or not, I'll probably never know.

Almost immediately after we crossed over into Kuwait, the entire sky opened up with enemy triple A and what looked like shoulder-launched SAMs. I have never seen such a beautiful yet

Hale cartoon showing a steely-eyed Wild Weasel character drawing a bead on Saddam using the two most used weapons; in the right hand is a 'shotgun,' aka the AGM-45 'Shrike' missile, and in the left is a 'magnum,' the AGM-88 HARM. (Kevin Hale)

so terrifying sight in my life. Nothing I have ever experienced or done prepared me for this.

Remembering all of the war movies that I've seen, the thing that struck me the most about last night's cacophony was the lack of sound. The barrage of anti-aircraft fire seemingly all around my aircraft looked intimidating but was completely silent. Although it was probably a lot further away than I thought, it definitely got my attention!

Chapter One

The first known US aircraft shot down by a surface-to-air missile (SAM) occurred on 1 May 1960. Francis Gary Powers, flying a more than 1,000 miles route overhead the Soviet Union in a CIA-sponsored Lockheed U-2 reconnaissance jet, saw several MiG fighters try to reach his altitude of well over 70,000 feet and fail. However, a Soviet V-750 Dvina, known to NATO as the SA-2 'Guideline', the telephone pole-sized SAM that would become infamous half a decade later in the skies over North Vietnam, could almost reach him. He didn't know about it and couldn't see it. (Note: The NATO – North Atlantic Treaty Organization – nomenclature for Soviet-era SAMs, radars and aircraft is used throughout this work, e.g. 'Guideline'.)

The SA-2 had a range of 25 miles and at Mach 4, could travel to its target in an incredibly short time. Not designed for low-altitude use, it was a deadly peril to anyone flying between 5,000 and 60,000 feet. Any aircraft wanting to avoid being a SAM target had to move into the low-level regime where old-fashioned guns became the biggest threat.

The SAM operator, under intense pressure coming directly from Soviet leader Nikita Kruschev, fired the instant Powers' jet was within range. With a cloud of noxious fumes and a bright orange glow, the SA-2 salvo of three missiles quickly leapt from their launchers and rocketed skyward. The missile tracking Powers detonated close enough that although the explosive warhead did not hit him, the concussive shockwave, magnified in the thin air at such a height, tore the spindly U-2 apart.

From that day on, SAMs have become a major threat to Allied aircraft. Fielding better, more advanced SAMs and finding ways to defeat an adversary's SAMs has become a continuing theme for air forces around the world.

In the United States' case, in its long tangle with North Vietnam, SA-2s were first photographed in April 1965. In July of that year, the first SAM killed a US fighter. From then on, increasingly more American resources were devoted to countering and defeating the deadly missiles.

In a never-ending game of threat and counter threat, more numerous and more lethal SAM systems have evolved. From the SA-2s of Vietnam, today's SAMs run the gamut from short-range, shoulder-fired IR (infrared – heat seeking) missiles like the SA-7 'Grail' and its descendants – SA-14 'Gremlin'/SA-16 'Gimlet' – to the extremely long-range, mammoth SA-10 'Grumble', capable of 'reaching out and touching someone' at 200 miles and from altitudes of 50 feet up to 100,000 feet. Many more SAM designs lie between the short-range SA-7 and the long-range SA-10.

Except for the IR-guided SAMs, the rest of these deadly aircraft killers use radar to detect and track a target and at least one additional, sometimes more, radar to provide fire control and/or missile guidance. Each radar emits energy in a specific wavelength to perform its job.

Generally, early warning (EW) radars provide advanced notification that an aircraft is out there. The radar can see targets at very long range; only the curvature of the earth can hide high-flying jets from its view. To scan the vast volumes of airspace at those distances, EW radars use longer wavelength frequencies like HF – high frequency – or VHF – very high frequency – for detection.

Each sweep of the radar takes a relatively long time to accomplish but scours a huge volume of airspace. Although good at finding the evidence of an incoming aircraft, EW radar data is too vague to provide the precise location of incoming target. Since the 'kill' envelope of a SAM's warhead is limited compared with the volume of the sky, much more accurate data is needed to target a SAM.

This is where the acquisition (AQ) and target tracking radars (TTR) come into play. For the Vietnam-era SA-2, the 'Fan Song' radar used much shorter UHF (ultra high frequency) wavelengths. Since the TTR operator knew in what area to look, he could rapidly acquire and refine the exact position of the intended target. Once the target was within the performance parameters – within the missile's range and height capabilities – of the SA-2, the operator fired the missile, often two or three at a time in a salvo.

Using another radar to track the SAM, the operator 'connected the dots' on his radar scope. The SAM followed the invisible beam of its radar like a blind bloodhound and the operator steered that beam to the dot being tracked by the first radar. When the dots merged on his scope, he could either command to detonate the SAM or in later models, sensors in the missile detected the aircraft and exploded the warhead. In many cases, this 'dot to dot' merge meant another American jet was severely damaged if not destroyed.

What makes many SAMs even more deadly is that they are mounted on mobile launchers and no longer have to be set up at a fixed, easily targetable site like an SA-2. Some, of course, do require such a site, but truck and tracked vehicle-mounted SAMs can easily 'shoot and scoot' to avoid being destroyed after launching.

One of the earliest methods of defeating SAMs by a fighter has been to 'take it down.' By flying nap of the earth sorties, aircraft avoid being seen by the radar beams of most SAMs. Of course, the counter to this tactic is simply to spray a wall of lead into the air and wait for the jet to fly into it.

Indeed, in Vietnam, the North often employed this tactic, called a 'flak trap'. By launching an SA-2, even if unguided, American aircraft had to honour the threat of the SAM and go low to avoid being targeted. Once the US aircraft was low enough, the Vietnamese used guns ranging from infantrymen's rifles or machine-guns to large-calibre, radar-directed cannons to fill the airspace with deadly metal fragments. The US lost more aircraft to this than to SAMs. (Anti-aircraft artillery was called 'Triple A' in the tactical vernacular, also sometimes written as 'AAA'. It was labelled flak by an earlier generation.)

Additionally, having to out-manoeuvre the SAM meant the heavily laden fighter-bombers used by US Air Force, Navy, and Marine Corps usually had to jettison their bombs to make their jets nimble enough to react. Of course, with no bombs to drop, the intended target was safe for another day.

The whole drama had to be re-staged for another mission, giving the defences another shot at the fighters, which might mean the fighters having to dump their bombs to avoid getting hit. This meant the mission was wasted, which meant it had to be flown again, meaning the defences got another opportunity and so on for the years of the Vietnam War.

Soviet P-35 'Bar Lock' long range acquisition radar. (DoD)

Together, SAMs and AAA formed a powerful 'one-two' punch for air defence. Add in a knock-out blow provided by fighter interceptors and a nation so equipped has an impressive system for keeping an adversary out of its skies.

The Iraqi air defences faced by the nearly 500,000 Allied ground, naval and air forces of the Coalition during Operation *Desert Storm* were thought to be some of the fiercest, most integrated of any nation in the world, much better even than those of the North Vietnamese.

At the heart of the Iraq integrated air defence system (IADS) was the French-designed and built KARI (Iraq spelled backward in French) Command/Control/Communications (C3) network. By providing a unified way of integrating all the inputs and centralised control of the reactions, KARI was a deadly threat to Coalition air power. Without destroying KARI and the component parts of the IADS, the Allies could not achieve air superiority.

Without air superiority, the ground forces necessary to drive Iraq from Kuwait were at much higher risk from the Iraqi Air Force. Without air superiority, General Norman Schwarzkopf, the overall military leader of the Coalition, did not have the ability to choose from all his options in dealing with Iraq's large ground forces. Air superiority was thus the first key to success in winning the war. Killing the IADS, therefore, was job one for the Coalition's air commanders.

In particular, the IADS of Iraq and its conquered territory of Kuwait had over 400 radar-guided surface-to-air missile batteries and nearly 7,000 shoulder-launched man-portable (MANPAD) IR SAMs. Add in the more than 6,000 AAA guns of various calibres and Iraqi skies were deadly.

Since Iraq had long been supplied and trained by the Soviet Union, it follows that her air defences used the Soviet model. The Iraqi strategic air defences used large EW radars such as the P-35/P-37 'Bar Lock'. These high powered, but low frequency and long pulse repetition frequency (PRF) radars were at fixed sites usually located at critical air bases or large cities.

The Bar Lock was also used by the Soviet-trained GCI (ground controlled intercept) controllers; technicians trained in deciphering the radar screen display and radioing height, speed, and heading instructions to the Iraqi fighter pilot. The pilot had to follow these instructions to the letter, since Soviet doctrine dictated very heavy reliance on ground controller instructions to obtain results versus the more free-ranging latitude used by most Western combat pilots.

Other EW radars were mobile but at the cost of detection range. Radars such as the Flat Face, Squat Eye, and Spoon Rest couldn't see as far as a Bar Lock, but did provide more precise target location data. This data was then sent via electronic data link or relayed via voice over the telephone or radio directly to individual SAM or AAA batteries.

The Flat Face radar consists of

Soviet P-15 'Flat Face' long range acquisition radar used most often by the SA-3 medium-range SAM system. (DoD)

Roland short-range Franco-German manufactured mobile SAM system. Here a captured Iraqi unit is the backdrop for a couple of US Army troops. (DoD)

a trailer-mounted pair of elliptical antennas attached one above the other on a mast sticking up from the trailer. It typically supported SA-3, SA-6, SA-8, and SA-9 Soviet-built SAMs. It could also be used in conjunction with the French-built Roland SAM system. The Flat Face supported various calibres of AAA like the ZSU-23, a tank-like, four-barrelled, rapid fire 23-mm AAA vehicle as well.

The Fan Song radar, known since its Vietnam days, primarily supported the venerable SA-2. Using two 'trough' antennas, one

Soviet 'Low Blow' guidance radar with TV-guidance back up in front of a battery of SA-3 'Goa' SAMs. (DoD)

vertical on the side of the control van and the other horizontal under the front of the van, the radar had a respectable 150-mile range if the target was at very high altitude. Most targets, however, weren't that high so a detection range of 40–50 miles was usually the norm. This was still a big enough picture to give the SA-2 with its 25-mile range a good look at the target prior to engaging.

While having a shorter range than the SA-2 or -3, the most deadly Iraqi SAMs were the newer generations of missiles like the SA-6 'Gainful', and the Roland. In comparison with the SA-2, for example, the 'Gainful' can turn using up to 15 g. The older, larger SA-2 can pull around 4 g, thus a pilot evading an incoming SAM, if he times it right, can outturn the SA-2 because fighters can pull up to 9 g. A manned aircraft simply can't do 15 g.

The Iraqi's SA-6 system actually consisted of several lightly armoured, tracked vehicles. One unit carried the acquisition and tracking radars and the three or four TELs (transporter erector launcher vehicles) held three missiles each. This self-contained SAM convoy can move quickly from one location to the next, making it a

Wheeled, very mobile, SA-8 'Gecko' short-range SAM built and supplied by the Soviets. (USAF)

constant threat just by its possible presence. The highly mobile point defence SAMs like the SA-8 and the Roland offer similar capabilities and were also widely used by the Iraqis. The over 6,000 anti-aircraft artillery pieces ranged in size from automatic rifles that could cause trouble down on the deck up to 130-mm radar-directed cannons flinging steel up to 50,000 feet.

Each of these radars contributed its piece of Iraq's air picture over its country and the newly acquired '19th' province of Kuwait to the Iraqi Air Force leadership. Each also had its own unique electronic signal pattern, dubbed a 'signature', that could be detected, countered and defeated by the Allies.

The final layer in the Iraqi IADS was their fighter aircraft. Mainly a mix of older and newer generation Soviet-built fighters, the Iraqis also used French and Chinese jets. They even carried some 1950s era British-built Hawker Hunters on their roster. All told, the Iraqi Air Force counted over 700 fighter and fighter-bombers at the start of the war in January 1991.

Typical SA-2 'Guideline' SAM site in the desert. (DoD)

Soviet built and supplied SA-6 mobile SAM system. Each TEL carried three SA-6 'Gainful' SAMs ready for launch plus a reload capability. (DoD photo)

Organisationally, Iraq split its IADS into three main elements. The first consisted of long-range SAMS, primarily SA-2s and -3s along with fighters to protect high-value ground assets like key airfields and air defence sites. These sites included the air defence headquarters in Baghdad and three large sector operations centres (SOCs), which covered the north, middle, and southern parts of Iraq. A fourth SOC, much less sophisticated, was set up to control Kuwait.

The Baghdad headquarters maintained strategic control of the country's air defence while each SOC had operational control of fighters, SAMs and AAA within its area and coordinated with adjoining SOCs for reinforcements if needed.

The second element of Iraq's IADS was the extensive network of long-range early warning and acquisition radars. Spaced around the perimeter of the country, these radars provided the first indications to Iraqi Air Force leaders of any Coalition air threats. They used longer wavelengths with longer ranges to provide that warning. Using extensive radio and landline communications, they had a very robust network in January 1991.

Soviet built ZSU-23 'Shilka' armored anti-aircraft artillery vehicle. Although only shooting cannons of 23mm, the ZSU-23 could put out an incredible volume of fire against low-flying aircraft. It was capable of shredding any jet caught in its sights. (DoD)

The final element of the IADS comprised the fire control and tracking radars associated with the SAM or AAA sites. Cued by the early warning radars, the operators of these systems fired up their shorter wavelength, higher pulse repetition frequency to generate the highly accurate data on any threatening aircraft. Once the target was acquired, the missile came off the launcher as the gunner pulled the trigger to send high-speed death to the 'aggressor' aircraft.

Not directly controlled by the Iraq IADS, but certainly important, were the point defence SAMs and AAA that the Iraqi Army fielded. These shorter range SAMs didn't have the extreme 'reach out and touch you' ability of the SA-2 and -3 missiles, but because they were developed much later than those two systems, their electronics and radars were much more capable. Additionally, these systems were highly mobile, usually mounted on a tracked or wheeled vehicle and capable of moving at a moment's notice.

MANPADs and automatic weapons carried by individual soldiers could also ruin a pilot's day if he was down low and ran across one of these. Since the Allies had long-planned to fight the war at 'in the weeds' levels to avoid radar detection, the proliferation of these low-tech threats was a real concern to Allied planners.

Chapter Two

After first encountering SA-2 SAMs in North Vietnam, the US military's air arms slowly and, at times, painfully developed means of countering the new threat. The US Navy was first off the mark by developing the AN/APR-23 radar homing and warning system ('RHAWS' – spoken of as 'RAW' gear), a small cockpit black box that listened to the three main frequencies used by the SA-2's radars. Upon detecting one of those frequencies, the box generated a line on a small 2½-inch cockpit scope. The line only displayed signal intensity, i.e., approximating how close you were to the SAM radar, and not a direction, but it was a start and not bad for 1964 technology.

Along with the RHAWS gear, the Navy started a project that produced the AGM-45 Shrike, the United States' first anti-radiation missile (ARM). The Shrike, still in the inventory during *Desert Storm*, was an air to ground missile that carried a sensitive radar seeker head in its nose to detect enemy electronic emissions. Once detected, it pointed via another display in the cockpit, where the signal was coming from.

A drawback to the Shrike, however, was its inability to be reprogrammed in flight. In other words, the earliest models only looked for a particular frequency. If it didn't detect that exact match, as far as the Shrike was concerned, there was nothing out there. However, SA-2s used several frequencies and could hop between those available, so even if the Shrike didn't see it, the 'Guideline' was just as deadly. Improved, later versions still had a relatively small frequency bandwidth search capability.

Another disadvantage to the Shrike was that it was a relatively short-range weapon. To deliver the missile, the launching fighter had to fly within 10 miles or so of the SAM, well within the SAM's kill range, meanwhile hoping the SAM stayed on the correct frequency for the Shrike to see it. The Shrike shooter also had to fly almost directly at the radar site in order to get the weapon 'into the basket' of its search ability.

If the SAM operator quit radiating after the Shrike fired or hopped to another frequency, the missile 'went stupid' and flew until it was out of propellant or battery power. Meanwhile, the SA-2 gunner could still fire at the fighter both while it was attacking and running (bravely!) away. The advantage definitely lay with the SAM.

The USAF was slower to adopt specialised electronics and SAM countermeasures. It was only after SA-2s shot down a McDonnell F-4C 'Phantom II' on 24 July 1965 that it began to notice the threat in a serious way. That same SAM inflicted severe damage to the other three members in that flight.

Two days later, AAA shot down a McDonnell RF-101 Voodoo reconnaissance jet sent to photograph the SAM site. The next day, AAA brought down five out of a total of forty-six Republic F-105 'Thunderchiefs' sent to pound the SAM site.

These losses in such quick succession brought about action within the USAF. By August 1965, the Air Force Chief of Staff, General John P McConnell, directed Brigadier General Ken Dempster to come up with a solution to the SAM problem.

The first result was the design and adoption of radar-jamming pods that could be carried by each fighter. Sets like the early AN/ALQ-72 emitted 'noise' in the frequencies most used by the SA-2s Fan Song radar so that the SAM operator, instead of seeing a nice crisp blip on his scope, had to look through a screen filled with static. If the radar and operator couldn't see you, then the fighter was relatively safe.

Another bit of electronic wizardry developed at this time was the first USAF RHAWS set, the AN/APR-25. Unlike the Navy's equipment, this scope displayed both the signal strength of the SAM radar, and thus how likely you were to be attacked, and a bearing line that showed the pilot where the threat was in relation to his aircraft.

The third result and most important to this book's premise was the idea of equipping fighter-bombers as radar 'ferrets'. By using specialised electronics, these ferrets would actively seek out SAM sites to destroy, or at least neutralise, them. Unlike the jamming pods and RHAW sets, this was an offensive tactic. The idea was soon dubbed 'Wild Weasel'.

The extra equipment needed for this new Weasel mission meant that a two-seat manoeuvrable fighter-bomber had to be used. The pilot did the traditional job of flying and dropping ordnance, but the backseat, stuffed with electronics, display scopes and the like needed a specialist crewmember. This second body needed to be an expert in electronic warfare; reading the 'beeps and squeaks' of the electromagnetic spectrum. In particular, he had to be quick in identifying the type of radar that was out there, where it was, and at what point in the detecting, tracking or firing sequence the SAM radar was.

Not many fighters of the day had a backseat much less carried such a specialised brain in it. Borrowing many of these first backseaters called electronic warfare officers or EWOs from the bomber force of the US Strategic Air Command, the Weasels began their first steps to combat. It was also at this time that the legend surrounding the Wild Weasel's cryptic YGBSM logo first appeared. Supposedly, the first EWO muttered, 'You gotta be shitting me!' when first told of his assignment to the programme. Enshrined in legend, most Weasel patches worn on flight suits carry some version of an agitated, cartoon weasel with YGBSM written underneath.

The first Weasel aircraft was the North American F-100F, nicknamed the 'Hun'. In a rush project, seven Huns were outfitted with the AN/APR-25 RHAWS and the new IR-133 panoramic display scope. The -133 could identify the Soviet-made Fan Song SAM radar and the Fire Can AAA radar and provide steering cues via antennas placed around the jet. The display showed which side of the jet was receiving a stronger signal and the EWO in the back would give directions for the pilot to turn.

The pilot, meanwhile, was busy scanning outside because although the first generation 'gee-whiz' Weasel gear would get him in the vicinity of a SAM, it couldn't pinpoint the site. The only weapons these first Weasels had were of the close-in type – rocket pods, iron bombs, or the two 20-mm cannons in the Hun's belly. This type of combat still gave the reach advantage to the SAM since it could shoot at around 20 miles while the F-100F Weasel had to get within one or so.

First flying in combat in November 1965, the untested Weasel concept made its first kill on 22 December of that year. Pilot Captain Allen Lamb and EWO Captain Jack Donovan were trolling near a suspected SAM site when Donovan detected the Fan Song's characteristic 'rattlesnake' growl in his helmet's headphones. The sensitive receivers in the Weasel picked up the different electronic emissions and besides depicting them on a cockpit display, translated the detected frequency into distinct sounds. A Weasel EWO quickly became adept at telling a Fan Song from, say, an air traffic control radar simply by the sound in his headphones.

Lamb, seeing the SAM's control van hidden under some camouflage netting, fired two rocket pods of unguided missiles at the site before moving his finger to the F-100's gun trigger and strafing the site. Accompanying Republic F-105Ds swooped in and finished off the SAM facility.

The rushed nature of this early Wild Weasel operation often showed in the jets' maintenance down time. The wiring for the various receivers and displays was not manufactured for the rugged conditions of combat and the extreme humidity of Southeast Asia, so it corroded quickly making the jet useless.

The Hun itself was far from the ideal platform to weasel in. The mainstay of the Air Force's bombing effort was the massive F-105, affectionately nicknamed the 'Thud'. Designed for the low-level, high-speed nuclear bombing role, it adapted well to carrying iron bombs instead of 'instant sunshine'. As described above, Thuds often flew with F-100s in a mixed flight while hunting SAMs. This type of flight was called an 'Iron Hand'.

The F-100, however, was a generation earlier in design concept and, while more nimble than the Thud, had a hard time keeping up in terms of speed. Thud drivers liked to cruise inbound to a target at 450 knots and be well into the 500-knot range when actually attacking. The Hun was pressed to keep up at 350 knots cruise.

Thus it was in May 1966, that the Wild Weasel II project, consisting of modified F-105F two-seat versions of the mighty Thud, first flew in Vietnam. The USAF also picked up the Shrike missile to add to its arsenal of anti-SAM weapons. The Weasel Thud usually flew with one or two Shrikes and external fuel tanks hanging from the wings. With only a half dozen machines in place, the Weasels usually flew in mixed formation with the single-seat F-105D 'vanilla' Thuds. The F model would find a SAM site and would launch a Shrike to kill the radar. If nothing else, the inbound Shrike made the Vietnamese gunner worry about living versus tracking the fighters. This distraction let the D models roar in low and drop iron or cluster bombs on the site, further adding to the destruction of this particular site.

Weaselling was, and is, an exceedingly dangerous mission. For example, two months after the initial six F-105Fs arrived in theatre at Korat Royal Thai Air Force Base, all but one had been shot down. Of the eight crews (one pilot, one EWO each) in that detachment, four were killed, two were shot down and made prisoners of war and two were wounded. Only four of the sixteen men in that first deployment to Korat completed the 100 missions required for a combat tour in Vietnam.

Nevertheless, the F-105F and an upgraded version, the F-105G (Wild Weasel III), proved itself as the best machine for the job of playing 'here, kitty, kitty' with Vietnamese SAM operators. If the SAM showed the slightest vulnerability, the Weasels pounced and laid waste to the site.

Such was their effect, that soon all strike packages flying into North Vietnam required Weasel support. A four ship of Weasels would precede the strike, hoping to get the Vietnamese to light up their SAM and AAA radars. If the Vietnamese did, the Weasels pounded them with everything they had. Even if they didn't destroy a SAM site, the fact that the Weasels made the radars shut down allowed the strikers to accomplish their mission. Perhaps not as satisfying as blowing up a SAM battery, but it was just as effective for the time required.

Similarly, another flight of Weasels would trail the main force in order to be in the target area as the bombers egressed. Often, having survived the cascade of bombs, a SAM might choose to tag one of the fleeing fighter-bombers. This last set of Weasels hung around to ensure that opportunity didn't occur.

Throughout the long, grinding years of the Vietnam War, Weasels performed their deadly mission. Many of them were shot down and died or were taken prisoner. Despite this, many of the Weasels pulled two or three combat tours during the War. The satisfaction of squaring off with a SAM site in order to protect fellow airmen was a big adrenaline rush to many of them.

Two Weasels won the nation's highest award for valour, the Medal of Honor, while flying the mission. Countless other awards for valour were also earned by the F-105 Wild Weasel crews but at the price of many lives.

Following the war, the Thuds soldiered on as Weasels, but the Air Force realised that the F-105's days were numbered due to the numbers lost in Vietnam (over 300 of all models) and the high maintenance requirements of the remaining birds. The F-4 had picked up the load from the Thud as a bomber during the latter years of Vietnam and the fighter side of the USAF soon was also equipped with mostly F-4s. It thus made sense to fashion the next Weasel out of an F-4 as well.

Indeed, Wild Weasel configured F-4Cs flew in the last year of the Vietnam War as Wild Weasel IV birds but with essentially the same electronics as the Thuds.

By the mid-1970s, USAF planners knew that they needed better tools for the Weasel to survive new threats and advances made in both SAM and radar technology.

Drawing heavily on lessons learned from the 1973 Arab–Israeli War in which a new generation of SAM, the SA-6 'Gainful', made its appearance known by shooting down a third of the Israeli Air Force in the first few days of the war, a project dubbed Wild Weasel V produced the ultimate SAM killing aircraft, the McDonnell-Douglas F-4G Phantom II.

An F-4G at rest, a rare sight during the war. (USAF)

APR-47 EQUIPMENT & ANTENNA LOCATION

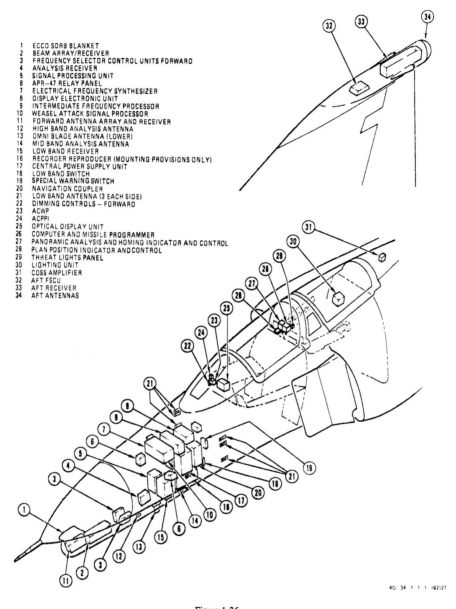

1   ECCO SORB BLANKET
2   BEAM ARRAY/RECEIVER
3   FREQUENCY SELECTOR CONTROL UNITS FORWARD
4   ANALYSIS RECEIVER
5   SIGNAL PROCESSING UNIT
6   APR-47 RELAY PANEL
7   ELECTRICAL FREQUENCY SYNTHESIZER
8   DISPLAY ELECTRONIC UNIT
9   INTERMEDIATE FREQUENCY PROCESSOR
10 WEASEL ATTACK SIGNAL PROCESSOR
11 FORWARD ANTENNA ARRAY AND RECEIVER
12 HIGH BAND ANALYSIS ANTENNA
13 OMNI BLADE ANTENNA (LOWER)
14 MID BAND ANALYSIS ANTENNA
15 LOW BAND RECEIVER
16 RECORDER REPRODUCER (MOUNTING PROVISIONS ONLY)
17 CENTRAL POWER SUPPLY UNIT
18 LOW BAND SWITCH
19 SPECIAL WARNING SWITCH
20 NAVIGATION COUPLER
21 LOW BAND ANTENNA (3 EACH SIDE)
22 DIMMING CONTROLS – FORWARD
23 ACWP
24 ACPPI
25 OPTICAL DISPLAY UNIT
26 COMPUTER AND MISSILE PROGRAMMER
27 PANORAMIC ANALYSIS AND HOMING INDICATOR AND CONTROL
28 PLAN POSITION INDICATOR AND CONTROL
29 THREAT LIGHTS PANEL
30 LIGHTING UNIT
31 COSS AMPLIFIER
32 AFT FSCU
33 AFT RECEIVER
34 AFT ANTENNAS

4G 34 1 1 (92)21

Figure 1-36

T.O. depiction of the location of the AN/APR-47's multitude of sensors
spread around the fuselage of the F-4G. (USAF)

APR-47 ANTENNA & RECEIVER LOCATION

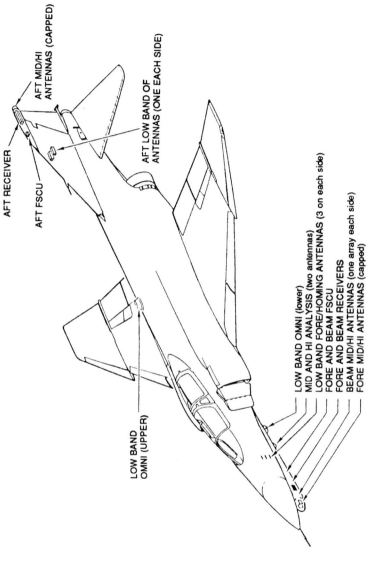

AFT MID/HI ANTENNAS (CAPPED)

AFT RECEIVER

AFT MID/HI

AFT FSCU

AFT LOW BAND OF ANTENNAS (ONE EACH SIDE)

LOW BAND OMNI (UPPER)

LOW BAND OMNI (lower)
MID AND HI ANALYSIS (two antennas)
LOW BAND FORE/HOMING ANTENNAS (3 on each side)
FORE AND BEAM FSCU
FORE AND BEAM RECEIVERS
BEAM MID/HI ANTENNAS (one array each side)
FORE MID/HI ANTENNAS (capped)

Figure 1-37

More of the same. (USAF)

The G-model was converted from the cannon-equipped F-4E. The heart of the new system was the AN/APR-38 Radar Attack and Warning System (RAWS). Using the beginnings of the digital electronics revolution, the 'brain' of the APR-38 was the Homing and Warning Computer (HAWC), which received, analysed and sifted through all the electronic emissions it detected. Sorting them through a pre-loaded threat priority program, it then selected the appropriate weapon to use against the emerging radar threat.

The system used fifty-two antennas placed around the F-4G's fuselage and wings. This 360-degree coverage gave the APR-38 a degree of accuracy only dreamed of in the earlier Weasel variants. At fifty miles from a target, the system could pinpoint its location within two miles and within two degrees in azimuth. If the F-4G closed on the intended target, by the time the jet reached firing range, the error distance was within six feet. Plenty close enough for government work and deadly to the SAM.

One of the initial issues with the APR-38 was the space requirement for its many black boxes. As hulking as the F-4 is, there is still a finite amount of room to place new equipment. There simply was not enough space for the new electronic wizardry gadgets and the internal six-barrelled 20-mm M-61 Gatling gun. So, the gun went and the black boxes went into the newly created void.

Even though the F-4G lost its gun, it still maintained its air-to-air capability by the use of its AN/APQ-120 on-board multi-mode pulse radar, which could detect other aircraft as well as 'paint' a picture of the ground for dropping bombs. The APQ-120 could fed targeting information to the AIM-7 Sparrow radar missiles the F-4G typically carried for long-range air-to-air fighting.

The F-4's crew tracked an adversary with the APQ-120, manoeuvred the jet within firing parameters, pickled off one or two Sparrows and as long as the radar stayed on the target, the Sparrow had a good chance of hitting. Ranges for this type of aerial combat were around ten miles or so.

Complementing the Sparrow's longer reach was the AIM-9 Sidewinder, an infrared seeking short range air-to-air missile. The Sidewinder detected heat from the target aircraft like the jet exhaust, or in more advanced versions, even the heat due to friction as the target pushed through the air. Ranges for this weapon were much closer than Sparrow use, typically in the one to two mile range.

Experienced survivors of Vietnam Weaselling set up the first 'schoolhouse' for the G-model Weasel at George Air Force Base (AFB) near Victorville, California. Already an F-4 training base, the first SAM-killing Phantoms arrived in April 1978. The 35th Tactical Fighter Wing (TFW) was the overall unit chartered to train new crews and operate the weapon system should America need her SAM busters again. The 35th comprised several squadrons, one for training and two operational. The training squadron's instructors could, of course, be used in combat operations if required.

By 1990, the two resident Weasel squadrons at George were the 561st Tactical Fighter Squadron (TFS) 'Black Knights', and the 562d Tactical Flying Training Squadron (TFTS) 'Gators'. The third Wild Weasel squadron had been inactive the previous year. Additional squadrons based overseas were the 81st TFS 'Panthers' at Spangdahlem Air Base (AB) in West Germany and the 90th TFS, the 'Pair o' Dice' at Clark AB in the Philippines.

A HARM climbs for altitude to increase its range in the thinner air. Somebody at the receiving end is about to have a very bad day. (Joe Healy)

Also by 1990, the APR-38 had been upgraded with a new digital processor, doubling its memory. This upgrade used essentially the same control interfaces, but vastly improved the amount of data that could be carried on-board. The increased memory enabled the crew to find and kill a threat, or multiple threats simultaneously, much more quickly. This new processor, the Weasel Attack Signal Processor (WASP), turned the APR-38 into the AN/APR-47 with double the memory.

By then, too, the most potent weapon ever carried by the F-4G and still in use today, albeit with many upgrades, was in service. The AGM-88, High Speed Anti-Radiation Missile (HARM) has an extremely sensitive radar-detecting seeker head capable of scanning a multitude of electromagnetic bands in milliseconds. The HARM overcame the Shrike's deficiencies by being both more versatile and much longer ranged, capable of reaching out more than fifty miles. The odds against a SAM got a little more even since the Weasel could shoot the HARM at the edges of most SAM ranges versus flying into the heart of the SAM's effective envelope.

Unlike the Sparrow in the air-to-air environment, the HARM was a 'fire and forget' weapon. So was the Shrike for that matter, but getting within ten miles or closer to a SAM site didn't leave much room for evasive manoeuvring. The primary target with all the targeting data was designated by the EWO and passed via circuits and electrons into the HARM's brain before launch. Once the pickle button, toggled by either the pilot or EWO, was pressed, the HARM launched from its carrying rail under the Phantom's wing and went to its target.

In an effort to increase the impact of the limited number of Weasel aircraft, both the Clark and Spangdahlem units paired the Weasels with non-Weasel aircraft. The 81st's jets, along with those of the 23d TFS's 'Fighting Hawks' and 480th's 'Warhawks', were mixed with General Dynamics (now Lockheed-Martin) F-16s. The 90th paired its similar F-4E, with Gs to double the Weasels' effects although the 'E' models could not carry HARMs.

In these mixed units, similar to the Vietnam-era Iron Hand flights of Weasel F-105Gs with single-seat F-105Ds, the F-4G/F-16 or F-4E teams relied on the Weasel detecting the SAM or AAA radar and guiding the flight close enough to employ weapons.

The G-model would designate the target and via either a data link or through pre-briefed code words, put the non-Weasel fighter in position to shoot. Even though the non-Weasel fighter couldn't detect the target, the 'G' model could, so the tactic of 'two for one' had its appeal.

This then is the environment in which Jim Schreiner and the other Weasels operated.

Chapter Three

Jim Schreiner, in 1990 a USAF captain, became a Wild Weasel pilot almost by accident. Following his graduation from Air Force pilot training in 1982, he was retained after winning his wings as what is known as a FAIP, or first assignment instructor pilot. Although most student pilots dreamed of flying fighter or attack jets after graduation, only a small percentage actually qualified for the available billets. Not everyone who did qualify could find an open fighter cockpit to fill. Many of those left empty-handed were given another shot by becoming a FAIP. By teaching the next three years' worth of students the basics of Air Force flying, a FAIP was more likely to be awarded a fighter upon finishing his tour.

Schreiner did just that, instructing in Cessna T-37s, the basic jet trainer familiar to nearly fifty years' worth of Air Force student pilots. Completing his instructor duties, he drew a cockpit in the remarkable Republic A-10 Thunderbolt II. The A-10 is *never* called 'Thunderbolt' by its pilots. Instead it is the 'Warthog', or just 'Hog' due to its less than sleek lines.

The A-10 was designed in the height of the Cold War as an anti-tank weapon to help fend off the expected hordes of Soviet tanks that the Western world feared would pour over the plains of central Europe. With an amazingly powerful and rapid-firing GAU-8 30-mm cannon, the A-10 could shoot forearm-length rounds through the toughest armour the Soviets could field. The Hog today also carries almost every air-to-ground weapon in the USAF inventory and in large quantities.

Schreiner checked out in the A-10 in late 1986 and was stationed at Royal Air Force (RAF) Bentwaters air base in the United Kingdom. While here, he progressed up the typical tactical fighter squadron totem pole. Initially assigned as a wingman, the lowest position because of lack of experience, he advanced to a four-ship flight lead. This is the most basic formation usually flown by fighters as it is the best combination of both offensive and defensive capabilities.

Offensively, a four ship of A-10s can deliver nearly 32 tons of bombs, rockets, and other deadly packages, not counting the devastatingly effective cannon. Defensively, each jet maintains a specific look out for threats depending on where it is placed in the flight. The A-10 is capable of taking enormous punishment and bringing the pilot back home anyway. The pilot sits in a 'bathtub' of more than 900 pounds of titanium armour and the vital areas of the jet are likewise protected. All in all, a flight of A-10s is a force to be reckoned with. Leading a flight was a good day for a fighter pilot.

Administratively, Schreiner attained a senior enough position to be named a flight commander within his A-10 squadron. A mid-level leadership role, the flight commander was responsible for scheduling the eight or so pilots assigned in all aspects of their flying, their training on the ground in subjects like escape and evasion, and processing all the paperwork needed to run a modern Air Force. With only three or so flight commanders in a squadron, the senior leaders relied on the flight commanders' judgement and input when making 'big picture' decisions.

All good things must come to an end, however, and by 1990, Schreiner's time in England was drawing to a close. By now he'd been in the service for nearly ten years. Typically, such a mid-level officer must do at least one tour, if not more, in a staff job at a headquarters or even (gasp!) in the Pentagon. To one who just wanted to fly and stay a warrior, such an assignment was like being given a prison sentence.

In Jim's case, the assignment team offered him one out; go to George AFB and learn to fly the ageing Phantom as a Weasel pilot. By this time, even the F-4G was showing its age compared with newer fighters like the McDonnell-Douglas F-15 'Eagle' or the F-16 as mentioned above. In USAF's budget planning, the costs needed to maintain the potent, but cranky, F-4G were becoming prohibitive and they planned to phase it out by the early 1990s.

It was a dying weapon system but until the final jet was parked in the vast aircraft boneyard outside Davis-Monthan AFB in Arizona, replacement pilots and EWOs were needed to man its cockpits.

Schreiner's choice was a 'take it or leave it'. Leaving it meant a desk somewhere so he took it.

Another pilot, (then) Captain Dave Lucia, and the last pilot to go through Weasel training, described what it was like checking out in the F-4G:

> I came to George following a tour as an ALO (air liaison officer – a USAF fighter pilot assigned to a US Army combat unit) with the 82d Airborne Division. I had jumped into Panama as part of Operation *Just Cause* and was ready to get back into a cockpit.
>
> Since I hadn't flown the F-4 before (I'd been an OA-37 and OV-10 forward air control pilot prior to going to the Army), I had to learn to fly the F-4E at the 21st TFTS there at George. My first flight was just a few days before *Desert Shield* kicked off.
>
> Compared with more modern jets like the F-16, the F-4 was like an old Cadillac. After cranking engines, the air conditioner wouldn't work until you were airborne so we did all our ground

Author Jim Schreiner (l) and his EWO, Maj Dan Sharp (r), pose beside a 561st TFS jet (note the squadron emblem on the jet intake) at George AFB, California. (Schreiner)

ops with the canopies up. I'd run the seat up to where I could look over the top of the canopy bow and feel the breeze in my face. That was a great feeling.

Another difference about the F-4 was that once airborne, it talked to you. You had to listen to what it was telling you. You could hear the wind noise change around the canopy as you manoeuvred the jet. You could feel it start to shake if you started pushing it beyond its limits. If you kept pushing, it could get away from you and stall.

I always felt that the F-4 required more pure airmanship – the skills needed to fly the jet smoothly – than does the F-16 where the computer does a lot of the work for you.

Ergonomically, the F-4's cockpit was horrible. The visibility was not very good. The side of the jet was about level with your shoulders so to see down or back you had to roll it to see.

The lights could be so bright on a night sortie that you put tape over them to blank them out. We stowed our stuff in various places, wherever there was room. I'd tuck my charts into the sides of the front instrument panel coaming. I'd throw my helmet bag with snacks and water and other junk in the space to the sides of the ejection seat.

Another aspect that took some getting used to was having another guy fly with you. Although I really learned to like the crew concept, at first it was strange. When first flying with a backseater, I tended to be more formal and use the checklists words, but once you got to know each other, you could tell what the other was thinking by just a grunt or a single word.

Even landing the massive Phantom presented challenges according to Lucia.

The forward viz in the F-4 was never great. With the [gun]sight, canopy framing and the 'Rhino's' long nose, it was nearly impossible to see ahead. During the landing, I'd again run my seat up as high as it would go to be able to see just a little straight ahead.

You could feel it as you got into ground effect and could touch down really smoothly most times. When it was raining, however, I always planted it firmly to avoid the risk of hydroplaning. (The

F-4, due to the nearly perfectly triangular positioning of the nose and main landing gear developed a reputation for this.)

Almost always, I got some sort of comment from the backseat about my landing.

After learning how to fly the F-4E, Lucia followed the well-worn trail over to the 562d TFTS to learn how to be a Weasel in the G model:

It was a demanding course. I went through the same academic courses as the EWO. We had to learn all the possible threat weapon systems out there, including the associated radar systems that went with those threats. And we had to know those down to the gnat's ass. We learned what noises each system made via the APR-47.

Some Weasel pilots even learned enough to tell from the noises what the threat was. That was standard for the EWOs, but not so much for the pilots.

The only Weaseling gear we had in the front cockpit was a small repeater scope. It fed a picture of what the EWO displayed on his much bigger PPIAC [Plan Position Indicator and Control] scope.

Some of the EWOs were good enough to tell if a site was a decoy or not just from listening to the difference in the gain. The hum from a decoy would be just a little different than that from an actual site.

Another trick EWOs had to learn was differentiating between friendly systems like the HAWK (Homing All the Way Killer – a USMC-operated SAM) and those that had been sold to other countries. [Iraq captured some HAWK batteries that had been sold to Kuwait prior to the Gulf War as an example.]

Jim Schreiner was a few months ahead of Lucia in the training pipeline. He had just finished his F-4G mission qualification when Saddam Hussein sent his tanks and infantry into Kuwait. From being a minor prince as a flight commander, Schreiner was back to being a wingman since he was once again the new guy in the jet.

Chapter Four

This is the first entry I have been waiting to make for some time. The events that led up to our being here are now well known, however, my personal thoughts and reactions are the reason I have started this journal. My greatest hope is that I am able to finish it.

On 2 August, Saddam Hussein invaded and conquered Kuwait. I knew we would respond but I had no idea that President Bush would act so quickly. I don't think Hussein did either.

I last flew on 6 August and until then we (our squadron) carried on business as usual. I was scheduled to fly again on the 7th and when I went home the day before, I fully expected to.

Around 1000, while I was preparing for my sortie, I noticed all the lines had been cancelled. [Lines are the flights listed on the board in a squadron's operations area. It lists take-off times, crews, and other data needed to see at a glance what the near-term flying schedule will be.]

Normally, the only time that happens so early is because of a serious aircraft accident or to signal the start of an exercise. Since we were already scheduled for a mobility/deployment exercise, I figured that's what it might be. I couldn't believe that the brass was considering sending the Weasels to war.

After all, George is scheduled to close at the end of 1992 and there is no follow-on base for the F-4G nor is there a replacement aircraft in the works. For all practical purposes, it has been decided that the Wild Weasel will retire.

At noon on the 7th, the squadron commander, Lt Col Walton, called us all in to tell us that we were going to deploy, ostensibly, to Mt Home AFB, Idaho, for an undetermined amount of time. I don't think anyone was fooled by that, and I don't think Col Walton thought we would. He was merely telling us what he was told to tell us, but the military has always been very secretive about what it's doing even when the truth is obvious. We were also told to pack our mobility bags, except this time with more than the minimum amount of holey underwear and socks.

I have been in the Air Force for almost ten years and I have never been told to do that. This was serious and everyone knew it.

I went home that night thinking that I was going to war tomorrow and knowing that I was not at all prepared either physically or emotionally. Who was going to take care of my house? How was I going to pay my bills? What was I going to tell my family and friends?

As I began drinking my normal after work beer, the whole concept of this situation was beginning to sink in. I had to get to work or I might drink myself into oblivion.

First off, I quickly jotted down a brief note to my mother telling her that 'I am leaving for a classified location where I may be going to war and, oh, by the way, here is my check book and will you please pay my bills while I'm gone?' Setting that aside, I began to pack my bag.

The basic stuff was easy; after all we had a list of exactly what was required right down to six pairs of white socks with no stripes. Were they kidding? Who cares what your socks look like when you're in the middle of a war? I guess they figure some important military secret will be given away if we're captured wearing socks with purple and black stripes on them. Well, being in the military, I knew that some things you don't question so I packed my six pairs of all-white socks that I had purchased several years back and that were still in the plastic bag.

However, six pairs of socks wouldn't be enough so I also packed my white socks with stripes. *Gee, I hope I don't get captured with those on!*

The sock situation all sorted out, I also packed everything else on the list plus civilian clothes, a book, magazines, and whatever else I could think of that I could cram into an A-4 bag. Sixty pounds and an hour later I had that finished.

Now the easy part. My next door neighbour, Chip Moore, works on the base as a civilian technician for our electronics branch. He is also in the National Guard and so is aware of how the military works. He knew something was afoot and so wasn't too surprised when I told him I needed someone to look after my house for an unspecified time. Still, the look of concern on his face made me a little more apprehensive.

His wife was also concerned, but for some reason Chip didn't want his wife to hear the rest of our conversation so we adjourned to my house for another beer. I told him what I needed done and he agreed to look after my house and wished me well.

Up to this point I was wondering what to tell my mother since I didn't know exactly where or when I was going, or how she would take this. She had always been concerned whenever she heard about an aircraft accident so I knew she wasn't going to like the idea of me going to war. What mother would? I took the easy way out and decided I would just let her know through the mail.

SCHREINER, (WEDNESDAY) 8 AUGUST 1990

I slept in since we were told to wait by the phone until called. As I was watching a press conference with Dick Cheney [Secretary of Defense] and General Colin Powell [Chairman of the Joint Chiefs of Staff (JCS)], I got a phone call to come in but I didn't have to bring my mobility bag with me.

I was beginning to wonder what was going on? At least we weren't going today so I was relieved. Now I could tie up more loose ends regarding bills and such.

During the day we were given several briefings on the current situation as well as some quick refresher academics on some of our newer hardware. Captain 'MikeBob' Conner, our squadron weapons officer, was happier than a pig in shit. He had orchestrated the entire day's briefings and he was in charge.

At around 1500, we were dismissed but told to return at 1600 for a briefing from the wing commander. That was all the time I needed to get my powers of attorney done, get extra soap and other toiletries, and finish some last-minute banking.

1608 and the wing commander still hasn't arrived. Oh well, Air Force regulations don't require superior officers to be on time for meetings with those of lesser rank. Besides, he probably had more pressing things to worry about.

1610 and we are called to attention for the arrival of the colonel. He told us 'warriors' to take our seats almost immediately. While he had always referred to us as 'the last of the warriors' as opposed to 'shoe clerks' and 'bean counters' as all the support people are known, he usually waited until he was seated before allowing us to sit. That small gesture made me feel a little special.

We were given a brief outline of how we were going to deploy and told that we were going to Dubai in the United Arab Emirates and that this place had little more than a runway and a lot of sand so we would be sleeping in tents and eating MREs [Meals Ready to Eat].

Oh, boy! I get to go to the fucking desert, get shot at, sleep in a tent with fifty other guys, eat freeze-dried food and, basically, have a shitty time. Oh, and by the way, alcohol of any kind is strictly forbidden in any Muslim country so forget about drinking any cold beer for a while. At least I would get to fly a jet over and get some more flying time in the F-4 before the shooting starts.

We will deploy out on Friday and tomorrow maintenance will load all the jets.

SCHREINER, (THURSDAY) 9 AUGUST 1990

I thought I was flying a jet over but thanks to some straphanger, I was bumped and now get to fly on a transport. Oh well, I guess nineteen hours in a web seat is better than fifteen hours in an F-4 cockpit…isn't it?

Maintenance has finally loaded all twenty-four aircraft with three external fuel tanks, three AIM-7Fs, and two AGM-88 HARMs. We couldn't hope for a better load-out. All the stories we heard about how we would be lucky to get Shrikes and *any* air-to-air missiles were just people talking out of their asses.

1600 – The final intell[igence] update and brief over for the flying aircrews. They are sent home into crew rest. Just as well I'm not flying, I didn't want to get up for a 0400 report time anyway.

Those of us not flying out in the morning are also sent home and told we will be leaving sometime tomorrow afternoon. So we just go home and sit by the phone and wait. And wait. And wait.

At 1900, I was called and told that the operation had been slipped twenty-four hours.

SCHREINER, (FRIDAY) 10 AUGUST 1990

We're called in and told by Lt Col Walton that we've been slipped twenty-four hours because our original destination has been cancelled. It seems Oman, the original destination of the [McDonnell-Douglas] F-15Es, 'Mud Hens' [officially Strike Eagle], refused to allow the F-15Es to land there, contrary to their original agreement, so the F-15Es took our place at Dubai.

Even though they said twenty-four hours they really meant forty-eight, but that doesn't matter because we've been put on seven days a week full-time. Oh joy! We've lost our weekends and we don't even have a union to bitch to, nor do we get any overtime.

Well, nobody said it would be easy and it is certainly not the first time I've had to work on weekends.

In any event, the plan now is for the twenty-four F-4s to leave on Sunday 12 August at 0800 and for us non-fliers to leave sometime Sunday evening. We're promised at least two hours' notice before we have to out-process.

Schreiner, (Sunday) 12 August 1990

0800 – Actually slept well the night before and awoke a few minutes ago. As is usual for the mornings here, it's cool and the winds are calm.

At precisely 0800, the stillness is broken by the distant roar of afterburner ignition. Even though George AFB is some ten miles away, the sound is very clear. It's an ominous sound, one that removes any doubt as to whether or not we are actually going to the Middle East.

I rushed outside with my camera knowing the planned route of flight will take each of the four cells of six aircraft somewhere overhead, even though they should be well over 10,000 feet by the time they pass.

Unfortunately, calm winds usually means morning haze, which doesn't burn off until well after 10 a.m. So even though I can hear the planes fly over, I can't see them. Up until this point, I don't think the sound of jet engines has ever made me feel so alone or so unsure about what will happen.

2000 – Since I haven't heard the phone ring all day, I figure I'd better call and find out what's going on. When I do, I'm told there is no airlift and none in sight, so just stay by the phone and we'll call you.

For the next few days everyone waiting on airlift is on pins and needles waiting for the airlift. We all know we're going, but not when. I can only imagine what people's families are going through. The emotional roller coaster must be awful. At least I don't have to deal with that.

Schreiner, (Wednesday) 15 August 1990

Col Abler, the Deputy Commander for Operations (the DO), has called us in for another situation update.

At this point, I'm expecting him to tell us that our deployment overseas has been cancelled and that our F-4s, which have been waiting in North Carolina, will return. I have obvious mixed feelings about that prospect.

On the one hand, like most fighter pilots, I was looking forward to going to war. After all, that's what I had trained to do for almost ten years. On the other hand, who in their right mind wants to be shot at?

The wing commander had told us that butterflies in the stomach was normal when going into combat. Butterflies, shit! I'd had birds flying around in my stomach.

Col Abler put any doubts I had about going to rest. He explained that the Air Force had finally decided where we were going and that airlift would finally be available, but he still didn't know when. It could be tomorrow or it could be next week. Great! Let's all get back on that roller coaster.

Chapter Five

What Schreiner and the other Weasels didn't know was the behind the scenes efforts by the United States' highest leaders to put together a coalition of Allied nations, including many of the Persian Gulf area nations, to deter further aggression by Saddam's forces.

With little effort in the early days of August 1990, Saddam's forces could have rolled further south into Saudi Arabia and after only 100 miles of combat through lightly equipped and inexperienced Saudi ground forces, found themselves in possession of the Saudi oil fields. Iraqi armour in those oil fields would have given Saddam control of more than a quarter of the world's oil supply. That was a threat that neither the US nor the rest of the industrialised world could accept.

With that threat in mind, the senior US military leaders had to put a credible defence into Saudi Arabia as quickly as possible. With the exception of one brigade of the Army's 82d Airborne Division who called themselves 'speedbumps', no American forces could get there faster than air power.

The first Air Force squadron presence would be the air-to-air F-15C, followed quickly by air-to-ground F-16s and the dual-role F-15E. To protect them in the event that shooting broke out, the Weasels had to deploy quickly as well. Unfortunately, the concept of American forces based upon Arab soil was a hard one for many of the Middle East's leaders to get their minds around. The thought that they might be next on Saddam's list eventually persuaded most of them to the basing.

This political chess game is what delayed the pawns that were the Weasels, waiting anxiously in North Carolina and California to continue east.

On 16 August 1990, the jets sitting on the ramp at Seymour-Johnson

AFB, North Carolina, finally got the word to 'go!' There was still confusion right up to the crews stepping onto the jets as to where they'd land. Many of them, in fact, didn't know where they'd touch down at the other end of the fifteen-hour flight.

Squadron commander, then Lt Col, George 'John Boy' Walton had taken command of the 561st only four days after the Iraqi invasion of Kuwait. The squadron had already been placed on alert for immediate deployment, so his spin up for command was, of necessity, brief.

As noted above, on 12 August 1990, Walton led the squadron to Seymour-Johnson AFB, North Carolina, to wait its turn for aerial refuelling support, and more importantly, final word on where they'd land.

The four days waiting in steamy summertime North Carolina quickly became old. Since the jets were carrying a full warload of weapons and fuel tanks, space for personal items was scarce. For peacetime deployments, each jet normally carried a travel pod on one of the underwing hardpoints. This pod was an empty casing for carrying aircraft and landing gear safing pins as well as spare flight suits and a change or two of civilian clothes. (Of course, coming back from exotic locations, the pods had been known to carry back a bottle or two of the local adult beverages.)

For this war deployment, however, there was only one pod for every two jets. Filled with the paraphernalia needed for war, there wasn't much room for four crewmembers' stuff. Thus, sitting in the American South in the summer soon overwhelmed the single flight suit and the few changes of underwear.

Finally, on 16 August, the 561st commander was told he'd be flying to Sheikh Isa, Bahrain. He'd never heard of the place, and for good reason. It had literally been completed in the previous weeks and wasn't marked on any published aeronautical charts.

Walton says he was handed a satellite image of the base as he was stepping to his jet. No information on runway length, tower frequencies, nothing, nada, zip. That single piece of paper was all he had to go on in taking his squadron to war. With four cells of six F-4Gs, he launched in the dark, early morning hours to start the long fighter drag.

A fighter drag is the name for getting the short-legged tactical fighters to the scene of the action many thousands of miles away. Most

A flight of Weasels getting gas. A very common sight during DESERT STORM. Gas was nearly always at the top of list of concerns for the crews. (USAF)

times, a dedicated tanker or two would provide both the needed fuel and the navigation services from start to finish during a drag.

The unforeseen demands of the massive *Desert Shield* airlift bridge with everything from fighters to monstrous C-5s shuttling constantly to and from the desert demanded a more efficient method of getting gas to the customers. In the Weasels' case, they flew a complex plan involving multiple sets of tankers.

Meeting up with their tankers near Plattsburgh, New York, each six ship had three Boeing KC-135 Stratotankers to draw fuel from. After draining nos 2 and 3 dry, they flew a loose formation on the remaining tanker until about the mid-Atlantic point where tankers flown from RAF Mildenhall in Britain took over.

This set of airborne gas stations dragged the Weasels to the Azores Islands where a third set rendezvoused. Near Sicily, a fourth cell of

Fighter drag: here a no-doubt tired Weasel crew approaches the boom of the
McDonnell-Douglas KC-10 'Extender' tanker for another in an endless
series of aerial refuelings required to get from the States to the fight. The
canisters on the inboard pylons are travel pods as mentioned in the text.
(DoD photo via Guy Aceto)

tankers joined up and flew them down to the Red Sea where a final set of tankers topped off the fighters.

This 15.6-hour flight strapped into the butt-numbing, non-cushioned, non-adjustable Martin-Baker Mark H7 ejection seat required each F-4G to fly the intricate, but vital, dance of aerial refuelling twenty-one times!

First performed in 1921 by a wing walker climbing out of one bi-plane onto the wing of another carrying a can of fuel, aerial refuelling has come a long way since then.

Tests and stunts during the 1920s and 1930s improved somewhat the techniques of keeping an aircraft aloft by transferring fuel. Indeed, in 1930, the record stood at 647.5 hours for a single mission. More than twenty-seven days in a cramped, smelly, extremely loud cockpit! As gruelling as the Weasels' non-stop flight from the United States to Bahrain was, it pales in comparison although the total distances covered were similar in both cases.

During the 1940s, the two main techniques of passing gas from a tanker aircraft to a receiver came into being. One, used today by US Navy and Marine Corps aircraft as well as many NATO and other foreign air forces, is the 'probe and drogue' method. In this procedure, the tanker trails a refuelling hose with a cone-shaped basket at the end. The receiver has a metal probe with an inlet valve and that pilot flies his aircraft into position to insert the probe into the basket. Once contact is achieved, the tanker turns on its pumps and fuel flows into the thirsty jet's tanks albeit at a slower rate than in the second method.

Most USAF jets, on the other hand, use the 'flying boom' method of taking gas. In this method, the tanker lowers a boom with a retractable pipe after the receiver aircraft lines up in position just below and just aft of the tanker. The boom operator in the tanker then 'flies' the boom into a receptacle in the receiver. On the F-4, the receptacle is located on the top of the fuselage several feet behind the rear cockpit.

The tanker aircraft has to fly a smooth profile with gentle turns while the receiver flies in close formation on the tanker using known points of reference to hold position. Each Weasel pilot had his own technique for determining what those points were, but as long as he got the jet in tight and held it there, the 'boomer' could plug the Phantom and pump gas. At night, specially placed director lights on the tanker's belly helped the receiver determine his position.

Another close-up of a Weasel driver concentrating on getting gas at 24,000 feet. Of note, is the older style 'bone dome' aircrew helmet. (DoD photo via Guy Aceto)

Although he did not fly one of the F-4G's to Bahrain, Dave Lucia described his technique for taking gas:

In the F-4, the canopy bow was right in your line of sight for looking at the tanker and gauging your reference points. I'd run my seat up higher than normal to be able to see over the bow just prior to the AAR (air-to-air refuelling).

I'd move into pre-contact position about 50 feet below the tanker, matching the tanker's speed and heading, then once stabilised and cleared into contact either via the radio if in peace-time or via visual signals if working under EMCON (emission conditions – no radio transmissions).

The boomer would then plug into the jet and I'd adjust my rearview mirror on the canopy bow to see the 'apple,' a bright orange painted ball on the boom just ahead of the end of the boom itself. If I kept that centred in the mirror, I knew I stayed within the limits of the boom and could stay on there with constant, minor control inputs.

Some of the tricks Schreiner used to get gas were similar.

I'd run my seat up high to see the director lights above the bow and use the mirrors to fly the apple. Unfortunately for me, when I ran the seat up, it was hard for me to reach the rudder pedals.

If I was down to around 3,000 lb of fuel it could take nearly ten minutes to fill both the internal and three external 'bags'. (Aircraft fuel is measured in pounds, not gallons. This convention makes it easier to do fuel burn/flight time remaining calculations vital to the relatively short-legged fighters.)

I'd have to keep trimming during that time as the AOA (angle of attack – essentially the angle between where the wing is pointing and where it is going) keeps increasing.

Self-portrait of the co-author at work in the cockpit of his F-4G. (Jim Schreiner)

Eventually, the AOA could become so great that the leading edge slats (airfoils on the outer leading edges of the F-4's wing, used to increase lift at slow speeds) would deploy automatically. Because they deployed so quickly, the jet's pitch changed drastically and it was easy to overcorrect into a PIO (pilot induced oscillation) and fall off the boom. Since getting gas and getting out of the way so the next guy could plug in is your goal, this is not a good thing to have happen.

I'd usually manually lock the slats in prior to AAR to avoid that happening. I learned about that the hard way during the war. Nobody had told me about it, and I'd never taken on that much gas during training so didn't see it then either.

Anyway, as we got topped off, the three 'full' lights on the canopy bow would illuminate once the externals were full and they didn't fill until the internal tanks were full, so you knew you were crammed with as much as you could take. Once I got the three lights, I'd disconnect and drop down to assume tactical formation again off the tanker's wing.

Normally, aerial refuelling is done at 310 knots. This speed is a good compromise for most jets in that it provides enough control authority to make the fine corrections needed to stay on the boom yet is not too fast that any errors magnify instantly into catastrophe.

However, human beings being fallible, sometimes the tanker crew flew a few knots too slowly resulting in higher AOA and thus drag or the refuelling had to take place higher than the desired 20–24,000 feet altitude range. Any or all of these factors might force the F-4G receiver to actually use afterburner while hanging on the boom. As the fighter grew heavier taking on gas, as described above, its AOA increased to maintain the required lift. Add in a slower speed and/or higher altitude where the 'lifties' were less effective, and the only solution was for the Phantom pilot to place one engine, usually the left, into minimum afterburner to compensate for the loss of lift and/or speed and jockey the other throttle with the many small adjustments to stay on the boom.

Naturally, using afterburner used a lot more gas since fuel flow in afterburner was more than tripled compared with non-afterburning, or military, thrust. Also, if the refuelling was at night, nothing gave away the element of surprise more than a sustained Roman candle streaking through the dark sky. Tactically, therefore, this was not a preferred option. It was better than running out of gas, however.

Major Tom Gummo was one of those who did fly the long hop with all the refuelling on that initial deployment. Gummo, a veteran F-4 driver in all its variants – C, D, E, and G models – was on the way to his first war. Unfortunately, his wingman's jet developed a severe oil leak and Gummo had to divert with him to Lajes Air Base in the Azores as a precaution.

Upon landing, besides the hassle of dealing with a sick jet, Gummo had to contend with a base and security police commander that hadn't quite made the switch to a wartime mode.

In 1990, the Air Force was in the midst of changing the aircrew personal sidearm; for decades it had been the puny Smith & Wesson .38 calibre revolver. Never known for its stopping power, it was considered a toy by most that carried it. The 561st, however, while delaying in North Carolina, had managed to acquire the new Beretta 9-mm semi-auto pistol. A little meatier in the 'oomph' department as well as carrying up to fifteen rounds per clip, it definitely was a step up from the .38.

The documentation to carry firearms was at George where the crews had given their gun cards, a bureaucratic requirement to prove the gun bearer was trained on the weapon, to the Security Police (SP) armoury in exchange for the .38s.

At Seymour-Johnson AFB, the crews managed to acquire the new 9-mm gun; even having the local SPs conduct a special training class and firing range exercise on the new gun. Of course, the paperwork on the new weapons was not up to speed, but in the rush to war, it wasn't considered a big deal.

Except, apparently, at Lajes. In addition to having to coordinate maintenance help being flown into the field since Lajes was primarily a long haul transit base and not a fighter field, Gummo had the issue of securing both crews' sidearms. Normally, they left the guns in the jet and depended on the SPs who guarded the flightline to ensure no one unauthorised rifled through the jets. The Lajes security police commander, however, wouldn't let them do that.

So, Gummo had to schlep the pistols to the base armoury and store them there. Normally, no problem, but since neither he nor any of the other waylaid Weasels had the proper documentation to carry the 9-mm guns, the armoury wouldn't release the guns back to the crews after the ailing F-4G was fixed, eight days later. Indeed, the officious SP commander tried to arrest the two crews for carrying unauthorised weapons. A phone call to the one star base commander cleared up the arrest, but not the issue of letting the crews get their guns.

After much gnashing of teeth, Gummo said 'screw it'. They flew on to meet up with the rest of the 561st and prepared for combat. In an unbelievable postscript, those guns stayed at Lajes for months, eventually being shipped back to George AFB to await the end of the war. Gummo and company used the dinky .38s after all. This was but the start of a frustrating war for Tom Gummo.

Meanwhile, during the initial drag from the States, another F-4G developed an in-flight problem and it and the wingman diverted into Spain. Walton eventually landed at the brand new Sheikh Isa Air Base with twenty jets, not sure if the war would start the next day.

Chapter Six

0730 – I answer the phone and am told that transport is here and to come in at 1300. I get to the squadron around 1230. Yeah, the transport is here, but it's not ours. I knew they'd fuck this up. Everyone jumping through their ass and, as usual, no one really knows what's going on. Oh well, hurry up and wait.

Finally, they send us through the out-processing line starting at 1500.

Shots, shots, and more shots. Throughout my career, I've gotten a number of different shots at recurring intervals. Back on August 3d, I got an overdue typhoid shot and my arm hurt for three days.

Last week I got a butt shot of gamma globulin (GG) – supposedly for hepatitis. Bill Beckinger, one of our squadron EWOs, told me that the shot was noted in my records and those were the last ones I'd need. He should know as that's his additional squadron duty.

But noooo! First, he forgot to note in my shot record that I got the butt shot. Second, he forgot to tell me I needed a tetanus shot. That fucker . . .

After much gnashing of teeth, I managed to get out of the GG shot, but couldn't find any proof for the tetanus vaccination.

Ouch! I'll be sore for another three days.

1700 – After two more hours of briefings, equipment issue and mostly waiting around, we walk out to the plane. We're in luck! We didn't get a [Lockheed] C-141 with web seats, instead we got the much larger [Lockheed] C-5 with real airline type seats. Damn! I was looking forward to those web seats.

As we were getting seated, the chief 'warrior,' the wing commander came aboard to wish us luck and see us off.

'But wait, Sir, aren't you coming with us?' Guess not on this load . . .

Soon after take-off, we are given our first of many in-flight meals. The ever popular 'box lunches' consist mainly of:

- 2, each, plain bologna or ham and cheese sandwiches, dry

- one can, Coke, warm

- one each, mustard and mayonnaise packet

- one each, candy bar, bite size

- one each, napkin

- one each, can opener, church key style; the kind found now in museums from the days before fliptop cans and twist-off bottles

We're off to war as part of the most powerful and modern Air Force in the world and they give us cold, dry sandwiches. American Airlines has nothing to worry about!

Twenty-nine hours and two stops later, we begin our descent into the island nation of Bahrain. Military Airlift Command (MAC) flies to thousands of different locations around the world; daily delivering people and cargo from Anchorage to Zaire, safely and efficiently. But then this. The C-5's navigator walks back and asks us if we know where we're supposed to land. You gotta be shittin' me!

You morons took off from Torrejon, Spain, some 3,000 miles away and you didn't know where you were going? I've been lost a couple of times and I've flown into airspace that I shouldn't have, but I've always known where I'm supposed to land!

Apparently Sheikh Isa Air Base in Bahrain is a brand new base on the southern tip of the island whose location is classified, but that's why they give us pretty pink covered approach plates that contain information on places such as this. I guess that's why these guys fly transports and why they put so many of them on an airplane. Hopefully, one of them has a clue.

Anyway, the landing was uneventful. It's 0800 local time on Saturday, the 18th of August and as I got off the aircraft the first thing I noticed after the wall of heat was the lack of anything around except a control tower and a few hangars. Boy, when they say 'bare base', they mean it!

No trees, no grass, very little vegetation of any kind, just sand and rocks. And people fight over this?

This definitely is a brand new facility. There aren't even any grease stains on the hangar floor. So far, I haven't seen any tents; that's always a good sign.

After waiting about an hour, we're met by one of the 561st's pilots. He'd arrived the previous evening with the rest of the Phantoms.

He took us to our operations building, which is also used by the Bahraini Air Force (BAAF) for their F-16 and F-5 operations. I ran into an old student of mine, George 'Lindy' Lindsted. I'd

A two ship over Bahrain. (USAF)

last seem him at Columbus AFB, Mississippi, back in 1983 when I was an IP [Instructor Pilot] there. He had gotten an A-10 out of there and was now an F-16 instructor on exchange with the BAAF. I would never have expected that.

After a few in-briefings, we were then taken to our new quarters, approximately three miles away. Our transportation consisted of one of dozens of Dodge pick-up trucks that had been in storage somewhere for some eight years. It seemed ironic to be riding in a 1982 truck covered with eight years of accumulated dust that had only 300 miles on it.

Our quarters were nothing if not cramped. They were designed to house two people each in a space something under 100 feet square. Each of the two floors had twenty-six rooms plus a small lounge and a shared bathroom with four stalls and four showers – all very reminiscent of a college dorm.

At least they are air conditioned and not bug-infested, and they sure beat the hell out of tents! Now if they only have beer at the O'Club.

For more practical issues, like refuelling and servicing the F-4Gs, Sheikh Isa's brand new status presented some unique challenges. Upon arriving and chocking the jets with sandbags, the first order of business that Walton had was to get gas into the Phantoms.

There were no fuel storage tanks on the base yet and only one refuelling truck. So that truck had to make many trips to and from the southern end of Bahrain where Isa lay up to the northern end to the port city of Manama for fuel. With each truckload only filling about one and half jets per load, the reader can do the maths to see that something better had to be found. Eventually, it was, but for the first few weeks in-theatre, getting gas was a major headache.

Sheikh Isa simply wasn't ready to refuel the jets and to do the other required maintenance just to keep them operational. With a long runway of 13,000 feet but only a single parallel taxiway, there was nowhere to park and work on the fighters that wasn't in the way. Not to mention exposed to the blisteringly hot sun of the Middle East in August.

Exacerbating the parking problem was the influx in the next several weeks of the entire 3d Marine Air Wing. With nearly seventy McDonnell-Douglas (now Boeing) F/A-18 Hornets, and Grumman

A-6 Intruder medium bombers, the taxiway was a traffic jam waiting to happen. The solution for the initial few months was to fold the wings, including those of the F-4s, and park the jets in short rows of four or five, leaving just enough room on the outside to form a lane for a taxiing jet to proceed. In peacetime, the proximity of the aircraft along with live munitions and cramped space was a recipe for disaster. The immediate threat of war sharpened everyone's mind to keep the danger uppermost and no serious accidents occurred.

SCHREINER, (SATURDAY) AUGUST 18 1990 D = 0

Welcome to the Sheikh Isa Officers' Club. Notice that I didn't say bar. This place is as dry as any county in the Bible Belt on Sunday. While alcohol is permitted off base – one of the few Arab countries to allow this – it is forbidden to drink on base anywhere. This has been decreed by the base commander who, while only a major, is given the equivalent rank of a two star

During the early days of the Weasels' deployment to Shaikh Isa, the crowded conditions are clearly evident in this photo. But there were no serious accidents during the entire deployment. (USAF)

general. What the hell, Libya's leader is only a colonel so I guess rank structure takes on a new meaning in the Arab world.

How about going off base then? Wrong!

We are restricted to base UFN – until further notice. Understandable, however, once the restriction is lifted we can only go off base in 'civvies', and only in a non-military vehicle. Ok, I packed a set of civvies, but did anyone manage to get their car into their A-4 bag?

Dinner is a treat to look forward to. On the first night, they served a rather bland salad – akin to coleslaw without the 'cole', i.e., no dressing. Some sort of mystery meat, I think it was lamb, and rice and vegetables. Actually, it wasn't too bad. And it was free.

The base is somewhat complete what with a barber, also free,

The US Marine portion of the Sheik Isa Air Base ramp. An extremely crowded operational area indeed. (Gary Rattray)

and a small shoppette where one can buy simple necessities. They don't take American Express, but they do take American dollars. The only problem is figuring the exchange rate.

Officially, it is somewhere around 3.5 to 4 dinars to one dollar but in reality it seems to be determined by whomever is sitting behind the cash register. And since all the coins and paper are in Arabic, I have no idea what I'm getting back.

SCHREINER, (SUNDAY) 19 AUGUST 1990 D + 1

Breakfast is somewhat unique if not simple – all the plain cheese sandwiches you want plus juice and coffee.

Not much to see at Sheik Isa. Flat, bleak and nearly featureless. The 'Weasel Dome,' the off-duty all-purpose hang-out of both air and ground crews is the large building in the distance. (Gary Rattray)

Not much happened today except for a few briefings.

Oh, and by the way, the Marines have decided they want to emplace some 100+ aircraft along with 5,000 troops here.

Great! The base was designed to accommodate 800 people and now we're planning to bring in over 6,000. No wonder so many other countries don't like us; we abuse their hospitality. I hope the Marines bring their tents.

SCHREINER, (MONDAY) 20 AUGUST 1990 D + 2

Nope, the Marine tents aren't here so they'll just have to move in with us. No problem, just double up. I'm glad I've got a bed because that floor looks awfully hard.

Of all the things we as Americans take for granted, toilet paper is probably high on the list. In most Arab countries, the use of TP is not considered clean, probably because they don't have many trees.

Rather, they will use their left hands for 'cleaning' and wash the left hand in water provided. More modern facilities provide a hand-held faucet in the stall. Presumably they use the 'butt wash' as they go along. How they dry afterwards is still a mystery to me.

The use of their left hand in this way is why it is considered an insult to touch someone else with it. One doesn't eat, wave, or write with the left hand.

In any event, I guess as a courtesy to those less civilised in toilet habits, such as ourselves, they have provided us with TP holders and a very limited supply of TP. Needless to say, four rolls every two days doesn't wipe very many asses. Hopefully, along with all the bullets, bombs, and missiles, someone will have enough foresight to send us some toilet paper.

As trivial as the toilet paper comments sound, the logistics involved for moving American, and later Allied nations, into the theatre were simply astounding. Nearly every soldier, Marine, and airman was flown in, as were thousands of tons of supplies – ranging from the aforementioned TP to parts to telephones. Airlift was quick, but

CODE WORDS	DATE: 21 FEB 91	ATO. K	MODE ONES ZULU TIMES

WOLFPACK	CANX ENTIR OPERATION	CHOP OFF-STATION	
CLAW	CANX MISSION	QUACK SYSTEM DOWN	0000- 22
REFILL	CHATTERMARK		
RIDGE	RTB	BASE COORDS 1100N 03100E	0100-
8/8000'	BASE #/ALT.	BASE FREQ 285.0	
FLAG	BADDLE DAMAGE ACFT	BASE HDG/SPD 80	0200- 13 0500L 13
SAR RADIO FREQS-----ALPHA 263.500		BRAVO 291.750	0300-

FUNCTION	CALL SIGN	OLY 04 CODE	FREQ	
				0400-
ABCCC EAST	ALLEYCAT	GOLD 15/TAD 250	331.05/356.375	0500-
WEST	REBEL	GOLD 15/TAD 07	331.05/371.225	
				0600-
ACE DIRECTOR	HAMMER	GOLD 1/GRAY1	289.925/7514	
RIVET JOINT	VACCUUM	GOLD 3	252.3	0700-
		GOLD 5	378.25	
		GOLD 4	341.7	0800- 50 1100L 50
(ZW) RED CROWN PIRAZ CHK IN		SILVER 7	391.25	
BF ZULU FAD 6 COMMON		SILVER 12	284.975	0900-
DHARAHN CRC	SHOTGLASS	RED 7	350.1	
KKMC CRC	BLENDER	CHERRY 7	370.75	1000-
AL JUBAYL USMC TAOC	COCONUT	CORAL 3	230.4	
				1100-
HVAAA EC COORD/P WEST/CENT/EAST		GOLD 8/10/12		
/S WEST/CENT/EAST		GOLD 9/11/13		1200-
(HF/AWACS) WEST/CENT/EAST		GRAY 11/12/10		
TANKER CONTROL/P WEST/CENT/EAST		CANARY 1/AMBER 1/YELLOW 1		1300-
/S WEST/CENT/EAST		CANARY 2/AMBER 2/YELLOW 2		
				1400- 63

AWACS C/S	WEST. COUGAR		CENT. BUCKEYE		EAST. BULLDOG		1500-
FUNCTION	CODE	FREQ	CODE	FREQ	CODE	FREQ	1600-
CHK IN /P	SCARLET4	335.125	CHERRY4	257.125	RED 4	373.875	1700-
/S	5	311.775	5	307.125	5	354.875	
OCA CAP /HQ	RUBY 8	A20.650	RUBY 5	A20.450	RUBY 2	A20.250	1800-
/P	VIOLET 1	236.825	PURPLE1	319.425	BLUE 1	229.95	
/S	2	347.55	2	377.05	2	310.6	1900-
DCA CAP /HQ	RUBY 7	A00.550	RUBY 4	A00.350	RUBY 1	A00.150	
/P	VIOLET 3	255.95	PURPLE3	301.05	BLUE 3	348.15	2000- 51
/S	4	240.625	4	354.425	4	370.275	
STRIKE /HQ	RUBY 9	A33.350	RUBY 6	A32.250	RUBY 3	A31.150	2100-
/P	SCARLET1	246.45	CHERRY1	274.375	RED 1	271.0	
/S	2	267.975	2	311.4	2	256.275	2200-
/T	3	306.9	3	349.5	3	392.3	
							2300-

MISSION DATA	TANKER (PR)	HAVE QUICK	TANKER (POST)	
MSN# 5403 W	MSN# 6656	20- 243.550	MSN# 6642/6643	0000-
C/S OLY 03	C/S Pike 56	19- 230.100	C/S Pike 42/SALAIN 43	
MODE2 5403	OFFLOAD	18- 227.100	OFFLOAD	0100-
MODE3 5473	MODE2 6656	17- 243.900	MODE2 6642/6643	
AREA Kuwait	MODE3 3032	16- 278.900	MODE3 3034/3037	0200- 12
TOT/TOS	TRACK RR Post	15- 374.500	TRACK RR Post	
ALT.	ARCT 0805-0945	14- 321.000	ARCT 0955/1150	0300-
REMARKS	ALT 23.0	RESERVE NET	ALT 21.0/23.5	
	FREQ Yel 15/16	FOR 35 TFW	FREQ Yel 15/16	0400-
	A/A TAC 16/79	RUBY 18-A19.3	A/A TAC 16/79	

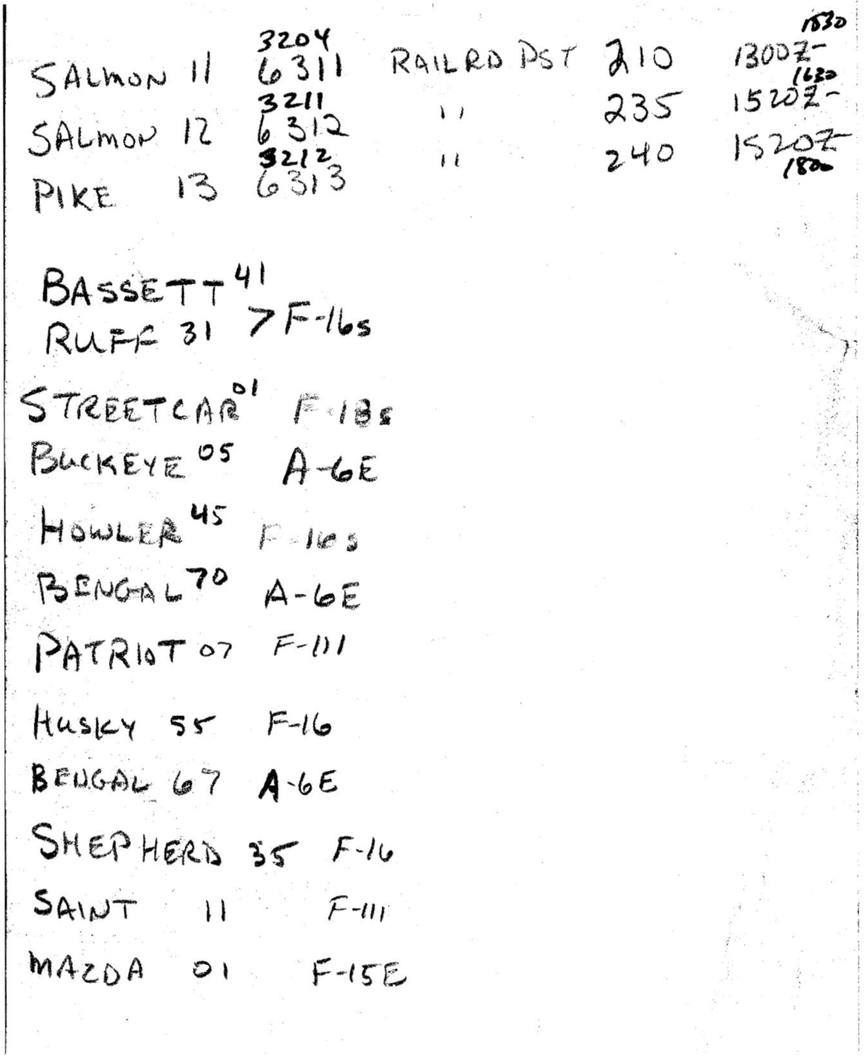

SALMON 11   3204   RAILRD PST 210   13002⁻
            6311
            3211
SALMON 12   6312   ''   235   15202⁻
            3212
PIKE   13   6313   ''   240   15202⁻

(handwritten notes: 1530, 1630, 1800)

BASSETT 41
RUFF 31   7 F-16s

STREETCAR 01   F-18s
BUCKEYE 05   A-6E
HOWLER 45   F-16s
BENGAL 70   A-6E
PATRIOT 07   F-111

HUSKY 55   F-16
BENGAL 67   A-6E
SHEPHERD 35   F-16
SAINT 11   F-111
MAZDA 01   F-15E

Listing of supported flights during a 'Weasel Police' mission of Joe Healy's. By knowing callsigns and times of various strike packages, the Weasels could cover many missions instead of being tied to supporting only one. But, it could make for a confusing situation if things got busy. (Joe Healy)

(Opposite) Just ONE page of the communications listing for a typical mission. Confusing enough when sitting at a desk at 1 'g,' but imagine trying to decipher it at night while keeping an eye out for the enemy. (Joe Healy)

expensive and couldn't take really big loads of divisions of tanks, armoured personnel carriers, trucks, etc. Bulk equipment and supplies used deep draft shipping, but at the expense of long sea voyages.

At what became Coalition headquarters in Riyadh, Saudi Arabia, the initial CENTAF (Central Command Air Force) planners lacked computer support and all planning had to be done with pen and paper. The use of desktop and laptop computers was relatively new to the military then and the logistics planning hadn't caught up to the technological reality. For many weeks, the crucial CENTAF computers were stuck at the US-based 9th Air Force Headquarters because the computers were considered low priority compared with 'bullets and beans' needed for war. The 9th AF became CENTAF when deployed into theatre and had become very proficient and efficient in using computers to generate an Air Tasking Order (ATO).

The ATO became the 'bible' for all military aviation in the area of responsibility (AOR). The ATO concept, still in use today, is designed to make the best use of available assets to strike targets deemed most important to the theatre commander. From that priority, all the support missions needed to get strikers to targets – AWACS (Airborne Warning and Control System), tankers, reconnaissance, etc. – are planned. The ATO is distributed on a daily basis to the tactical units who take their fragment, called a 'frag', of the ATO and build their local plans to meet the ATO tasking.

Obviously, the ATO is a massive document and building one by hand is a cumbersome, time-consuming effort. Of course, any change to the ATO (and there were dozens, later hundreds, of changes every day as aircraft availability increased or higher priority targets were discovered) involved 'pen and ink' changes that sometimes weren't caught in time. As a result missions were flown when not required or, worse, when no one in headquarters was expecting them since they weren't on the 'new, improved' ATO.

With the computers left in the States, the ATO concept was in jeopardy. So bad did the situation become that Brigadier General 'Buster' Glosson, a 'get the job done' individual, who served as the principal operations director for the duration of the war, purchased some desktop computers from a store in downtown Riyadh with his own money. He was eventually reimbursed for those computers.

KUWAIT	POLICE

✗3 F-4 FLIGHT LINEUP/MISSION DATA WORD: **5431**

CALL SIGN	STEP **-5**	START	TAKEOFF	JOKER **11**	BINGO **10**
SCHLITZ **35**	1590	1610	1690	D2 **8**	

AREA/RANGE–TIME	FREQ/SECONDARY FREQ	TANK C/S	FREQ/SEC
1800–1830 1930–2000			

CONF	GW	MAC	TEMP	PA	MINGO	MAX ABT	TRACK	ALT	ARCT
					—	165			

NWLO	T.O./DIST	LAND IMMED 45 A.S./DIST	LAND NORMAL 165 + A.S./DIST	ARIP	ARCT OFFLOAD
175	4.0	180+ 45	165+ 45		

POS	PILOT	IP/WSO		AC – SPOT	CREW NO'S
	Lt Col. Bubba Osborne		238	07y	I 42
36	✓	KAD	263	70Y	70
					II. 5436
				A31,150	III. 5436

REMARKS

RED 4
YELLOW 1/3
YELLOW 15

N

D5
D6
△ 1800 1830 1930
W
E
D4
D3
1754
D2 1924
△ 1325
D34
S

'Line up' card used by most fighter crews; it is a short-hand way to annotate the highlights of any mission. This one depicts one of Joe Healy's missions including the 'flow' of his flight over the target area. (Joe Healy)

SCHREINER, (TUESDAY) 21 AUGUST 1990 D + 3

This *is* a red letter day! Kellogg's Corn Flakes is served for breakfast for the first time. This is, of course, in addition to the ever-present cheese sandwiches. They even put the flakes into a sterling silver bowl to go along with the silver flatware. Is this how to fight a war or what?

Today will also be my first sortie in over two weeks. I didn't think we would fly this week but I guess maintenance has gotten its act together.

Originally, the sortie was planned to go up north, about twenty-five miles from the Kuwait–Iraq border and see what types of radars were on the air. Oh boy! The first Wild Weasel sorties flown in the Middle East and who knows when the shooting will start.

However, as is typical of higher echelon decision-making, no one above the rank of major can decide whether or not we should fly that close to the border. So rather than take a chance our plan is disapproved. Oh, well, I guess we'll just have to practise BVR (beyond visual range) intercepts.

Now I just have to remember not to squeeze the trigger and fire off a live air-to-air missile at my wingman. That logic doesn't apply to F-15s, I guess. [One USAF F-15 wingman shot down his flight lead during the late 1980s while flying with live AIM-9 Sidewinder missiles. The wingman forgot his jet had live weapons, hit the pickle button, and just had time to yell, 'Lead, break right, I hit a Fox 2!' before the AIM-9 hit his flight lead. The pilot survived; the wingman did too, but with a new body orifice.]

Apparently, no one has told the crew chiefs that the war hasn't begun yet because one of them took my picture and another told me to come back with all my missiles expended. He also told us (me and my pitter) that we were the best.

That made me feel good and since my crew chief was psyched, I didn't want to spoil it and tell him what we were really doing.

Chapter Seven

SCHREINER, (TUESDAY) 21 AUGUST 1990 D + 3

The sortie went as planned with no unusual encounters and after we landed we told the crew chiefs what we did and saw. Even though they don't fly, they are always very interested to find out what we did and how 'their' jets flew.

The heart of the jet; here a F-4G crew chief preps his 'baby' at sunset before the crew appears to 'borrow it.' (USAF)

A crew chief 'owns' a jet and is responsible for every aspect of its care and maintenance. He or she babies the airplane, nagging the backroom shops and technicians to fix or replace the items that he doesn't do himself. The aircrew, on the other hand, simply 'borrows' the jet, often flying whichever one is assigned, and thus has less responsibility for that one jet other than how it performs during that flight.

Even at George on the hottest day I can't ever remember sweating as much as I did today. It's so hot out there and the arming crews took longer than normal to arm us up. I must have lost four or five pounds in water; I can imagine how much our over-worked ground crews lose.

Every day more and more transports show up and offload their cargo and passengers. Where is everyone going to sleep? Even in the officers' quarters, we're sleeping three and four to a room. We

An F-4G in its protective revetment is prepped for another DESERT STORM mission. Note the difference between this photo and its look of permanence compared to the early days during Operation DESERT SHIELD as on page 50. (USAF)

even have females living on the same floor and using our bath-rooms.

I like having women around, especially good looking ones, but I still don't like the idea of women in a combat zone. I still haven't gotten used to walking into the men's room and find women there. I guess walking in there or down the hall butt-naked is out of the question.

SCHREINER, 22 AUGUST 1990 D + 4

A new concept in harassment – ALERT!

Here we take eight guys and four airplanes, load them up with special equipment and make them sit around for twenty-four hours waiting for the war to start. At least they let us sleep even if it is in sleeping bags on the floor in the operations building.

Before going on alert, however, one must eat a good breakfast and today the dining hall introduced another new treat – eggs! Yes, hardboiled eggs still in the shell. And fresh? It took me ten minutes or so to peel one out of its shell so aside from the fact that I expended more energy in shelling the egg than I got from eating it, yes, it was pretty good.

On a more dismal note, an Iraqi tanker has decided to run our naval interdiction (we don't call it a blockade, yet) and President Bush has ordered the Navy to stop the ship. Does that mean sink it or just scare them into submission? I guess we'll find out. The big clue will be the klaxon going off at 3 a.m.

What Schreiner couldn't know when he began sitting alert is that the big brass in Riyadh and Washington, DC, didn't know if Iraq was going to roll further south into Saudi Arabia. Every day the ATO was built as essentially a defensive document, detailing each new squadron arriving into a plan to stop Saddam's tanks from gaining the Saudi oil fields. A big part of the effort would be SAM suppression so that the other fighters could start taking out the Iraqi armour and infantry units.

As part of that planning team, Larry Henry (then a brigadier general), a former Weasel EWO and Weasel Wing Commander, was eventually brought in to plan the kick in the door to Saddam's air defences, more formally know as 'Suppression of Enemy Air Defence', or SEAD.

As such, Henry had to develop the plan to best employ not only the Air Force's F-4Gs, but also the General Dynamics EF-111A 'Spark Vark' radar jamming jets and the EC-130 Compass Call radio communications disrupting aircraft based on the venerable Lockheed C-130 Hercules. After HARM-shooting US Navy Grumman EA-6B jammers, Navy and Marine Corps F/A-18 Hornets and the British RAF's Panavia GR1 Tornado with its ALARM (Air Launched Anti-Radiation Missile) arrived in theatre, Henry had to factor these players into the SEAD mix as well.

The first dedicated Weasel to serve on the CENTAF planning cell in Riyadh was Lt Col Jim 'Beagle' Keck. An instructor EWO in the 562d TFTS, Keck had been at a Red Flag exercise at Nellis AFB outside Las Vegas when the Kuwaiti crisis erupted. Recalled back to George AFB, Keck recalls going through the mobility line, grabbing his bags and catching a transport to Riyadh.

Upon arrival at CENTAF HQ, Keck was told, 'Congratulations, you are now the chief of electronic combat operations. Plan how we beat the SAMs.'

Keck was a good choice as a planner. He knew both how to Weasel and how to integrate them into an air campaign.

Initially, Keck and the rest of the CENTAF staff had to prepare for a defensive fight; the very real possibility that Saddam's forces would roll further south loomed over all other considerations. Even though US and Allied forces were flowing in an ever increasing rate into the area, ground troops, especially the heavy armour needed to thwart Iraqi operations, would take time to arrive.

Keck's task was to keep the fighter-bomber and tank-killing fighters alive long enough for those Coalition armoured forces to arrive by using Weasels, Compass Call, and Spark Varks to hold off the Iraqi ground forces. Heavy with mobile SAMs and operating with numerical superiority, until late September, Keck and CENTAF never knew when the expected Iraqi push would happen.

He planned the probable routes and timing of the electronic combat operations to lead any strike packages and to cover those packages' withdrawals from a target. Backing up the strikers were many tankers and AWACS radar control surveillance aircraft. All these components had to be woven into a coherent plan daily in case fighting broke out.

As mentioned earlier, a lack of computing power made writing an ATO a cumbersome task. Even after an ATO was completed, the lack of common data communication capability meant that for many weeks, hard copies of the ATO had to be hand distributed to each of the scattered flying units. Keck would often jump into a Lear C-21 fast jet transport and take copies to the tactical units. The US Navy likewise had to fly a copy of each daily ATO to the carrier, later carriers, in the Persian Gulf to see what the latest air plan was.

For Keck, however, this courier duty had some advantages. When calling on the Weasels, he managed to scrounge some flights despite having worked an eighteen-hour day in the CENTAF planning cell.

Keck would continue to plan and fly even after the war began in earnest.

SCHREINER, (THURSDAY) 23 AUGUST 1990 D + 5

0600 and the klaxon never went off. I wonder what happened to that tanker? Apparently nothing. Anyway, it's a balmy 92°F outside and I still have 1.5 hours of alert to go. I think I'll go outside and watch the sunrise.

This place is really starting to get crowded. The Marines have finally started to put up tents, but as of yet, there aren't nearly enough. Some of the troops have been forced to sleep in the hangars and those are the lucky ones. The rest have been forced to seek shelter (shade – same thing) wherever they can. I'm told that several have already succumbed to heat stroke and one unfortunate even managed to get himself bitten by a scorpion. Unlucky . . .

0800 and I'm off alert and onto breakfast. Guess we've over-taxed the kitchen staff because the Corn Flakes are no longer kept in a silver bowl but come right out of the box. And the cheese sandwiches now come assembly required.

1130 and it's 'uh oh!' I was afraid this might happen. The shits! Either I got hold of a bug or there is something in the water. At this point it doesn't matter because I've got the shits and still don't have any toilet paper. Maybe I'll learn to use the butt washers after all.

I'm saved! I found some paper and none too soon. After deciding that excusing myself from academic training every ten minutes is getting disruptive, I've decided to head back to the dorms. Normally, waiting for the bus in 100°F heat is bad enough, but when you're ready to explode, it can be excruciating. Finally, the bus arrived and I took it to the flight surgeon's clinic.

I'm told by the medical staff that they check the water daily and while there is a lot of chlorine in the water, it is safe to drink. Oh, and by the way, heavily chlorinated water can cause temporary intestinal malady. Now they tell me! Fortunately, Kaopectate is not in short supply.

SCHREINER, 24 AUGUST 1990 D + 6

Yes, Kaopectate works as advertised and none too soon because I'm scheduled to fly again. I didn't really relish the thought of wearing a diaper while flying.

The rumour mill is still getting in gear. Seems Saddam has not only ordered all the embassies in Kuwait to close but since Americans won't allow any food into his country, he has promised to eat all American pilots he captures. I guess the 'Butcher of Baghdad' intends to live up to his name.

Now that we've settled in, our squadron is flying sorties up north along the border to gather ELINT. [Electronic intelligence – The F-4G's multitude of radar receivers, in addition to displaying a real time picture to the crew, could also record on something akin to an eight-track tape called a CONRAC, all the collected signals. These signals could then be replayed and studied by intelligence personnel to see what radar frequencies the Iraqis used.]

We've also been tasked to lead a two ship of Marine Harriers and drop them off at King Abdul Aziz Air Base in Saudi Arabia.

We definitely got an 'Unsat' in radio procedures on this sortie. First off, 2, 3, and 4 were on the wrong check-in frequency and so naturally, lead couldn't find us. It came out in the debrief that he'd briefed one frequency but really meant something else.

It would seem that the Marines don't see the need to acknowledge radio frequency changes since they only answered one out of four channel changes. I guess they haven't figured out how to talk and fly at the same time.

They (the Marines) also briefed that since they didn't have any radar missiles, they would split off if we got into a nose to nose radar missile fight. Normally, I would agree except they did have heaters and could have helped in a fight. I thought jarheads were all dick and no forehead anyway.

In any event, the flight otherwise went smoothly without any altercations. We did manage to pick up some enemy surface-to-air missile radar signals, but we stayed well out of their range.

I decided that wearing the web belt and canteen while flying is definitely not the way to do it. Also figured out that aircraft #246 has a shitty air conditioning system, even for an F-4. I must have lost five pounds in sweat and it wasn't a physically demanding sortie.

1830 and it's dinner time in Bahrain. The usual chicken and rice is standard, but what's this? Coke and not Pepsi? Boy, that's a switch!

Tom Gummo also commented on the monotony of the food, 'For the first several months, it was curried chicken and rice or chicken and curried rice.'

Both men agree, however, that they had it much better than the ground troops in the field who subsisted on water and MREs (not-so-jokingly referred to as 'Meals Rejected by Ethiopians') for months on end.

SCHREINER, 24 AUGUST 1990 D + 6

Intel still hasn't pinned down the locations of the Iraqi SCUD missiles with their chemical warheads and an attack by them was what everyone feared most. Supposedly the Patriot batteries set up north of us would be able to down any Iraqi missiles but if they didn't, it wouldn't be the first time a multi-billion dollar weapon system didn't work as advertised.

By 1900, everyone in the dining hall had settled down to the evening meal. The conversations ranged from when we would get to go home to whether or not there was any other kind of salad besides the chopped salad with lemon wedge.

At 1903, what sounded like an air raid siren went off.

In about as much time as it took to register on everyone, chairs were flying and as if on cue, everyone headed to the door. Some were putting on their gas masks if they had them or dived under tables. Any fire marshal would have been proud because the entire building had been evacuated in under a minute.

Once outside, it was obvious that something was wrong. Not only were we the only ones evacuating a building, but other people in line at the shoppette or waiting for the bus were standing around like nothing had happened.

At once we realised we'd been fooled. Apparently, one of the kitchen workers had set off the fire alarm. It sure sounded like an air raid siren to me! And everyone else apparently . . .

In any event, we went back inside and had a good laugh.

Some time later in the night, we had what was apparently an infiltrator come ashore near the weapons storage area. What happened next is still not clear but the two most prevalent rumours say that A) the infiltrator was spotted by the Bahrainis in the guard towers or B) the Bahraini guard in the tower was seen signalling the infiltrator and both were arrested by the US security police. I don't know what the final outcome was but it does show how vulnerable this base is to a terrorist attack.

I bet a terrorist would do himself proud in Allah's eyes if he could hit such a ripe target as us. Some fifty-plus F-18s, some AV-8Bs, A and EA-6s, and, of course, our twenty F-4Gs all parked so close to each other on the ramp that a single can of well-placed CBU [cluster bomb unit] would pretty much end our participation in Operation *Desert Shield*.

More frightening is the fact that all of the aircrews, myself included, are billeted in several buildings only a few hundred yards from the Persian Gulf. Not only that, but with a large flow of construction workers going on and off base, who knows whether one of those cement trucks is loaded with explosives or not.

I'm told that the Marines plan to use 10 per cent of their men for base security and that motion sensors will be set up around the perimeter, especially along the beach. In any case, I'm sleeping with my weapon.

SCHREINER, (SATURDAY) 25 AUGUST D + 7

Woke up this morning with a sore throat – great! I guess you can catch a cold even in the desert.

I told the scheduler to take me off the schedule for tomorrow's flying schedule. I just hope I'm not DNIF [Duty Not Involving Flying – term used by the flight surgeon to temporarily take a flier out of the cockpit while an ailment is resolved] when the shooting starts. I think I'd be less scared if I were one of the first to go into action than if I hear how tough it was and then had to go.

We've been here a week so far and all I've seen of Bahrain is either from the cockpit at 20,000 feet or from inside the fence of Sheikh Isa Air Base. WHEN are we going to be allowed off base?

Side note: Pepsi appears to be winning the cola wars here since there was no Coke at dinner tonight.

SCHREINER, 26 AUGUST D + 8

My cold is complete. My sinuses are congested and I can't clear my ears. I guess it's a good thing I removed myself from the schedule.

You can definitely tell we're on a wartime posture. Normally, when I go see the flight surgeon for a cold, I get my blood pressure taken; have to fill out forms, and have fancy prescription bottles filled. This time, after I told the Doc what I needed, Actifed and Afrin, he tossed it to me in a small plastic bag and I left. I don't even have to go back when I'm well to get back on flying status. I just fly when I'm ready. I like that system!

SCHREINER, 29 AUGUST D + 11

My sinuses are cleared and I'm ready to fly. Our four ship is scheduled to fly a night mission up near the border to gather ELINT.

Oh boy! Strap on a high performance jet, fly to within thirty miles of the enemy with highly sophisticated and lethal missiles and then just drone around punching holes in the sky, never exceeding 400 knots or 3 g.

At least it'll be at night so it will only be 86 degrees and not 111! Oh, and we'll try a new tactic to help hide our intentions and maintain surprise or at least deception.

Normally, when a flight takes off anyone listening on the open radio frequencies soon knows how many, what type and the formation's call sign as well as a rough guess of the flight's destination long before the actual take-off. Tonight, instead we'll do all of our ground ops, including take-off, using only pre-briefed times and light signals.

Everything seemed to be working pretty well until I found my scheduled jet was broken. We had to step to a spare and I ended up taxiing five minutes late, but still everything was comm out.

Okay, we're all armed up and ready to go. We all turn our exterior lights to bright and flash to signal tower that we are ready. Tower, in turn, is supposed to turn off the runway lights momentarily for our approval to take-off.

Once again, the fucking jarheads involved are either asleep or drinking coffee because they missed our signal. Lead gave them a 'zipper' [double click on the radio mike, commonly used to signal acknowledgement or, in this case, to get Tower's attention]. No problem, Tower finally catches the cluebird and dims the lights, then back on.

But now a C-130 is on ten-mile final with clearance to land. What to do? Tower's solution: 'Uh, C-130, I need you to do a 360 turn so four F-4s can take-off.' So much for deception! Why not call Saddam direct and tell him we're coming?!

Fortunately, we didn't have to deal with any Marines so the mission went smoothly until after landing. You guessed it, the jarheads are involved.

From about 100 miles out, we'd been following two Marine F-18s also headed for Isa AB. They had to know we were there but maybe after landing their brains went dormant because no sooner did they pull off the runway when they decided to stop, blocking the taxiway, forcing our 3 and 4 to wait on the active runway.

Even when lead pulled in behind them with his taxi light shining on them, they didn't move. It took a radio call from lead to get them to move. Now we all drink the same water and eat the same food, so it can't be that . . .

Chapter Eight

W hile Schreiner and the other Bahrain-based Weasels began their 'Groundhog Day' life in the desert, events outside the wire were proceeding. As the Coalition military and political leadership realised that Saddam was not going to proceed further south, they began thinking beyond a strictly defensive 'stop 'em at the wire' mentality and changing into an offensive, 'push 'em back into Iraq' mindset.

As the CENTAF planners looked at that scenario, they realised they'd need many more offensive air assets, including more F-4Gs. Gen Henry and 'Beagle' Keck, among others at Riyadh, sent in the request for forces to the Joint Staff back at the Pentagon for more Weasels. They naturally assumed that the reinforcements would come from the 562d TFTS at George AFB, the sister squadron to the already deployed 561st.

However, the call went instead to the 52d Tactical Fighter Wing at Spangdahlem Air Base in West Germany. Here, the Weasels were split into three squadrons, each consisting of a dozen F-4Gs and a dozen F-16Cs. The 23d, the 81st and the 480th TFS all used the F-16 Block 30 versions as extensions of the Weasel force.

Equipped with the ALIC – avionics launcher interface computer, a bolt-on device that let the F-16's computer interact with the Shrike and HARM missiles and use the missile itself as a highly advanced radar threat warning receiver – the F-16 flew in a pair with the F-4G. This pair used the Weasel's extensive ground threat detection capability with the more powerful, digital air-to-air radar of the Viper to be a much more efficient team than either platform working alone.

The drawback of the early ALIC was that it only allowed the F-16 to shoot pre-briefed shots. Quick reaction or 'pop up' threats like mobile SAMs could only be dealt with by the F-4G. Still, the pairing effectively doubled the number of SAM-killing missiles carried to a fight.

(Then) Captain Sid 'Scroll' Mayeux, an F-4G EWO with the 23d TFS 'Fighting Hawks', described how the F-4G/F-16 hunter/killer team worked.

> To start talking about a mixed F-4G/F-16 flight, you have to first understand the difference in the two missiles we had at the time, the AGM-45 Shrike and the AGM-88 HARM. The Shrike, an improved version of the Vietnam-era missile, was essentially a bottle rocket. Its seeker head had to be pre-programmed before take-off for a specific threat, i.e., radar frequency. It would only look for that one frequency, and in the later variants, that band-width. If it didn't see that particular one, it was useless to you. Also, its max range was only around twelve nautical miles, depending on your altitude. At that range, you are well within the envelope for most SAMs. Thankfully, Shrikes went out of the inventory not long after *Desert Storm*.
>
> The HARM, on the other hand, could be re-programmed while airborne based upon whatever indications we picked up via the APR-47. It could also be set to always look for a particular threat emitter, for example, an SA-3, but had the capability to 'flex' to another target if you told it to. It's a much better missile with a much longer range. Since it's still used today, exact ranges are best not talked about.
>
> Most HARM and Shrike shots occurred in one of several modes:
>
> - Pre-briefed, where the missile goes to a specific reference point and looks for a specific threat. Called a 'PET shot' for 'pre-emptive targeting'.
>
> - Range known shot meant that the missile was programmed to fly a specific bearing and range spot and attack whatever emitter it found there.
>
> - Range-unknown – in this mode, the missile came off the rail in 'rabid dog' mode, looking for any emitter in range. Once

acquired, it homed in on the first signal and went to that point or if there was no signal, it flew until it ran out of propellant or battery power.

- Self-protection – fired at the unexpected, unknown target threatening to kill the Weasel in the very near future if not killed first.

Now, to employ the hunter/killer team effectively, besides selecting the different missile modes, each missile type required specific manoeuvres to shoot. For example, a Viper carrying Shrikes might have one programmed for the SA-2's Fan Song radar on the left wing and another Shrike programmed for the SA-6 on the right wing.

If we wanted the F-16 to shoot the SA-2-programmed Shrike based on APR-47 indications, we'd do a left turn, call 'Slapshot' and move out of the way in a descending turn. The F-16 pilot would select the left hand Shrike, pitch his nose up 30 degrees, and pickle the Shrike.

The Shrike comes off the Viper's wing and turns on its seeker. If it picks up the specific frequency it's programmed for, it will home in on it. If it doesn't, or the SA-2 goes 'down' before the Shrike arrives, the missile goes 'stupid' and will fly to nowhere until it runs out of propellant and falls to the ground. The F-16, meanwhile, pitches back onto us to rejoin on our wing, ready to shoot the next Shrike if need be. He also keeps his APG-66 radar in an air-to-air search mode, looking for any fighter threats to our flight.

If the Viper was carrying HARMs, we could use our targeting system to pass info via the ALIC to the F-16's HARM and retarget his missile. From there, we could radio the F-16 something like 'Slapshot 350', which meant 'Turn to the heading 350 and shoot'. The HARM would take it from there based on the threat radar we, in the F-4G, had detected along that axis.

Lt Col Ed 'Victor' Ballanco was the Chief of the 52d TFW's Weapons and Tactics division when *Desert Shield* kicked off. He and his team had been demonstrating a new concept in Weaselling around NATO and USAFE (USAF in Europe) even before the desert confrontation kicked off.

The concept, geared towards fighting the perennial Soviet invasion of central Europe threat, involved using Weasels as part of an integrated campaign to defeat the Soviets' IADS instead of using a piecemeal approach to fighting SAMs. By combining EF-111s, EC-130s, and F-4Gs, each asset brought something different to a fight, but together they could present a formidable counter to the expected Soviet onslaught over a wide area.

One of Ballanco's ideas was to use Weasels at much higher altitudes than previously envisioned. In Vietnam and in the training since, much effort had gone into preventing the enemy IADS from seeing a Weasel by flying down on the deck. At low level, as discussed earlier, a search radar can't see an incoming enemy attacker until the jet is nearly on top of the SAM. The trade-off for this tactic was that AAA could be just as deadly. The 52d's 'road show' briefing tried to sell the idea of operating the F-4G up high, in 20,000 feet and above arena.

The higher altitude extended the reach of the F-4 by not requiring as much fuel as low-level ops did. The J-79s engines guzzled JP-4 fuel down in the weeds, but were much more efficient at altitude. If the Phantom didn't have to carry two external drop tanks on the wings, then it could carry two more HARMs.

The HARM too offered much greater range than the Shrike and iron bombs of earlier Weasel missions. Combining the HARM's extended range with that of the F-4 up high and the Weasel assets could cover more ground and kill more SAMs per sortie. This idea translated very nicely when Ballanco was told to deploy to Sheikh Isa and plan a Weasel campaign using the twelve jets the 52d would deploy to augment the 561st.

Unlike his plan, however, the Weasels detailed to the Gulf would fight as F-4G flights only. The idea of mixing Phantoms and Vipers was shelved for this geographically smaller fight. The 52d's F-4Gs would all deploy under the banner of the 81st TFS Panthers.

By Ballanco's own admission, when he arrived in theatre, the electronic combat planning was well advanced and he didn't need to do much in Riyadh. Instead, he gradually assumed the lead in planning at Isa; taking the plans formulated by CENTAF and turning them into a usable document for the crews.

When I got to Sheikh Isa AB, we used the ops building of one of the Bahraini squadrons. We had two US squadrons crammed into part of the building normally used by one much smaller Bahrain squadron, so space was at a premium. We didn't even have a place to do Top Secret planning or to store any TS documents. A C-21 from Riyadh would drop off the ATO and after we got what we needed from it, we stored it in a safe. There was no control of TS material for a while, but eventually we got our arms around that problem.

Once we arrived from Spang, Lt Col Walton and his weapons officer, Brad Ellico, gave us their plan based on using the 561st's jets. We then found out what CENTAF was planning and tried to make sure everyone was talking to each other. Interesting to me was that the Navy and Marines were even more vocal about knocking the SAMs out in the initial stages of any war than were some of the Air Force types.

Steve Johns (then a captain) was another of the Spangdahlem-based 81st TFS Weasels to get the call to deploy:

When the war kicked off and the George guys flew in, we figured we weren't going to go. By September, I thought that maybe there might not even be a fight. We were sitting at the Spangdahlem Officers' Club drinking Tanqueray and Tonic (T&Ts) the drink of the 80s. Vinnie Quinn (VQ), Ken Spaar (Momar), Dan Shelor (Gramps), our Director of Ops and a few other squadron mates were sitting at the bar, and we joked about 'give us a call when the war starts'. We were planning on continuing with our festivities; deployment was not in our thoughts.

On 4 September, my wife and I had been at a wine festival until getting home at around 0200. At 0630 on the 5th, I got a phone call at home from Gramps who was at the squadron, recalling me.

By 10 September at 0530, Johns was in the backseat of the 81st TFS's DO (director of operations, number two leader in a squadron) Lt Col Dan Shelor's F-4G. Johns said on the intercom, 'I don't fucking believe it' as they rolled down the runway headed to war.

Shelor agreed as he led his six-ship of F-4s on the flight south to the Gulf. Like the initial deployment from the States, the Germany-based crews were woefully unprepared for where they were flying to.

Johns recalls:

We took off not knowing exactly where we were headed. We did
not have clearance to penetrate French airspace to head to the
Med, so we planned orbits at the German/French border
awaiting clearance. We'd been faxed an approach plate shortly
before take-off with hand-written frequencies on it and we didn't
have clearance to enter Saudi Arabia or Bahrain before launch.

We met up with the tankers who were dragging us down. They
were concerned with the Libyan SA-5s that we'd pass on the
drive to the Gulf. But with a full load of HARMs, we used our
number 1 and 3 to monitor the APR-47 for any SAM activity and
kept 2 and 4 in the APQ-120 for any air-to-air activity.

Thirty minutes later, another half-dozen of Spang's F-4Gs took off
for Sheikh Isa.

Upon arrival after the butt-numbing flight of nearly eight hours,
the 81st found itself seemingly unexpected. After much shuffling of
gear and turning to setting up some tents, they settled into the daily
grind of life at Sheikh Isa with their jets ready to fly the next day if
need be.

Not everyone was pleased by the additions to the base population.

SCHREINER, 5 SEPTEMBER 1990 D + 18

We've been told that twelve more Weasels will be brought in
from Spangdahlem. Great, just what we need, more people.

Why is it that every swinging dick in the Air Force thinks he
has to come to Operation *Desert Shield* or his career will be
ruined? As if it's not crowded enough, the rumour is that those
of us living in these 'luxurious accommodations' will have to
give them up so lieutenant colonels won't have to double up.
Needless to say, that's *bullshit*!

Yes, sports fans, morale is starting to sag. The scary thing is that
we all carry loaded handguns. The only good thing about this
whole fucked up situation will be when it's over.

And later:

Just when I thought it couldn't get any worse, CINCCENTCOM, General Schwarzkopf issued general order #1 forbidding alcohol consumption to all troops in the region, whether on or off base, even in legal drinking establishments. He also forbade the use or possession of any pornographic materials, the use or possession of any personal firearms even though the USAF-issue .38 is a piece of shit.

Let's see how can we keep morale down? Don't let people go off base and no drinking. Don't want to offend the Bahrainis. We can defend their country but we're not allowed to enjoy ourselves while waiting.

SCHREINER, 8 SEPTEMBER 1990 D + 21

At least there is still flying. Today, I flew my first low level in over a month. To be honest, I had to reference my radar altimeter because it's hard to judge height over nothing but sand. Talk about desolate. Even Death Valley is a garden spot compared with the Arabian Desert. I'm surprised anyone could live here.

It's gotten to the point that I don't mind hot-pitting the jet anymore, just to get a chance to go flying. Anything to relieve the boredom. Rumours are still flying rampant about when the shooting is going to start but nobody here knows for sure.

The changes that have occurred on this base in the last three weeks are amazing! Something like thirty-six F-4Gs, forty-eight F-18s, eighteen A-6s and EA-6Bs, twenty AV-8Bs, and several helos and Marine C-130s are parked on the taxiway. We have well over 100 personnel tents set up – finally everyone has a cot and a roof over their heads even if not all the tents are air-conditioned.

The base defences are all up with the inclusion of HAWK (Homing All the Way Killer, USMC SAM system) missiles. The security seems complete what with all the towers and lights all manned and turned on.

They're even checking all incoming vehicles for explosives, although I'm sure the SPs are also looking for alcohol.

We even have a 100 bed US Army field hospital complete with

some of the ugliest nurses I've ever seen. Some of them look like they were mothballed after the Korean War and just re-commissioned. Boy, are they ugly! I wouldn't fuck them with my roommate's dick.

Schreiner, (Sunday) 23 September 1990 D + 35

Lt Gen Horner, CENTAF commander, visited us. He had told the wing commander that the Weasels were so valuable that he couldn't afford to lose a single one. Of course, he also said in a published interview that the F-15E is the most valuable asset in theatre. I guess next week, he'll come out for the F-117. So much for his credibility.

Well, I've managed to catch another cold. This time I'm not so worried about missing out on the first combat sorties. First off, it seems less and less likely that we will go to war anytime soon. Second, the 'fear factor' I mentioned earlier doesn't seem to be a player.

I've been flying steadily since we arrived and I'm finally getting comfortable in the airplane as well as with the local area. Any fears I may have had have evaporated. I suppose all that could change once I put my foot on the first rung of the ladder when the shooting does start.

Things here at 'Shakey's Pizza' have settled into a definite routine. It's not so much the boredom as the lack of freedom. Back home, my off time was pretty much mine to do with as I pleased. I could drive anywhere or eat and drink anything I wanted. I could play my stereo, use my computer, work on my car or just watch TV. All of these things are unavailable to me now and that stinks. I guess I'm giving up some of my freedom so others can have theirs. Oh, well, things could be a lot worse.

Despite what I have read in the various newspapers, I truly believe what Mr Bush is doing is right. Some people say that we are only here to save 'big oil' and they are the only ones who will benefit.

Others say we have no business being here, threatening war. To those people I say 'Look around and see what you have. Wake up! If you think things would be "peachy keen" if we weren't over here and Iraq controlled 40 per cent of the world's oil production, then you must be smoking rope.'

If we hadn't stopped Saddam at the Saudi border, I doubt he would have stopped of his own volition. Must we learn again and again that if you don't stop despots in places like Kuwait and Munich, then they will continue to grab power until a very costly, devastating war is inevitable.

Sorry for the soap box stand there, but those people who don't realise that sometimes you have to fight for what you believe in just annoy the shit out of me.

SCHREINER, 28 SEPTEMBER 1990 D + 40

We've done some pretty ridiculous things in the past but this takes the cake. Twenty-two crews, myself included, stepped to twenty-two jets, started them and taxied onto the runway. We had take-off clearance and so performed all of our line up checks, then ran the engines up to full power.

And then we taxied off the runway and back to the chocks.

The reason we did this, we were told, was to gauge an Iraqi reaction to a mass taxi of not only our fighters but all the other Air Force fighters in theatre. The speculation was that our generals wanted to see if the Iraqis would scramble to meet a perceived threat and also to see how effective the Iraqi intelligence network was.

But then Saudi Arabia refused to play, citing fear of being too provocative. Well, shit! Of course we're being provocative; we want the Iraqis to start something so we can finish it.

We even sent the battleship *Wisconsin* up the Gulf to the Kuwaiti coast just to see if Iraq would be stupid enough to fire on it.

They weren't and they didn't. I guess we'll have to try something else to get this war started.

Related to this ruse was the ramping up of larger and larger sized formations consisting of various US and Allied tactical aircraft, called

LFEs (large force employments) that ranged nearer and nearer the Saudi/Kuwaiti and Saudi/Iraqi borders. These LFEs were vital training for the mixed forces to practise going to war together. There were enough potential threats coming from the Iraqis should shooting start, that unfamiliar procedures or inexperienced aircrews mixing in large strike packages didn't need to create their own.

For example, if the target was a factory complex that required a bomb-dropping force of twenty F-16s, there probably would be a four ship of Weasels assigned for SAM suppression, a four ship or two of F-15C 'Eagles' to counter any air-to-air threats, a pair of EF-111A Spark Vark electronic jammers, an E-3 AWACS providing air surveillance and threat warning, an RC-135 Rivet Joint platform with its signals intelligence and warning capability, rescue helicopters either airborne or on alert, escorting A-10s for the helos, and, of course, the key to all of these aircraft, an armada of tankers endlessly circling to provide the vital fuel to each.

All of the assets mentioned are USAF with at least a common frame of operational reference. Imagine operating with the different needs of the US Navy or Marine Corps not to mention those of the Allied nations like Britain's RAF. Obviously, practising LFEs was a necessary step in taking the war to Saddam in the future.

Previously, however, these LFEs had been flown deep in the interior of Saudi airspace or over the waters of the Persian Gulf away from the watchful eyes of the Iraqi long-range radars. Now these practice attacks went right up to the border in an attempt to stir up some action.

Another reason for these feints was the opportunity to discover any Iraqi IADS components previously unknown or to get the Iraqis to light up their known radars in order to determine what modes they'd use when the shooting started. Most militaries use different frequencies and techniques for training than for combat operations. Keeping these differences secret from prying sensors could be the difference between Iraqi success or failure in the looming conflict.

Steve Johns, the recent 81st TFS EWO arrival, recalled the situation:

> We'd do the LFE feints toward Iraq to get them used to the idea, so that when we did press across the border for real, they'd be conditioned to our flights and not be looking as closely, perhaps.
>
> Meanwhile, the accompanying F-4Gs were gathering all the

EOB (electronic order of battle) emissions we could so that intel could then update the most recent Iraqi changes.

We'd fly two goes a day; a morning push and an afternoon one. You usually flew on one or the other every day from Saturday through Thursday. Friday being the Muslim holy day, we couldn't fly then due to concern over host nation sensibilities.

The routine got real old, real quick. Little things to make life easier or more convenient became big issues. For example, in one care package sent from the States, I got a State Farm insurance insulated coffee mug. You know, the plastic insulated ones they'd put out for promotional purposes. But such things were so scarce at Isa that my mug became a prized, jealously guarded item.

I wrote a thank you letter to the company and three weeks later, I got another package from them, but this one had fifty of the mugs. That was such a great morale builder. I still have my mug to this day.

Anonymous care packages addressed to 'Any serviceman or woman' flooded into the Gulf area during the build-up and in the war. Many contained notes saying 'thank you for serving' and the like along with many trinkets, children's drawings, etc. So numerous were these packages that the sender usually was not thanked due to the sheer volume received. The troops would not have had time to thank everyone and train for the upcoming fight.

In addition to the generic care packages, loved ones and friends not deployed sent very specific items to help with morale. More than one mailed Listerine bottle's contents were replaced with scotch or bourbon to slip through the draconian Muslim customs efforts. Creative approaches like that also did a tremendous amount of good for the morale of those stuck in the desert.

Another, more serious method for enhancing morale was Lt Col 'John Boy' Walton's 'hard' four ship concept for his crews. Developed not long after arriving in Bahrain, the hard four ship rule meant that just as a crew consisted of the same pilot and EWO, the basic tactical Weasel formation (the four ship flight) would also consist of the same four crews. With the constant practice of the LFEs and the same crews flying in each formation, each crew then knew what its wingmen would do in any given circumstance without any extraneous radio calls or hesitation, thus making threat reactions quicker and more lethal to the Iraqis.

SCHREINER, 20 OCTOBER 1990 D + 65

For the first time since early August, I actually had more than one day off in a row. Through a quirk in the scheduling plan, our normal alert duty was pulled by the Spang boys and my four ship had a 'down' day.

That night, several of us went to the Al Bandar club for some recreating. Since we can now drink – although limited to only two – it's amazing how big the beers are there. Because they are so big, it takes a while to drink our limit. I'm glad they're broken down into easier to use containers when they're brought to us. I haven't had that much to drink since I left for Stalag Isa.

Maybe it just seemed like a lot since I haven't been drinking regularly and lost my tolerance. The one good thing about not having any alcohol for such a long period is that it's given me time to test out several of my theories about the long term physio-logical effects of booze on my body.

First, I have not lost any weight by not drinking beer. In fact, I may have actually gained; must be all the chicken.

Second, my visual acuity, or lack thereof on some days, is about the same as it has been for the past few years. I guess I'm just getting old.

Third, I seem to have about the same amount of energy as I did back home. On the other hand, I'm just as willing to be lazy now as I ever was.

The final question remaining is whether or not I will start drinking my usual three to four a night when I get back home.

Well, the Marines continue to exhibit gross buffoonery every now and then. Yesterday, the Secretary of the Air Force, Donald Rice, paid us a visit.

Naturally, 'quiet hours' had been established for his arrival and subsequent speech out on the flightline. But, as with most dignitaries, he arrived about twenty minutes late. When he did finally pull up to review the Bahraini Honor Guard, two Marines decided it was time to fire up their F-18s, no more than 100 feet away. After all, quiet hours were over.

It certainly was humorous to see Fish Face, the wing commander, squirm and try to think of a way to stop the noise. It must have been a humbling experience to be a wing commander in charge of some thirty-six F-4s and countless personnel and have no control of two jarhead pilots and their jets.

The fact that the Marine two-star didn't seem to care even though he was standing right there must have made it all the more frustrating for Fish Face. Such is the life of the wing commander, I guess.

Schreiner, 22 October 1990 D + 67

The first officer has received an Article 15, unfortunately he was my backseater.

Yeah, he fucked up. He was found in the bathroom by an SP major, drunk and passed out. That meant he was drinking on base, which is prohibited, and he was drunk, which meant he had more than the two allowed.

What I can't understand is our ops officer, who previously said he didn't give a shit about his 'mediocre' career, did not try to intervene even though he was there and probably could have told the major to stuff it or at least sweet talk him out of it.

So what we have is:

a) A full colonel that is so worried about his job that he makes ridiculous rules and puts incredibly tight restrictions on us.

b) A Lt Col ops officer that is supposed to watch for his people but doesn't.

c) An SP major who is just being himself in arresting a crewmember.

d) A captain now with an Article 15 in his record, which will probably keep him from going to pilot training and may have just ruined his career.

Yeah, the Air Force, it's a great way of life!

For my first nine and half years in the Air Force, I never once regretted what I was doing or contemplated getting out before retirement. And most of the time, I really enjoyed what I was doing. But after seeing some of the shit that has happened since we have been here, I have to admit to second thoughts.

It would not surprise me at all if, once this situation is resolved and we all go home, that a lot of people put in their papers to get out of the service.

SCHREINER, 2 NOVEMBER 1990 D + 78

Went out to see the HAWK battery today. Located a few miles north-west of the base, the Marines have set up operations that command a good view of the southern portion of the island.

I thought I was bored, but they are out in the middle of nowhere with nothing to do except sit around and play games – at least until the shooting starts.

More rumours of war; apparently an F-15 was cleared to fire on an Iraqi jet that intruded into Saudi airspace. He didn't and I don't know why.

The papers are saying that war is imminent and that President Bush is ready. At least he said he told Congress he probably wouldn't give them any notice before launching an offensive. Can't say I blame him knowing the propensity of that 'august' body for leaks.

Rumours on rotating home range from a partial rotation this month to us staying here until next May. I wouldn't mind being here as much if we were treated like adults instead of like children.

Not three days after we were cleared by our beloved commander, Col Fish Face, to go downtown in taxis at our own expense, he rescinded that approval, claiming that accountability is too difficult and we wouldn't be able to get back in an emergency.

Personally, I don't see how the absence of up to eight aircrews could be that detrimental when they are otherwise 'off duty' anyway and we have twelve times that number at Stalag Isa anyway. I guess it's all part of the harassment program.

I do know, however, that Fish Face allows himself to go down-town, in a government paid for rental car, and that he plans on rotating home this month, with or without his troops. That's the sort of leadership I look for.

SCHREINER, 4 NOVEMBER 1990 D + 80

The double standard definitely exists in the Air Force.

As I wrote about a couple of days ago, my backseater will receive an Article 15 for getting drunk, as will his roommate even though he wasn't falling down shit faced. Even the two other card players, who weren't drinking and don't anyway, will receive Letters of Reprimand. Fish Face said he wanted to 'nip this problem in the bud' and make an example of these indi-viduals. Ok fine, rules are rules, but . . .

Several nights later at the same facility, the Al Bandar club, one lieutenant colonel ops officer, not the one mentioned above, became somewhat inebriated – a violation of the rules. This had to be obvious to Fish Face as he was there at the dinner and heard the Lt Col give a little speech.

This same Lt Col attempted to prevent several individuals, 'not from his squadron', from getting on the bus for the return to base. Most of his squadron crews witnessed his performance and his less than professional conduct. Yet this individual received not so much as a wrist slap for his 'wilful' disregard of the rules that are ending the careers of the two junior guys. Nice . . .

Chapter Nine

In November 1990, President Bush authorised the build up of US forces past the 200,000 mark with another 130,000 troops, acknowledging it would take until after the turn of the year to get them all into place. With that pronouncement, the sand-bound Weasels knew a little more about their immediate future.

SCHREINER, 13 NOVEMBER 1990 D + 89

Several days ago, Secretary of Defense Cheney announced the troop rotation plan – there isn't one. We'll be here until it's over.

However, Lt Col Walton has told us we're 'double digit short', meaning under a hundred days.

I flew a CFT (composite force training – LFE but with multi-national participation) today with twelve F-16s as the bombers – actually they prefer to be called strikers. Four F-15s acted as escort and at least six Mirage F1s from Qatar acted as red air, i.e., the bad guys. One of Iraq's biggest air-to-air threats is their F1s so I was anxious to engage these to see how they look and fight.

The good news is they didn't fight well and we actually got some kills, which is pretty unusual. The bad news is they are difficult to distinguish from our F-16s until rather close so visual ID will be a problem. I just hope the Iraqi F1s fight as poorly.

In November, the 'Weasel Dome,' a huge, pressurised tent, started operations. Run by civilian contractors, the Dome provided a big boost to morale by being a place to get snacks, quick meals, and even beer in a rowdy, but homey environment. Many off-duty hours were passed under the red and white striped plastic, with both flight crews and maintainers mixing in the vast open space with its cheap plastic tables and chairs. Still, it beat nothing by a long way.

It was also in November that Schreiner crewed up with EWO Major Dan Sharp. Also a new guy to the Weasel, Sharp and Schreiner had gone through F-4G upgrade together at George AFB, but were each assigned with a more experienced crewmate once finished with training. Now that Schreiner's first EWO had run afoul of demon rum and the Air Force, and Sharp was available, they were crewed together again. It turned out to be a good match. They'd developed the cockpit coordination and intimacy vital to flying and fighting the F-4G during training. Now, when survival itself was added to the mix, the habit patterns previously established came back in a hurry.

Schreiner, (Thanksgiving) 22 November 1990 D + 98

When I first arrived, I didn't think we'd be here for Thanksgiving. A few weeks after arriving, Gen Horner said he was planning on being home for Thanksgiving so I felt pretty much reassured that I was right.

Well, here we are. From what I hear, however, Gen Horner is, in fact, home, but we are not. [Authors' note: Gen Horner did not, in fact, go home, but such was the power of the rumour mill that many thought he did.]

Yesterday we were informed that twelve more Weasels and eighteen RF-4Cs would be arriving by the end of December. I guess the President was serious about the extra 200,000 troops.

In any event, we've been told that we'll have to make room for all those extra crews. It probably means that all of the O-5s will move into this building while us captains will be crammed ten to a room in another. It's barely tolerable now with two roommates, but when the move occurs I'll have absolutely no privacy whatsoever.

I'm losing more and more control. It's ironic that just over a year ago, I was a four ship flight lead and flight commander in charge of ten other pilots deployed at our forward base. Now I'm just a piss-ant wingman with very little responsibility and seemingly less authority. It is so damn frustrating!

SCHREINER, 8 DECEMBER 1990 D + 114

The billeting situation here at Stalag Isa has taken an interesting turn and fortunate (for me anyway) twist. It seems my room is slightly smaller than the rest in this building, so rather than have to give it up, we've been allowed to stay while all the other captains and lieutenants have had to move to the 'slums', another building with ten to twelve people per room.

This has caused some ill-feelings, especially among those who had to move out this past week. However, the fact that the women were also allowed to stay – seven women in three rooms – has almost everyone up in arms. They could easily be moved to one of the larger rooms in the slums, thereby freeing up three rooms here.

Of course, there are no sit down toilets in the slums and that's one of the arguments Col 'Chairborne', a non-flyer, used to justify their staying. To their credit, they (the women) realise the unfairness involved and said they'd move out, but neither they nor we were asked for our opinions. It seems the women aren't as 'equal' as they'd like to think.

SCHREINER, 22 DECEMBER 1990 D + 128

Flying on Christmas – there's a concept!

The brass seems to think that Saddam may decide to attack over the holidays. That is a definite possibility if he is unwilling to pull out of Kuwait and he thinks we are going to fight. If I was him and going to take on a superior force, I'd certainly launch a surprise attack rather than wait for the first blow to land.

As a result of this logic, we have gone back to a seven days a week flying schedule and all of our jets have been fully loaded with either four HARMs and a centreline [fuel tank] or two HARMs and three bags. We now have two four ships on alert – one on one-hour readiness, the other on two-hour.

Of course, our Christmas Eve party was cancelled. Actually, I'm not surprised and many of us thought it stupid to crowd all

Locally produced aircrew aid - a series of pages containing the most useful/often referenced information a busy fighter crew would need. Here the artwork of EWO Kevin 'Grinch' Hale decorates pilot Tom Gummo's copy (Tom Gummo)

WEASEL AIRCREW AID

of us into one hotel downtown and have it be a ripe terrorist target.

As an added bonus, we now have our very own Patriot missile battery set up on base. It's claimed these missiles are capable of shooting down Scud missiles. Let's hope we don't have to find out.

Col Patton, our DO, has said that he believes that 15 January is a 'watershed' day. We'll either go to war that day or start going home. With Saddam's increasing intransigence, the latter seems unlikely since 15 January is the date President Bush has given him to get out of Kuwait.

The only way I can see us going to war on the 15th (16th local time) is if we are already fighting. I don't think we would dare attack the day after the deadline because, for one, Saddam would probably be expecting it and, two, I'm not sure we are going to fight without Congressional approval. The way they do business, it will be several days, at least, before they even consider that action, if they ever do.

It would surprise me if Bush decided to launch an offensive without the 'Declaration of War' and I'm still not convinced we are going to get it. There are many lily-livered assholes who would rather wait for the sanctions to take effect, no matter how many years that takes.

I just hope their number is not large enough to keep us here. I came here to fight, not sit on my ass. If we aren't going to do anything, then let's get the hell out. I've already wasted four months of my life and would rather not waste any more.

In mid-December, the routine feints at the Iraqi KARI air defence system increased in both number and size. Huge armadas of aerial

CONTROLLED BAILOUT

- FLY HEADING SOUTH FORM CH 123 AT MIN OF 2000' MSL. BAILOUT OVER SOUTHERN END OF ISLAND PRIOR TO FEET WET.

JETTISON

- JETTISON HUNG LIVE ORD FEET WET. (IF UNSECURE JETTISON THE RACK) SOUTH OF ISLAND.

LAME DUCK

- NORDO AIRCRAFT RECOVER TO PT INDIA. FLY STRAIGHT IN AND CONFIGURE BY 10 NM PRESENTING A NONTHREATENING FLIGHT PATH. FOR RWY 15, FLY STRAIGHT IN TO 33 THEN AT 2 DME TEARDROP FOR LEFT BASE TO LAND RWY 15.

Bailout notes in the aircrew aid (Tom Gummo)

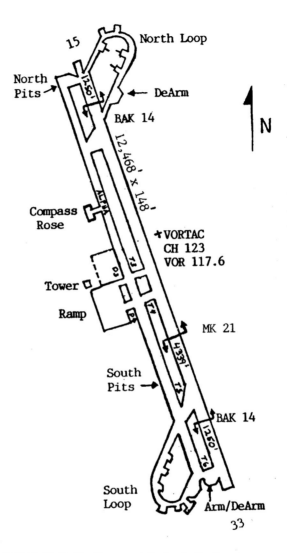

North Loop

15

North Pits →

← DeArm

BAK 14

12,468' x 148'

Compass Rose

ALPHA

1,567'

N

✦VORTAC
CH 123
VOR 117.6

Tower

Ramp

MK 21

4,339'

South Pits →

BAK 14

1,250'

South Loop

Arm/DeArm

33

N2555.3 E05035.4
ELEVATION 100'

3 (Ch 1)

Aircrew aid depicting Shaikh Isa's runway, taxiway and areas of interest to the crew. (Tom Gummo)

hardware – everything from tankers, AWACS, air-to-air fighters, mud movers, Weasels, USN EA-6B jammers, to U-2 high-altitude surveillance jets – moved *en masse* right up to the border, both to see if Iraq would react and to lull them into a false sense of security for the day when the armada did not turn back.

On 26 December 1990, another twelve jets from the 52d TFW were ordered into place as 'battle loss replacements'. Major Bart Quinn, pilot and assistant DO of the 480th TFS, also flew to the desert from the dark wetness of a German winter. These jets and crews also served under the 81st's flag. The 561st, 81st, and the RF-4C reconnaissance jets flown by the Nevada Air National Guard comprised the 35th Tactical Fighter Wing (Provisional) for the war.

SCHREINER, 5 JANUARY 1991 D + 142

Finally, I feel like part of the team. Today, I was let into the inner circle of the planners and now I know there is a method to our madness. We have a plan, although obviously, I can't elaborate here. Maybe when this is all over, I can say what I know.

The best part about it is knowing that everyone, including myself, will be allowed to fly 'contingency' missions if and when they ever occur. I had known for quite a while that I'd be part of the MPC – mission planning cell – but was afraid that it would be a permanent position and I wouldn't be included in mission prosecution.

Funny, I never thought I would be worried about not going to war, but I had visions of being one of the few members of our squadron that would have to put up with all the bullshit of the past four and half months but would be benched for the big game.

As I write this, I am suffering from one each, cold, standard issue. I say standard because about ten days before it started I was given the mandatory flu shot and I've always suspected those shots caused more illness than they prevented. At least I'll be over this by the 15th.

The question is will the 15th be any different from any other day? So far, Iraq has not removed one soldier from Kuwait. Obviously, Iraqi troops will not be out by the 15th, but if they

FREQUENCIES

PRESET	UHF	AGENCY
1	318.25	GROUND
2	364.15	TOWER
3	358.15	APPROACH
4	317.25	APPROACH
5	273.20	BASE OPS
6	274.10	WEASEL OPS
7	373.50	F-16 OPS
9	375.50	MONSOOR GCI
10	278.20	MONSOOR GCI
11	273.50	MONSOOR GCI
14	360.60	DHAHRAN APPROACH
15	351.20	DHAHRAN APPROACH
16	341.70	DHAHRAN APPROACH
17	318.95	DHAHRAN MILITARY
18	275.80	BAHRAIN TOWER
19	344.0	BAHRAIN CENTER
	287.45	TOD GENERATOR (HQ)
	338.10	METRO (MIDDLE EAST)

1
(Ch 1)

Aircrew aid page with most commonly used radio frequencies at Shaikh Isa
(Tom Gummo)

started to leave, I seriously doubt there would be much support for an attack by us. How long would we allow him to drag his feet before we did anything? I just hope we're not here next Christmas asking these same questions.

Planner Ed Ballanco shed some light on the planning process involved in briefing the crews. Intimately involved in fleshing out the plan since his arrival in the theatre, Ballanco worked on translating the ATO plan developed by the 'Black Hole' folks in Riyadh into a concrete mission planning document for the crews of the 35th TFW(P):

> While everyone saw the daily 'training' ATO and flew the *Desert Shield* sorties based on that, we were developing the *Desert Storm* ATO at the same time.
>
> We had to constantly revise the targets set and the order of hitting them as additional forces flowed into the theatre. With more assets, we could hit a wider variety and more dispersed set of targets. However, the Weasels were a finite asset and could only cover so many targets at any given time so we had to do a lot of coordinating with both Riyadh and the supporting units like an F-16 wing based in Qatar.
>
> I worked with a team of intel officers, weapon school graduates and the like in a trailer there at Sheikh Isa. With all the comings and goings of those folks and not letting anybody else in, we acquired the nickname of 'Secret Squirrels'.
>
> Because we couldn't divulge the plan, but we did want some of the ideas to be practised before the war kicked off, we were able to put some of the concepts into the training ATO. One of those concepts was the fact that the ATO process was just too cumbersome.
>
> We had somebody go to Riyadh and bring a hardcopy of the next day's ATO back. This was before the days of widespread e-mail and classified systems. We had one classified fax machine, but it took literally hours for an ATO to be transmitted and we just didn't have that kind of time.
>
> We also put the planned ROE [Rules of Engagement] and SPINS (Special Instructions) into the training ATO so that crews

CONTENTS

	PAGE
FREQUENCIES	1
HAVE QUICK	2
AIRFIELD DIAGRAM	3
NORTH DEPARTURE	4
SOUTH DEPARTURE	5
LOCAL TRAINING AREAS	6
SOUTH AREA	7
NORTH ARRIVAL	8
SOUTH ARRIVAL	9
Shaikh Isa Arrival	10
Bahrain Intl Arrival	11
TACTICAL INITIAL	12
ILS/DME RWY 33	13
TACAN 1 RWY 33	14
TACAN 2 RWY 33	15
VOR/DME RWY 33	16
South Loop	17
DEARM/HOT PIT REFUEL (NORMAL)	18
MASS LAUNCH & RECOVERY FLOW	19
DIVERT	20
DIVERT AIRFIELDS	21
ALTERNATE AIRFIELDS/FUELS REQ'D	22
BAILOUT/JETTISON/LAME DUCK	23
AIR REFUELING TRACKS	24
ATC Radar Out Departures	25
ATC Radar Out Arrivals	26
Aircraft Turn	27-29

SRJ/DOV

Aircrew aid Table of Contents (Tom Gummo)

could become familiar with those, but we didn't let it be known that those were *the* ROE and SPINS.

Back to hand-carrying the ATO, we found that it could take the better part of twenty hours to break the ATO and determine what the Weasels were tasked to do. Errors could creep in during that kind of process, not to mention if there were changes made to the ATO.

Since it was such a time and labour intensive process, we had to eventually get the mission leads 'read' into the process so they could both help and add their inputs to the final planning. Eventually, we let the four ship flight leads into the plan and just before the war kicked off, were able to tell all the crews.

Chapter Ten

I departed George exactly five months ago and tonight we go to war! It's about time! If any bad guy reads this before tomorrow, I'm dead meat. H-Hour is now 0300 local time tomorrow. That could, of course, change or be called off but I think that unlikely.

Fish Face told us that it is normal with all the adrenaline in our body to have a knot in our stomach before we go into combat. He also said that if you didn't feel something wrong then there was something wrong with you. Well, I'm here to tell you that I'm as healthy as a horse! At least I'm in the first wave, so I don't have to listen to someone else's stories before I go.

We also were told to start taking our anti-nerve agent pills just in case. Great! As if I wasn't edgy enough . . .

The opening assault on Iraq had more than 2,000 aircraft in it. The first attack consisted of a unique US Army McDonnell-Douglas (now Boeing) Apache helicopter SEAD mission. Led, at extremely low level, by USAF MH-53J Pave Low helicopters, the Apaches took out via Hellfire missile and devastating 30-mm gunfire, two Iraqi early warning radars perched 400 miles west of Kuwait. This Task Force Normandy opened up the first gap in the Iraqi air defence network to allow the fast-movers into Iraq proper without giving away the element of surprise. Nearly completely successful, the doomed radar technicians did manage to get out one warning phone call. That call triggered a massive, blindly fired AAA barrage over Baghdad and started Iraqi F1s rolling down runways to meet the assault.

Following the attack, USAF EF-111As flew into the radar hole provided to set up their jamming orbits, thereby covering further offensive strikes ever deeper into Iraq.

Several unique 'silver bullets' added to the shock of the opening attack. Forty-four Northrop BQM-74C Chukar decoy drones – normally used as targets in weapon system trials back in the States – salvoed into the night from a secret, remote base near the Iraq border. The brainchild of Gen Henry, these decoys looked like attacking jets on the Iraqi air defence radar screens and the scope operators light them up like Christmas trees. This, of course, is just what the Weasels wanted. To kill SAMs, AAA, and associated radars, those radars had to be emitting. The decoys definitely achieved that goal!

Another silver bullet was the first mass use of the Lockheed F-117A Nighthawk. Its radar deflecting shape, combined with meticulous mission planning to avoid radar detection, made it nearly invisible to the Iraqi KARI system. Some of the F-117's first targets were the Sector Operations Centers and the Intercept Operations Centers as well as the Baghdad headquarters of the Iraqi Air Force. These strikes were designed to cut off the head of KARI before it could direct the body into action against the non-stealthy attackers still inbound. The F-117s succeeded in isolating the central command from the outlying facilities, thereby degrading the overall effectiveness of the KARI system.

Unlike the sharply angled F-117s, the F-4Gs were highly visible to Iraqi radars. The radar cross section, for example, of the Nighthawk is around .05 metres squared. The Phantom, on the other hand, showed up as a hefty 6 metre squared radar blip. The analogy would be the difference between a hummingbird and a billboard.

Schreiner's first experience at war is described in the Introduction. Continuing the narrative from that first mission:

It seemed that no sooner did we lock up a SAM radar to shoot than he knew we were locked and shut down. But then another radar would come up, always just a little more north, luring us further into the lion's den. I doubt this was a coordinated, deliberate action on the part of the Iraqis, but more likely the result of radar operators too frightened to stay on the air long enough for us to shoot them. But, of course, that meant that they couldn't engage the attackers we were supporting.

As we proceeded further north through the triple A barrage for what seemed like an eternity, we finally did manage to get two radars up long enough for us to shoot.

Whether or not our missiles ever hit them is something probably only God will ever know but judging from all the explosions on the ground, I would say we were successful in providing cover for our bomb-dropping friends.

During the hours leading up to the mission, I was concerned that I might not be able to stay awake, or at least become tired during the mission, as we weren't scheduled to land until after 0500. I needn't have worried. There was so much adrenaline flowing that I had no trouble staying alert. It wasn't until after the debrief that I 'came down'. This was a day I'll never forget; the day I won my gold star. [USAF combat pilots used to sew tiny stars on the cuff of their flight suit, one for the first 500 hours flown, then another for each additional 500 hours of fighter flight time.

Conditions were nothing if not cramped. Here a 'go' of F-4G crews receives an intel briefing before stepping for a mission. This room also served as their locker room. Note the rack of flight helmets on top of a row of life support stands. (USAF)

These stars were sewn using silver thread. Combat time changed the thread colour to gold and this was a highly respected, and thus coveted, symbol of professional fighter aviation.]

Other Weasels flying that night had very similar, yet very different, experiences. Jim Uken recalls:

Although I'd been intimately involved in the planning for the night, it was still sobering to be sitting in the ops briefing room – we called it the 'Church of What's Happening Now' because it consisted of two rows of four benches much like church pews – and getting the mission briefing.

Brigadier General Glenn Proffitt, by now the air division commander for us, stated, 'Gentlemen, tonight we ride.' After that we suited up in life support and went to the jets.

In the pitch dark, I noticed the American flag flying over the last revetment and lit up with light-alls. This in itself was unusual because we weren't allowed to fly the US flag in deference to the Bahrainis and their sovereignty on the base. However, with 2,500 Air Force and 5,500 pumped up Marines, they didn't say anything. Of course, the fact that armed SPs and Marines were guarding the flag probably also helped.

That night, the 561st took the Iraq/Baghdad area and we in the 81st supported in Kuwait itself. They flew sixteen jets and we took eight in the first wave. Conversely, the 81st took the lead over Kuwait with sixteen jets and the 561st contributed eight. The jet configuration for each area was different. The Iraq-bound guys flew with two HARMs and three bags because they had a much longer drive than we did. We carried four HARMs and a centreline [tank].

We took off, just like all the CFTs we'd done so far. We hit the tanker as per the ATO and turned north-east. At H-Hour, as we fenced in, I said to my pilot, who was the 81st squadron commander, 'This is surreal. The war's started but nothing's happening.' Indeed, for the first one to two minutes it was pitch black outside. We flew into Kuwait for around five to seven miles and then the world turned on. The amount of AAA visible was amazing.

We were tasked to shoot all the SAMs that could threaten three strike packages heading to Ali al Salem SOC, Ahmed al Jaber airfield and Kuwait International Airport where the Iraqis had deployed some air assets and SAMs. Fourteen Marine HARM-carrying F-18s were to provide cover for simultaneous US Navy 'alpha' strikes against the southern Iraqi airfields at Basrah, Basrah West, and Shaibah.

We were supposed to go to about the centre of Kuwait and react to whatever was radiating. I was looking for Republican Guard SA-6s in particular as well as tracked AAA. While doing that, an SA-2 came up right underneath my four ship. We all split in four different directions.

Next, SA-6s times a bunch came up and we were completely reactive. There were so many SA-6s up that I could only display the top fifteen on the PPIAC scope. We shot our sixteen HARMs in something like ten to fifteen minutes. I shot at three SA-6s and an SA-2, then our second four ship of F-4Gs relieved us.

We were supposed to call the Marines to let them know it was safe enough for them to press, but with all the activity, we couldn't say that. To their credit, they still pressed on to cover their buds coming in from the carriers.

One of the funny moments looking at it now, but not so much at the time, was hearing our # 3 jet call 'Wounded bird, egressing south.' That meant that he had damage and was heading south. We were all worried that we'd already had our first loss.

A few minutes later we heard, '3's back in.' Then, '3's wounded bird, egressing south' followed again by, '3's back in.' A third '3's wounded bird, egressing south' and then '3s back in' had us scratching our heads. We found out at the debrief that each time # 3 had shot a HARM, he hadn't bumped the nose of the jet to miss the HARM missile's exhaust gases. This usually caused a compressor stall in the engine on the side where the HARM was launched from and he had to leave thinking he had a bad jet. We trained to turn the nose, but in the excitement he forgot. Once he had power, he turned back into the fight. Then he did it again and again.

The best moment of that first night was after we landed. After clearing the active and going through de-arm, the entire two-mile length of the taxiway was two and three guys deep with cheering airmen and Marines. That was a good feeling . . .

Kevin Hale (then a captain), an EWO in the 561st, recalled that he was 'cotton-mouthed' the whole time from take-off to touchdown. He was in Captain Jack Patterson's pit in the seventh jet, call sign Lonestar 43, of the sixteen headed to Baghdad.

We were briefed to expect twenty per cent losses. That is a sobering statistic.

We hit the tanker as fragged [directed by the ATO portion or 'frag'], then flew in a long trail formation with about seven nautical miles between jets. I was in the back, head down running the scopes when Jack said, 'Ooh, look at that.' There were tracers everywhere!

Jack jinked and turned the jet, but all that cost us altitude and airspeed until we wound up at about 12,000 feet. We had to climb back up and that was a long climb . . .

We heard the first MiG call as we were heading north from the south of Baghdad. At around 0320, we saw a spear of burning smoke pointed right at us. That was awe inspiring.

Off to work: a two-ship of F-4s begins its take-off run. (USAF)

The 'burning smoke' was F-15C pilot Captain Steve Tate's AIM-7 Sparrow kill of an Iraqi F1 sent to intercept the string of Weasels. Detected by the E-3 AWACS' long-range radar, the controller aboard the Boeing-built jet vectored Tate's flight into position. Tate acquired the F1 on his radar, locked it up and called 'Fox One' as he pickled the Sparrow. Seconds later, the unlucky Iraqi pilot died in the fireball.

Major Bart Quinn led an eight ship of 81st TFS F-4Gs in support of F-117s and F-111s attacking the Salman Pak chemical and biological warfare (CBW) production and storage site located to the south-east of Baghdad. His strike package was a few minutes behind the opening attacks on Baghdad. Such was the importance placed on destroying the stocks of biological and chemical weapons stored at the target area, that even though the initial wave would undoubtedly stir up the air defences, Salman Pak had to be hit to prevent those stockpiles from being disbursed and used against Coalition forces.

One of the concerns for the F-117s was the belief that the Iraqis had

Moving into position so the 'boomer' can plug the jet and start pumping fuel. (USAF)

moved at least one battery of the Kuwaiti I-HAWK (Improved Homing All the Way Killer) SAM from the conquered country to the Salman Pak area. The HAWK's continuous wave targeting radar could track the Nighthawks better than the more common pulsed radars, so the F-117s were a little nervous about being vulnerable. Quinn's flight was briefed to watch for the HAWK.

Additionally, two SA-3 sites were located to the north-east and north-west of the target area and were a real concern to the non-stealth F-111 Aardvarks who would go in at low level to hit the CBW bunkers.

Says Bart Quinn of the mission:

The F-111s were going in fairly low in order to lob their laser-guided bombs into the entrances of the storage bunkers. The theory was that the bomb would penetrate the door and fry any 'bugs' inside, thus destroying them immediately. The problem was that there were dozens of threats in the immediate area, including an SA-8 at the F-111s' release point. The -8 is a fearsome weapon particularly at low to medium altitudes. We had to make sure we got anything that could target the strikers.

During the mission planning, the EWOs, led by mine, Ken 'Howdy' Hanson, divided up the threats among the flight, taking the highest priority ones in order depending on what stage of the strike we were on at any given moment.

Vinnie Quinn [no relation], our Fighter Weapons School graduate, took a look at my chart and just muttered 'Schweinfurt'. [During World War II, the ball bearing plants located in that German city were a prime target of the American heavy bomber campaign. The Germans knew it was valuable and had placed unbelievably heavy concentrations of flak and fighter airfields in the area to protect it. The first such mission cost sixty bombers, each with a crew of ten. It became known as 'Black Thursday' because of the horrendous losses.]

Victor Ballanco told me that the computer models estimated that we'd lose 30 per cent of our force that first night. That gets your attention in a hurry as I briefed the fifteen other guys in my Weasel mission.

From the beginning, fuel was a concern. The planning was tight the whole way in and out. I told everyone that we just did not have the gas to deal with any MiGs encountered or if anyone went down, there could be no RESCAP [Rescue Combat Air Patrol], we just had to leave whoever it was and press.

Stepping to my jet, I couldn't get the APR-47 repeater scope on my dash to dim. It was so bright I couldn't see the other instruments. Rather than go to another jet and risk missing the take-off, I taped my right flight glove over the scope and told Ken what I was doing. The -47 scope was my primary threat warning receiver, but I knew Ken could take care of us and there was no way I was going to miss this flight.

We met our tankers as fragged, about 100 miles south of the Iraqi border. The tracks were designed to be that far to keep the Iraqis guessing about our actions. Unfortunately, that's a long drive when fuel is tight. To their credit, those tankers flew us much closer to the border than they were supposed to, thus letting us get as much gas into us as possible. I really appreciated that from them.

The whole time on the tanker and heading north, the flight kept expecting to hear the 'abort' code word. But since I knew that the first bombs had already dropped, I knew we were going.

We were in a line astern formation, with me at about 20,000 feet and the rest of the jets stepped up in altitude into the high 20s. As we crossed the border, I remember saying to Howdy 'This is it.'

At about that time, I caught some chatter between my # 2 and # 4 about air-to-air missiles. I wasn't exactly sure what they were referring to, but I told them to 'disregard and press'.

About then, I saw off my left wing a large, green explosion. Looking like liquid metal, the first thought I had was that it was a flare the Iraqis had set off to see us. Of course, it was really AAA. From then on, the fire was just constant.

At Nasiriyah, I saw a cloud, which was unusual because the night was clear everywhere else. That cloud was actually the remnants of the 57-mm AAA gunpowder. I realised I had to go through that cloud and the intense, continuous barrage AAA.

I was scared, but what I remember most is that I didn't want to fuck up or make a mistake that cost somebody else. My throat was so tight it hurt; it was like my adenoids were growing. I said to Howdy 'Here we are at the cradle of civilisation and we're gonna blow it up.'

As we got to the target area, I called 'Buntari', which was the code for the Weasels that they were cleared to fire.

It was about then that Derek Knight, in my # 4, saw a MiG taking off below us. But, as briefed, we couldn't do anything about it due to fuel.

We set up an orbit between the Euphrates River to the south and the Tigris to the north. In the orbit, we always had at least an element facing toward the target area and the threats.

Outside it was just mayhem. SAMs were going off unguided, just long streaks of flame, the AAA tracers with their greenish flashes and sparkles. I could see cars driving along roads, and the city lights were still on. I peeked underneath the glove hiding my APR-47 scope and it looked like a bowl of Cheerios had been spilled on the screen, so thick were the threats of SA-6s and -8s.

Howdy shot at the SA-8, which went down at the right time, but we don't know for sure that we killed him. I forgot about the HARM's exhaust and didn't have the motors in mil. [Mil = military power – full power without using afterburner.] Using mil kept them from air starvation in the event of ingesting missile exhaust, but I just forgot until I had one flame out. I quickly got it re-lit and pressed on.

After the war, one of the F-111 drivers contacted Howdy and thanked him for taking out that SA-8 since he had to fly right at the SAM's position to loft his bombs. That was nice thing for the guy to do and made us feel good about the job.

That 'F-111 driver' was then 1st Lieutenant Craig 'Quizmo' Brown. He was flying as Ram 44, the last jet in a four-ship of F-111Fs attacking the CBW site. His version of the story makes for an interesting tale in its own right and a much different view of the same events:

We were supposed to hit the site after the F-117s had actually taken out the CBW bunkers. Since the facility was an anthrax production and storage site, our job was to provide the compliance with Geneva Convention requirements that any attack on a CBW site be rendered 'unapproachable' by the enemy in order to safeguard him.

Anthrax, a living micro-organism, is deadly even if only a

small number of its spores are inhaled. Unlike most chemical weapons, anthrax has a long-lasting effect on an area. Dispersed easily by the wind, the spores can live a long time in the ground waiting for a mammal host. The ever-increasing mass of Allied ground troops looked like a lucrative target and this particularly repugnant and deadly threat had to be taken out in the first wave of attacks.

Brown continues:

Unbelievably, we had to haul our load of four CBU-89 Gator mines, an anti-personnel, anti-armour area denial weapon and bomb, so that we prevented the Iraqis from entering the site and being infected by their own biological weapons. [Each Gator unit contains seventy-two magnetic anti-tank mines and twenty-two anti-personnel mines. The Ram four ship of F-111Fs thus carried over 1,500 mines to blanket the area. A most effective area denial weapon indeed.]

We pushed from the tankers at about 0130 local, using timing only to deconflict us from each other, and pushed across the border in the dark. We went in at 400 feet up to the border, then descended to 200 feet with about eight miles or one minute between each succeeding jet. We used 480 knots and stayed low as we got inside Iraq.

We crossed almost all of south-central Iraq on a north-easterly heading and turned for the initial point [also called IP, it is a pre-briefed point just prior to the target that allowed a final reference to find and attack the proper target] where we pushed it up to 570 knots.

For many miles into Iraq, it was like flying over Nebraska. Town lights were on and we could see car headlights on the highways as we crossed them. It was very surreal.

The F-117s were supposed to have already bombed the anthrax bunkers by the time we hit our TOT [time over target] so we flew in our full chem. gear suits except for the mask. We had those in our helmet bags tucked to the side. As we neared the target, we turned off the ECS [environmental control system – the air conditioner] so we wouldn't risk getting any 'bugs' in our cockpit while over the target.

Ahead of us, the F-15Cs had done an air-to-air sweep to make sure the skies were clear of any Iraqi fighters and by the time we approached the target, they were pretty far away. On the strike freq, we could hear Bud and Miller flights talking about various SAM and AAA sites, so we knew they were working, which made us happy since a captured HAWK battery was situated at our turn point for the run to the IP. The Iraqis placed a lot of confidence in that system, so they hadn't located any other long-range SAMs in the area. If they [the Weasels] took out the HAWK, then a big corridor all the way to the target opened up.

Once we hit the IP, we closed up our spacing to only four miles or thirty seconds between each F-111F to be on and off the target in the shortest amount of time, thus complicating the Iraqis' targeting problems and giving each of us a better chance of getting through. We heard lots of 'Magnum' calls, meaning the Weasels were shooting their HARMs.

I also saw the fireball of that F-15 kill on the Iraqi F1 above me.

Right at the IP, I heard Bud lead call my lead, Ram 41, telling him 'We got a couple of SA-6s, a couple of -8s, but we're Winchester [ordinance expended] and good luck.'

My lead acknowledged and pressed on. It was then that we really saw a wall of AAA. It was like you saw on CNN only worse. I watched it get thicker as we flew. It looked like flying in a tunnel where the tracers formed the ceiling just above us. I kept wishing we could set the TFR [terrain following radar] to lower than 200 feet to get us out of the fire. I even wanted to lower my seat, anything to get lower.

We had focused a lot pre-war on the MiGs and larger SAMs but not so much on the AAA. We quickly learned to respect it as well. We didn't know it at the time, but our ECM [Electronic Countermeasures] pod had failed, so we weren't jamming anybody and were highly visible to any enemy radars and we were getting tons of indications on our RWR [Radar Warning Receiver].

About thirty seconds from the pull point we got some pretty solid SA-6 indications but never a lock indication. Right then I saw a missile launch at my right, two o'clock. I watched the missile, looking like a Space Shuttle launching, fly across from my right to left, exploding at my ten o'clock about where I thought Ram 43 would have been. That all happened in much less time than it takes to tell, just a few seconds. I couldn't tell if someone had been hit or not, but I had no time to worry about it as my WSO [Weapon System Officer], Major Lee Monroe, was down in the scope on the target and I was weaving between the AAA.

At the pull point, I climbed to loft my bombs while Lee stayed in the radar to make sure we stayed on target. Just as I hit the pull point, I saw we'd been locked up by that SA-6, which was now at my six o'clock. I had to use the normal 4-g pull for two seconds but I put out a ton of chaff and broke the lock. At about 45 degrees nose high, right as I felt the weapons release, the SA-6 locked us up again. Instead of the planned post-release 135-degree slicing turn to the left (planned that way to take us down the Euphrates River to avoid threats), I pumped out boatloads of chaff, pulled between 5–6 g and continued my roll for 180 degrees, anything to break his lock.

While all this is going on, I heard/felt a 'thump', but I didn't know what it was. We were now inverted and pulling the nose down hard to get back to low altitude. It worked, so I rolled upright with the nose low and transitioned back to TFR flight at 200 feet with the target and all threats behind us.

What we failed to realise was that our extension to the west in our threat reaction had taken us away from the safety of the river. Then, at our twelve o'clock, we saw the brightly illuminated runway and taxiways of Shayka Mazhar airfield, one of the Iraqis' largest MiG-23 bases. I just couldn't believe it and froze for what seemed like forever. We screamed right down the centreline and it was like looking at a 'normal ops' base back home except the jets taxiing were enemy MiGs.

Fortunately for everyone involved, we were over and past the airfield before they realised we were there and could shoot at us. I just kept pumping out chaff in the meantime. I puked out so much I probably FOD'ed them out. [FOD – foreign object damage – what happens when a jet engine sucks in anything but air.]

Checking behind us, I could see some of the lights going off, if a little late as we left.

It turned out we had only released one CBU-89 on the primary target, probably due to a bad setting or a quick-pickle on my part during the threat reaction. We hit our secondary target, a road/rail junction, dumped the bombs and headed for the 'delouse' point [pre-designated area where either fighters or AWACS would ensure that only friendlies were exiting the area]. Exiting there, we climbed up, found the tankers and flew back to Taif, our base.

Unfortunately, the pain wasn't over yet. Remember, we had hit an anthrax storage site and there was a very real possibility that we'd flown through some of the bacilli during our run. The risk of contamination to us and the ground crews was very real.

After landing, therefore, we had to taxi through a water spray to clean the jet off, taxi back to the ramp, put our masks on and wait for life support to scrub the outside of the canopy and canopy rail to ensure it was anthrax free. Those guys are in full chem. gear so it was good that it was cool there early in the morning.

Once they'd done that, we popped the canopies and tried to stand up. After a 5.5-hour mission and another hour on the ground, I was numb from the waist down and couldn't move my legs. There just wasn't any blood below my waist and they had gone to sleep for a few hours. Our head life support technician, TSgt Ted Poe, picked me up under my arms and heaved me upright. The blood rush to my legs really hurt, but it was good to finally stand.

We found out at debrief that the F-117s had aborted their drops due to weather so we 'gatored' the target, but with no anthrax in the air. They had to go back later to take out the storage bunkers. After debrief, I went and had breakfast and went to bed. I thought my war was over until the next evening when the duty airman shook me awake, telling me 'You're on the schedule.'

It was then that it hit me and I thought every mission would be like this one. Fortunately, they were not. We had some scary moments during the rest of the war, but none like that night.

As an aside, one thing we did that I'm sure ticked off the Weasels was, on later missions if we felt threatened by an Iraqi SAM or AAA radar, we would make a bogus radio call like 'Coors, magnum!' Instantly, the offending radar would drop since they were quick studies and knew that a beer call sign

coupled with the word 'magnum' meant that their life could be
very short if they stayed up.

Continuing Bart Quinn's opening night story from that mission:

Up at the Tigris, we got lit up by the I-HAWK located at the spot
intel said he was. The indication was in the forward right quadrant of the -47 scope and we were headed north. We immediately
received launch indications from it as well. I saw a missile launch
on the ground and after the booster burned out, there was no
relative movement between the missile and us. That's bad
because that means it's tracking us. About the time I yelled for
Howdy to put out chaff, I could feel the bundles being ejected as
he also worked the ECM pod as well, trying to get the SAM to
break lock. I kept us out of burner because I didn't want to give
the AAA gunners a visual on me and make their job easier.
    At what I judged to be the last minute, I booted in full left
rudder, pulled the stick full aft and rudder rolled us around the
missile. It went by us and I looked back where I saw the flame go
by and then it exploded.
    Glad that was over, I looked at the instrument panel and saw
we were at 13,500 feet and only doing 230 knots. Low and slow
was not where I wanted us to be, so I hit the burners to get high
as quickly as I could.
    We shot at the HAWK site and, again, he went off the air at the
time of impact that the APR-47 counted down.
    Out of missiles, we still had time on station to cover the strike
package, so we stayed in the orbit. Even if we couldn't shoot, we
could still scare the SAM operators so that they would stay off
the air. It seemed to work out anyway. We did about three of
these 'square-ish' orbits that took about fifteen to twenty
minutes.
    The whole time we're there, the AAA is just unbelievable. You
can hear/feel the 'vvvummph', 'vvummph', of the smaller
calibre stuff and the concussion from the big rounds like 85 and
100-mm jolted the jet like a kick in the side or bottom depending.
    Finally, our time over, we're heading south as a single ship,
everyone making their way home on their own more or less. I
queried the flight to see if anyone had missiles yet and out of the

sixteen we carried, we shot fifteen with one guy having a hung missile that wouldn't leave his jet.

Egressing south, I used the APX [IFF – Identification Friend or Foe – interrogator] to see if we had all the F-4s and I only picked up six. I thought we lost one, but eventually we found him way out to the west of us where he'd been forced to manoeuvre to avoid AAA and SAMs of his own.

Continuing south, I saw more SAM launches, but I think they were unguided because they never tracked. I've always thought their intent was to scare us with the SAMs and force us down into AAA range, which historically has a much higher kill ratio compared with SAMs.

We got back to the tankers at about 0500. I was very relieved that we had everybody back safe. I had only about 1,200 lb of gas at that point so it was nice to get some insurance before flying back to Bahrain. Thinking, 'Man, I'm glad that's over' I then realised that was only ride one and it might be a long war.

Ken Hanson, then a captain, echoed Bart's comments about that first sortie:

The F-111 driver saw a picture of us in the *Stars and Stripes* newspaper after the war and sent me a copy of his radar cockpit tape. It has the radar picture from his jet as he flew the mission plus all the comm both inside his jet as well as the common frequency we were all on.

You can hear he and his WSO talking about how 'clean' their RWR was. We like to think it was due to us making the Iraqis keep their heads down. But we were up at 24,000 feet and these guys took it down to 100 feet, at night, in the midst of some of the heaviest flak in history. That crew nailed the CBW site and definitely earned their Silver Stars [actually Distinguished Flying Crosses].

Gary Rattray (then a major) was the EWO in the # 3 jet of Quinn's leading flight. Crewed with pilot Mike 'Diesel' Deas, he recalls some of the same in events as well as ones deeply personal to his crew.

As we crossed the border, I remember seeing lots of AAA. There were all different types – 'whip' lines of closely spaced red balls weaving back and forth; groups of three red balls, slightly space apart; and then the shots that just looked like one flash. What was interesting to me was how detached and analytical I felt at the time.

Even though this was my first time in combat, I remembered the descriptions of the different types of AAA. I knew that the 'whip' ones were smaller calibre stuff that couldn't reach us, so it was no threat. The 'three red shots' were 57 mm that unless they got lucky couldn't reach us either. Finally, the single shot flashes were the bigger guns like 85 or 100 mm that could reach us, so they were the ones to really key in on.

During training, we practised where the EWO is supposed to maintain the visual look out for everything aft of the '3–9' line – that is, everything behind the wing – while the pilot was responsible for seeing all the threats from the wing line forward.

For the war, however, we figured that the major threat to us at the higher altitudes would be SAMs or AAA and not enemy fighters since we had lots of air-to-air assets in the theatre. So 'Diesel' and I worked out a contract where I would mainly stay 'heads down' in the radar and AN/APR-47 looking for threats and he'd do all the visual scanning. This actually worked to my advantage because after seeing all the AAA, I forced myself to stay in the equipment so I couldn't see a lot of the outside stuff and get scared. Mike didn't have that luxury and I heard him over the intercom with some 'Oh shits!' and the like.

As it was so dark outside, I actually had better SA on the 'big picture' than did he. For example, as we were going in, the first wave of strikers were coming out. We'd been briefed on their timing so we knew when they'd be approaching us southbound as we were headed north just south of the border.

Now the border was the line where guys could turn on their lights heading south to increase the chances of not being run into by one of the hundreds of jets airborne.

I could see what I described to Mike as a 'train' of jets coming south, but just then I felt the jet break left in a 4 g turn and felt Mike punch out three flares that lit up the entire night sky.

Looking up from my scope, I could see somebody with their lights on up and to our left, exactly where the friendlies were egressing south. But the sudden appearance of a set of lights startled 'Diesel' and he threat reacted as he'd been trained – to turn into the threat to minimise the time and angles that an enemy could use to shoot you down.

Now the other jet (an F-16) saw us react into him so he reacted to us and broke into us, popping flares. I could just see this shaping up as a 'blue on blue' fight, so I jumped on the radio saying, 'Friendly, friendly, friendly!' to try and defuse the situation while at the same time telling Mike that the other guy was one of ours.

Eventually, both jets turned back onto their respective courses, but I have no doubt there were three soiled flight suits from that encounter!

At the target area, it was much as Bart described it. We (nos 3 and 4) had been assigned to the north-east quadrant of the F-111s' target area. At the end of our station time, we were still working an -8 with a good chance of getting him, so I told Mike to keep heading north. I eventually got enough good data to shoot, but at about the same time, I feel Mike threat react to the left again, puking flares.

I asked what was going on, but he interrupted me with a request for the next nav point that was on our way out. I gave it to him, but missed his call that 'his light was burnt out' and I watched us swing through the southerly heading. All this while, we are still in afterburner and descending.

After passing the heading by about 30 degrees, Mike asks me specifically for the exit heading so I give that to him. Once again, we turn past it by about 30 degrees, still in 'burner and dropping.

I finally figure out that he can't see his ADI (attitude-director indicator) so he doesn't know when to roll out on the correct course. So I tell him to turn back south and when to roll out so we finally start heading out, but by this time we've done three 360-degree turns in afterburner, and are down to about 13,000 feet over the target area!

We're heading out and by using the APX I realise that everyone made it out since we're the last ones. Historically, it's usually the last one in a flight who gets shot down, so I'm not thrilled to be there just then.

As we egressed and climbed, we realised that our fuel state was serious and we discussed cleaning up the jet by punching off all the externals and reducing our drag. Mike decides to keep the pylons and the centreline tank since their drag is minimal, but to dump the two outboard 'bags'.

He hesitates punching them saying, 'Well, I don't really know what's underneath us and where they'll land.'

I replied to him that we (the Coalition) have just dropped thousands of pounds of bombs on him and he's shot thousands of rounds of AAA that will come back down. I don't think two empty 370-gallon fuel tanks are going to make much difference!

Cleaning them off, we climb to our best fuel burn altitude and speed and head to the tanker track but we are way below what we need. We realise that we've got, maybe, one shot at the tanker before we have to divert to KKMC [King Khalid Military City – a vast base in northern Saudi Arabia]. We relay our status to Bart who talks to the tanker.

To that crew's credit, they turn north and leave their track to

Hot pitting: taking on gas and changing out crews while leaving the engines running. A great time saver, it is nonetheless a dangerous procedure if done carelessly. (DoD photo via Guy Aceto)

come get us. Considering this was the opening night of the war and nobody really knew what the air threat was, this was a courageous move on the tanker's part.

I ran the hottest intercept I've ever run as we meet the tanker head on and Mike does a great job to roll out underneath the boom. The boomer, in turn, sticks us on the first try and we start taking gas. We had about 200–300 pounds remaining before we would have had to divert.

After getting home, everyone else in the flight taxies to the 'hot pits' so the jets can be turned for another mission. Since we'd dumped our tanks, we had to take it back to the revetment so new tanks could be fitted. Bart good-naturedly ribs us over the radio about being 'special', but it was great to have everyone get back in one piece.

We were credited with killing that SA-8, by the way. And we flew another mission that night, but it was nowhere nearly as exciting as that first one!

Major Joe Healy was the EWO in the # 6 Phantom of Quinn's flight that night. Crewed with pilot Captain Jim Hartle, he recalled some the moments from his first combat sortie:

That night, I recall looking at the sunset wondering if it would be my last. Melodramatic, maybe, but I watched it settle below the horizon and had the thought. I knew what we'd be facing, but I didn't know how good or bad the Iraqis would be.

After the mass briefing, we split up for our flight briefing, but much of it was 'standard', so we didn't take long there. Then it was off to life support to put on g-suits and survival vests, grab our helmets and bags and head out.

We got to the jet about 0100 and I can recall how surreal the revetment and ramp looked. It was all stark shades of bluish-white and black. The only light came from the gasoline generator-powered light-alls and they put out a blinding white light that washed the colour from everything. In the shadows where the light didn't reach, like behind the landing gear and the opposite sides of the HARMs, away from the light, it was absolutely pitch black.

As the crew chief helped me strap in, he said, 'God bless you,

Sir.' I was so engrossed with my own thoughts that the realisation that there were other people concerned about our welfare somewhat surprised me and made me feel good. I thanked him and he moved to the front to help Jim.

While doing start up, we talked to the crew chief via an intercom system. He could see the tail surfaces react as the pilot checked flight controls, tell us of anything wrong with the engines or any leaks once we'd cranked up.

Just before we started taxiing, I told him that the second HARM 'is for you'.

Normally, during peacetime sorties, it's custom for the crew chief to snap a quick salute as we taxi past, and we'd do a quick return of his salute. On this night, as we turned onto the taxiway out of the revetment, all seven of the ground crew were lined up and in unison, popped the sharpest salutes I've seen in my career. I got a little lump in my throat a little as I returned the salute. I said a quick prayer as we lined up on the runway and then we were off.

It was about twenty to twenty-five minutes to the tankers and we were fragged for the third in the three-tanker cell. Naturally, as we were closing in on the cell with them heading north, our tanker starts his turn south early, leaving us in a tail chase. We called him and he turned around for us.

Getting our gas, we headed north in a radar trail with the next jet about two miles in front of us. Looking outside, I can see absolutely nothing, no lights, nothing, just inky blackness, the only lights visible being the stars. For a moment I thought, 'What combination of intentional and accidental events in the course of my life brought to this point in time and space?'

About ten minutes after crossing the Iraqi border, I see three bright red lights come up, then wink out at our nine o'clock. It took me a second to realise it was AAA. I calmly told Jim, 'Triple A, left nine o'clock. No factor.' I didn't see any more for a few more minutes, but that changed the further north we flew.

A few minutes after the first AAA we got a scare. Our number four in our flight (and number eight in the formation) called, 'Budweiser 04, contact! Nose 40, angels 24', which meant he had picked up an air-to-air contact on his APQ-120 radar and that the contact was 40 degrees off his (and our) nose at 24,000 feet.

A different look at two George-based F-4Gs about to take off at dusk. (USAF)

Close up of impending doom. (USAF)

'Hunter-killer' element of an F-4G leading an F-16CG, combining the outstanding SAM killing capabilities of the Phantom's APR-47/HARM combination with the remarkable air-to-air capabilities of the 'Viper's' digital air-to-air radar and dogfighting agility. (DoD photo via Guy Aceto)

Although this photo is over Nevada, it does show the F-4G's typical load-out towards the end of the war when SAM and radar targets were scarce. Here, HARMS occupy each of the outboard stations while CBUs take up the inboard. Not shown is the belly tank underneath the fuselage center. (DoD photo via Guy Aceto)

Flagships of the 37th TFW and the 561st TFS. Note the wing king's jet carries the colors of all the squadrons on the tail fin while the squadron commander's has his unit's color only. (DoD photo via Guy Aceto)

A Weasel driver maneuvers his jet into position behind a tanker to get gas over the bland background of Saudi Arabia. The refueling door located a couple of feet behind the EWO's rear cockpit is open, ready to plugged by the tanker's boom operator. (USAF)

It ain't pretty; a nose-on view of the 'Double Ugly', one of the many nicknames of the famous Phantom. Here an F-4G at George AFB carries 'wall to wall' HARMs under the wings. (USAF)

Oil well fires in Kuwait, set by Saddam Hussein's forces in a failed attempt to slow down the Coalition forces. (Ken Hanson)

Getting gas over the mountains of the western United States. This jet is from the Weapons School at Nellis AFB, Nevada. (USAF)

F-4G's front cockpit. Note the limited forward visibility due to the canopy framing, the APG-120 multi-mode radar screen directly in front, etc. The APR-47 repeater scope that relayed the threats being detected is the square box to the right of the radar scope. (Ken Hanson)

The F-4G's rear cockpit. It was here that the Weasel EWO fought the deadly electronic duel with air defenses. Flight instruments line the top row followed by the APR-47 controls. The visor sticking up at an angle is the display for the APG-120 radar. The green bag on the seat is Hanson's helmet bag, used to carry everything from charts, checklists, to water and snacks. (Ken Hanson)

The EWO's APR-47 console showing the radar detection screens in a test mode. But it does give some idea of what the EWO saw. (Ken Hanson)

The PPIC scope in a test mode. This was the primary threat display used by the Weasel crew. (Ken Hanson)

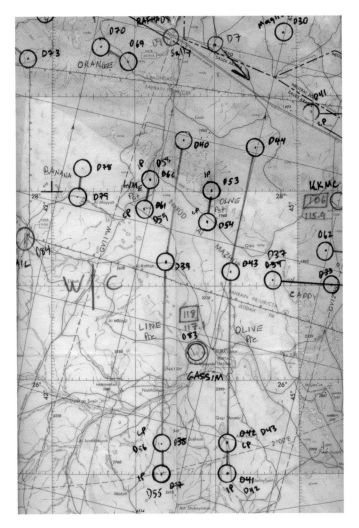

One of Schreiner's maps showing the most often used A/R (aerial refueling) tracks in northern Saudi Arabia. (Jim Schreiner)

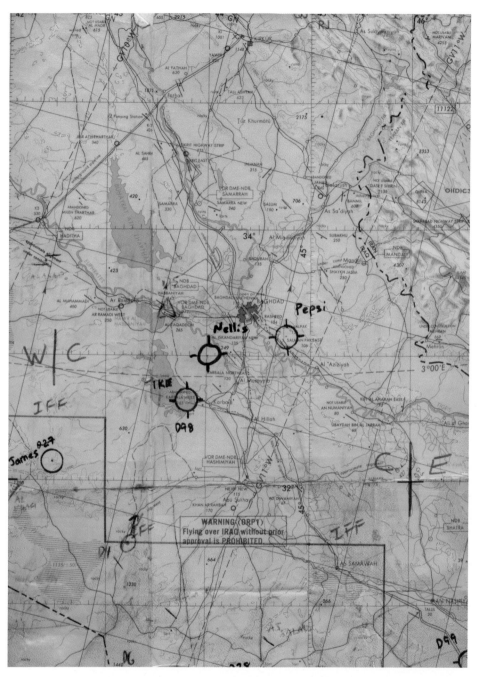

Another showing central Iraq and Baghdad labeled as 'Nellis'. As such, referencing it during air to air communication gave everyone a common point of reference. For example, a call of 'Bogey, Nellis, 020, 20 miles' told everyone who was in on the plan that there was an unknown aircraft north of Baghdad at twenty miles. 'Pepsi' was the code word for another location on the map as well. (Jim Schreiner)

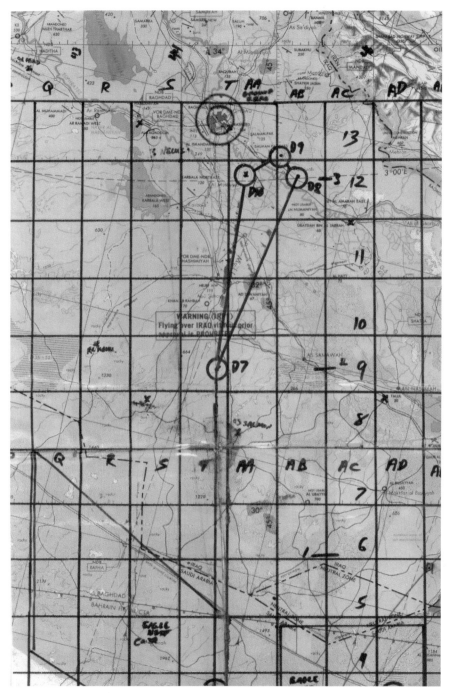

Grid map used over Kuwait. By dividing up the area into smaller chunks, more precise control of aircraft and munitions was possible. If a pilot was told of enemy activity at 'M9' then like the board in the game of 'Battleship', he could look at the grid reference that corresponded. Superimposed on the grid is one of Schreiner's Weasel Police patrols. (Jim Schreiner)

'Three bags and two HARMS.' (USAF)

A four ship flying over the coast of the tiny nation of Bahrain. (USAF)

A mixed 'hunter-killer' team of Spangdahlem's line up of F-16CGs and F-4Gs. (USAF)

'Contact!' It only takes a few minutes to fill up. (USAF)

BREAK! An in-bound Phantom delivering close-range destruction via the CBUs on the inboard pylons turns violently to avoid a simulated threat in this training sortie. (DoD photo via Guy Aceto)

The aftermath of a HARM strike on an Iraqi SA-2 SAM site. Here, intelligence inspectors as well as the curious view the results post-war of a very successful mission. (DoD photos via Guy Aceto)

Another intimidating photo of Clark AB-based Weasels taxiing. The sheer brutishness of the Phantom shows up well here. (DoD photo via Guy Aceto)

I had set the strobe of our radar to level so that it was sweeping out ahead of us at our altitude. At his call, I looked down at my scope and there was the radar return!

Mindful that my best friend was ten nautical miles closer, at the front of our formation, I thought 'Aw crap! There's somebody coming straight at us, head on! How did he get by AWACS and the F-15 CAP [Combat Air Patrol]?'

At the same time I told Jim, 'CW [continuous wave] on! Switches air-to-air', which told him that I was going to lock this guy up with our radar and he should reconfigure his armament switches from HARMs to the AIM-7 Sparrows we carried in the two aft missile bays.

I was going to lock this guy up, light up his RWR and, hopefully, he'd do a 180 and run away to the north (and maybe into an F-15). We knew that was the Iraqi tactic if they were lit up. If he kept coming, we'd shoot him in the face if someone ahead of us didn't do it first.

The contact had not responded to IFF interrogation, which, of course, an enemy aircraft wouldn't. At the same time, I realised it looked just a bit odd. 'Oh, good! Maybe…please let it be . . . ' I thought. I said to Jim, 'Wait a minute, let me lock him up.'

I did and 'Yes! It is!' I thought. Our Vc (pronounced 'Vee sub cee') or overtake velocity was the same as our groundspeed, which meant the object was stationary in mid-air.

Only one thing did that and looked that way on radar. 'Miller Zero One, ahh, Budweiser Zero Two, contact *chaff*! Contact is chaff!' I told Bart and everyone else in the formation. There was a noticeable pause and then I could almost hear the sighs of relief from the other jets. The call was then echoed a few times through the formation, 'Contact chaff' and 'Roger, understand chaff'. [Chaff is a bundle of metal-coated strips put out by aircraft on both sides as a decoy to searching radars. Harmless in itself, but can be effective as a distracting tactic.]

At one point, we were slightly west of a highway and I could see cars absolutely flying down the road with their lights on, all of them heading south. Then I started to see lots of AAA – some of it white flashes, mostly it was bright red like automobile tail lights, and I could see bright spots in the distance that flew up at an angle without losing speed like AAA; those were SAMs.

One SAM on our left side was so close I could see its exhaust flickering like a candle as it went by. At the same time on our right, I saw some lime green tracer going under us.

With all that light, I could see an undercast beneath us, which I thought odd since the weather forecast was for extreme clear. It wasn't until the next day that I realised the AAA was so heavy all the smoke from the individual bursts had merged into a continuous layer!

After the ground fire started getting heavy, it seemed there was no way we would avoid being hit. I got this irrational thought momentarily that a hole was going to open in the floor right between my feet and I'd be looking down at the highway and the ground lights through it. Of course, if a hole *had* been blown in the floor, it probably would have done serious damage to me too!

I found myself thinking, 'So far, so good. We haven't been hit yet.' Then, 'If we do get hit, we might get knocked down right

Unique air to air shot showing the underside of an F-4G. The load out here is HARMs on the outboard stations, AGM-65 'Maverick' short range air to ground missiles on the inboards, a centerline fuel tank and two AIM-7 'Sparrow' air to air missiles in the aft missile wells. (USAF)

away, or be able to limp south and punch out or we might make it back across the Saudi border.' This whole thought process seemed to go on for two or three minutes, but was probably only ten seconds or so, I don't really know. Finally, I said to myself, 'Screw it, do your job and deal with a hit after it happens' and got back to work:

As soon as we got within LOS [line of sight] of Baghdad, the APR-47 lit up. We were tasked to hit a line of four SA-8s north-east of Salman Pak that were lined up roughly east to west.

Sure enough, I found them as predicted, and shot at one of the centre ones. As the time of flight counter for the HARM counted down, at '0' the site went 'dotted', a pretty good indication that we'd killed it.

I targeted the second HARM but it wouldn't fire. I ran through the checklist again, Jim confirmed that the proper station was selected and the master arm was on. I handed the target info to the missile via the hand-off button and pickled again. Again, nothing happened. I tried probably five times to shoot that second missile, but it never would launch. The amount of cussing in my cockpit was pretty colourful that night. Later we found out, there was a software failure that kept the missile from launching.

As we turned south, I had a pretty good view of Baghdad. It was just a solid layer of AAA flashes, tracers – sparkling and churning everywhere.

Looking toward Kuwait during egress, I saw what I can only describe as a green, rolling vapour that covered a patch of the desert. I don't know what it was, but that's what I saw.

After the post-strike tanker, I said to Jim, tongue in cheek, 'That wasn't so bad.' We landed back at Isa just about dawn. Turning off the taxiway into the revetment area, all the maintenance guys were cheering, waving, and pumping their fists into the air! Many had waited for our return even though their shifts had ended. As soon as we met at the bottom of the ladder, I shook Jim's hand as well.

After landing, the crews from each jet debriefed the maintenance troops with any snags encountered with the jets while flying, then headed off to the intel debrief. Here they gave the bare facts of times of HARM shots, results as indicated by radars going down at the end of the missiles' time of flight or not, any explosions or SAM launches noted, as well as the altitudes of the AAA. They turned in the tapes from the Phantom's CONRAC system so that they could be replayed later to see what frequencies and problems the crew might have encountered but not debriefed verbally.

By taking in all this information, the intelligence officers could pass on to the ATO planners at CENTAF headquarters which targets were destroyed and which ones still need attention. Also, the threat briefing for the next crews to fly could be updated with more precise data.

Steve Johns, up from his duties at Riyadh, flew in the second 'go' of the war. He attended the mass oh-dark-thirty briefing given to all the crews the night before, but he had to wait for daylight and his turn to fight. Being second is rarely a good thing, and waiting to hear how the first wave did just gave the butterflies more time to get their act together in a man's stomach.

Says Johns:

We'd been told to take our anti-nerve agent pills, but they made me sick so I quit after the first one. When it was my flight's take-off time, it was broad daylight.

My pilot, Scott Swanson, and I had been briefed to go against an SA-2 site in Kuwait. It had already popped off a couple of shots at the first wave, but nobody could say whether they'd killed it or not.

So after we hit the tanker and fenced in, we put the position on the nose and sure enough, I got an active SA-2 radar on the APR-47. It went just like training in the cockpit.

I said, 'SA-2 on the nose, give me station', which told Scott that I had the SA-2 located and I needed him to select one of the underwing points carrying a HARM so I could target it against the SAM.

He confirmed, 'Master arm on.' This meant that the master arm switch – essentially a safety switch on his instrument panel that allowed power to the firing circuits – was switched on.

Then I handed off the target to the missile, that is, fed the target via the AP-47 to the HARM so that it knew what and where I wanted it to look after launch.

I made a quick countdown, 3, 2, 1, then onto the radio, 'Lonestar 33 is magnum!'

The SA-2 stopped transmitting at about the time the time of flight counter said the HARM reached the spot, so I thought I was a hero and nailed it. But later flights were shot at by the same site, so obviously he survived.

Captain Vinnie 'VQ' Quinn and his EWO, Major Ken 'Momar' Spaar, also flew in the first daylight mission of the war. Tasked with protecting twenty-four F-16s attacking the Shaibah Airfield near Basra, Iraq, Quinn led his four ship inbound:

In the same area, I knew there was a four ship of Weasels protecting some Marine F-18s hitting Tallil further to the west of us and a two ship north-west of Kuwait. There were gonna be a lot of airplanes around in a short period of time.

The mission started out with a problem in that we couldn't get our centreline to fill up so we pushed already some 2,000 pounds short of gas. To make our TOT, I couldn't follow the planned route, which drove us around some known threats. Instead, we had to go in a straight line from the tanker. That line took us over the Al Faw peninsula. All was quiet there except for one AAA gun at the very tip of the peninsula. There he was, this one guy, plinking away. I thought it was kind of comical.

As we crossed the border, I remember seeing all the trenches and smoke and thinking that looks just like something out of World War I.

As we got closer to the target area, we were briefed about an SA-2. Sure enough, we started seeing missiles in the air, but at the same time, Momar was telling me about being tracked by Iranian SA-2s off to our east. I was trying to think how I'd handle that situation with my flight if we started getting shot at from both sides. Fortunately, we didn't have to do that.

Spaar continues the story.

We could see the contrails from the SA-2s; that was something we'd never encountered before. At the same time, there was a dirty brownish-grey haze building up below us. At the time, I didn't realise that the haze was actually smaller calibre AAA.

So for this SA-2, we picked up a strong enough signal to shoot, so 'VQ' selected a missile, his habit always being the right one first. I locked up the SA-2 and shot. The HARM came off and tracked across our nose to the left, flaming out our right motor.

Quinn continues:

I pushed the nose over to start the engine restart checklist and saw the same haze below us. I didn't know what it was either, I thought it was just some cloud as well. I got the engine restarted and we continued.

We fired four HARMs on that sortie, two at SA-2s and two at SA-3s. They gave us credit for destroying one of each.

Paul 'Baloo' Gregory (then a major), EWO with the 81st, flew his first mission on the afternoon of 17 January 1991. A Weasel since 1983, this was his first time in combat.

We took off in the late afternoon and headed to the KTO [Kuwait Theatre of Operations]. At 1900, after hitting the tanker and fencing in, I picked up an active SA-2. My pilot, Captain Vince Cooper, used the technique of selecting both stations since we were carrying two HARMs and three bags. This was our standard way of operating since we felt it gave us more flexibility quicker should we need to get both missiles off in a hurry.

Anyway, I handed off an SA-2 to the left hand HARM, and pickled it off. It whooshed off and went up for altitude as they're designed to do, as it sped away. At the same time, we got a flashing 'fail' light on the second missile, so it was useless now. At the end of the time of flight, for the HARM the SA-2 site went 'dotted' meaning the site had stopped radiating.

I don't think we got him because I found out later that several guys shot HARMs at this same site plus the site was fragged by strikers several times, dropping iron bombs and CBU.

After the war, four of us drove out to the site to see what it looked like. The Fan Song radar antennas had holes in them and most of the missile launchers were empty. Some guys went back later and unbolted the Fan Song guidance antenna from the remains of the site and took it back for display in front of the squadron at Spangdahlem.

When we landed and went through the de-arm area, the de-arm crew asked us if we knew that the second missile was burned out. Obviously we didn't. In fact, besides the flashing 'fail' light, neither Vince nor I saw or felt anything unusual after the first HARM shot.

The following week, a very smart McAir [McDonnell Douglas, the F-4's manufacturer] engineer named Larry Scott came to Isa as part of a Tiger Team to investigate the problem. I had worked with Larry previously when we were both on the F-4G Test Team at George a few years prior to the war. He figured out that some of the jets would send a fire pulse to each station if more than one was selected. He wrote up the problem and recommended that crews select only one station at a time. He also worked with the software engineers at Warner Robins Air Logistics Center on a software fix for the APR-47.

I gave him one of the HARM umbilical cables from one of my shots later in the war. That cable fed the data to the missile from the underwing pylon; when the missile fired, the cable separated and stayed with the pylon. We used them as our souvenirs for our shots.

In those first eighteen hours of *Desert Storm*, Weasels flew seventy-nine sorties and fired 125 HARMs to kill a confirmed fifty-six radars at SAM and AAA sites. Especially hard hitting in the more concentrated KTO, the F-4Gs destroyed any sort of coherent Iraqi IADS there. Although there would be more excitement in KTO missions as the war progressed, the overwhelming firepower of those first waves of Phantoms secured air superiority in Kuwait from SAMs.

The SAMs and AAA in Iraq itself, on the other hand, were much larger targets to destroy to the same degree. More time and many more sorties were needed to defeat Saddam's forces there.

Chapter Eleven

For the Weasels, daily life started into the grind of war with no end in sight.

Flew two more combat missions today. The first was an abortion. The weather was dogshit and after having to leave my first jet because it was broken, I stepped to the spare and rushed through the pre-flight. With the rush, my situational awareness rapidly fell behind.

As we approached the target area, our navigation system, the ARN-101, 'ARNY', locked up. At this point, I was so out to lunch that I decided to abort our mission and RTB [return to base]. In retrospect, I could've continued to the target area and gotten my missiles off. I felt bad about leaving early. I essentially failed, but luckily, no one died as a result.

Last night's mission was a different story. After starting engines, my backseater, Dan Sharp, was unable to get the ARNY to work. On to another spare.

After wasting ten minutes reviewing the 781 [the aircraft's record of maintenance documentation] and pre-flighting the jet, I discovered that only one of the three external tanks had fuel. This would have created a serious imbalance problem on take-off, not to mention being almost 1,000 gallons short of fuel. And we needed every drop for this mission, so it was on to the third, and hopefully, final jet.

Schreiner was flying as the # 2 of a four ship, call sign Longhorn 31, flight led by Major Steve 'Teach' Jenny and EWO, Captain Mark 'Gucci' Buccigrossi. Schreiner was Longhorn 32. The mission for the flight was to provide direct support for a cell of Boeing B-52 'Stratofortresses' dropping some fifty-four bombs weighing 750 lb each on the dug in positions of one of Saddam's vaunted Republican Guard armoured divisions.

The B-52, nicknamed since its Vietnam days as the 'BUFF', for Big Ugly Fat Fucker, had paid a fearsome toll to North Vietnamese SA-2s in that earlier conflict. Planners for *Desert Storm* wanted to ensure things went better for this fight.

The Longhorn flight would go in ahead of the BUFFs and target and kill the SA-2s and any other SAM that had the altitude range to reach the bombers in their high 30,000 feet track. It was a high priority, do or die mission for the Weasels.

By this time, 3 & 4 were long gone and lead, tired of waiting for us, decided to take off without us. I could tell he was pissed because as he taxied by, he twirled his hand above his helmet, telling us to hurry up. At the time, he didn't realise we were on our third jet.

Sweating profusely by this time, I rapidly completed the pre-flight and got the jet running. Fortunately, everything worked and we were out of the chocks in record time.

I called tower for take-off clearance and was told to wait for three aircraft landing. The last one was an emergency and might take the barrier and close the runway. Luckily, he didn't and we were off, but twenty minutes late.

Tom Gummo was the near permanent SOF [Supervisor of Flying – the tactical director of ground operations responsible for solving any problems and monitoring safety during them] due to an injury suffered not long before the war kicked off. Frustrated at missing the action, he recalled the Marines and Navy using Sheikh Isa as their primary divert base when carrier-based jets had a problem. It was good for them to have an alternate that was longer than 1,000 feet and not pitching with the waves, but the many aircraft emergencies did tie up the runway for extended periods of time, making a shambles of scheduled F-4G ops.

(This page and opposite) The much improved Weasel end of Shaikh Isa's runway. The revetments and ramp improvements are much in evidence .

Schreiner continues:

I proceeded direct to the tanker as fast as the Phantom would go
without using afterburner – about 540 knots groundspeed. Not
bad considering a 50-knot headwind and all the shit we were
carrying.

It was a little sporty at the tanker with him flying in and out of
a cloud layer. The fact that I was a little nervous didn't make it
any easier. After taking a full load of fuel, we proceeded direct to
the target area.

Schreiner and Sharp made their target time and rejoined their flight.
At about 0207, Buccigrossi detected an SA-2 in search mode short of
the BUFFs' intended target. Needing to deal with this threat but not
wanting to strip all Weasel coverage from the bombers, he directed
Longhorn 33 and 34 to continue while 31 and 32 dealt with this
problem.

Said 'Gucci', 'We picked up the SA-2's signal – first in search mode

and then rapidly switch to targeting. We then pickled a HARM at it.'
Schreiner's view of the event was:

> At the TOT for the BUFFs, we saw many explosions on the
> ground as they salvoed. At the same time, we picked a '2 bar' on
> the SA-2 from the APR-47 ['2 bar' was shorthand for saying the
> system had picked up strong, reliable indications of an SA-2D/E
> SAM, an improved version of the original SA-2.]
>
> It went from range unknown to range known to tracking indi-
> cations to a firing indication in about as much time as it takes to
> read this sentence. Lead said he was working the signal so we
> didn't shoot, although, in retrospect, we should have because it
> was the only chance we'd have.

Buccigrossi continues his part of the story:

> We were at medium altitude at around 350 knots. There was a
> cloud base around 1,800–2000 feet AGL [above ground level]. We
> picked up an orange glow below the cloud deck at our nine
> o'clock. Popping through the undercast, we saw two SA-2s
> tracking toward us. Teach and I both saw them, so as he rolled
> the jet, I put out chaff and hit the switches for the ECM pod.
>
> Both missiles continued towards our six o'clock but climbed
> while we descended fairly rapidly. I watched the missiles
> explode behind us.

Seconds after avoiding that first pair of SAMs, the Longhorn flight
was targeted again. Longhorn 31 saw a second pair of missiles arc
upwards toward them from their two o'clock position. Again, they
evaded the SAMs, trading altitude and airspace for distance from the
warheads. The missiles guided to just behind them and detonated with
no damage to their jet.
Buccigrossi continues:

> Immediately after those two exploded, we saw a third set on our
> left side, so away we went again, down and around, to avoid
> these guys. The missiles couldn't turn hard enough to stay with
> us, so for the third time in about ninety seconds, they tracked
> behind us and exploded.

The good news was that in less than two minutes, we'd avoided six SAMs and made that site shoot his whole wad, so they wouldn't be able to shoot again at the BUFFs until they'd reloaded and that would take them too long.

The bad news was that with all our turning and burning, we'd dropped down into AAA range. I looked down at our gauges and saw that we were below 10,000 feet and under 300 knots. I told 'Teach' to climb or speed up and he said, 'I'm working on it.'

From Schreiner's cockpit:

I looked in the direction of the launch indication on the scope and saw a sight I'd never hoped to see. SA-2 missiles were headed towards us!

I immediately selected AB [afterburner], rolled the aircraft inverted, and pulled. All this while keeping the SA-2s on the beam.

I was at 25,000 [feet] when I started for the deck and levelled at about 10,000. It was a standard manoeuvre we'd practised in training but for safety reasons weren't allowed to try at night – amazing how physics and the airplane work the same at night as during the day.

As I did this, I told Dan to hit the chaff and ECM pod. Apparently, the combination of all three did the trick because one by one, I watched them arc harmlessly away and self-destruct at the end of their life.

After we avoided the SAMs, I rolled level and saw a blue glow outside. Our -47 wasn't showing any threats, so I couldn't figure out what the glow was.

Then I realised I was still in afterburner, and the glow was the flames from my engines. What a perfect advertisement for our position! So I pulled the throttles back and started climbing so we could work that site again.

Longhorn 31 had also used a lot of gas avoiding the six SAMs, and being as they carried only one 'bag' they were short on gas and couldn't hang around. They RTB'd, flying due south into Saudi Arabia where they landed at a base, got gas, and flew back to Sheikh Isa.

Schreiner and Sharp, having taken a spare configured with three 'bags', had more gas and stayed in the area, even after the B-52s departed, trying to nail the SA-2 site that had gotten their attention so dramatically. Schreiner continues:

> We'd point our nose at the site and the scope would 'go dotted', meaning the site wasn't active, but the APR-47 was giving us a bearing and range on the estimated position it had on that site. If we turned our tail to him, we'd get lit up again and get a solid lock on him.
>
> The HARM could be fired from either cockpit and could even be fired while pointing away from a target (it would position itself after launch to find the target indicated), but with no need to shoot since he was out of SAMs, we decided to not waste the round. If we could keep the bad guys from doing anything effective without expending ordinance, we considered that as effective if not as satisfying.
>
> We finally bingoed out and turned for the post-mission tanker track. The weather remained marginal to bad on the return trip and staying on the tanker was very disorienting.
>
> The combination of clouds, stars, and the tanker turns had me thinking we were upside down more than once. I was glad to get off the tanker and RTB; we arrived back at Sheikh Isa at around 0315. It had been an exciting night, and we wound up flying again early that morning.

Likewise, Jenny and Buccigrossi found themselves immediately back in the saddle after returning from their exciting sortie. Handed a mission planning package while their jet was being rearmed and re-fuelled, they led another four ship, this time to Baghdad. They flew as lead because they had the only operating APQ-120 radar in that flight and had to be the pathfinder for the rest.

As a result of their efforts in protecting the B-52s and avoiding the six SA-2s in those few seconds, (then) Major Steve Jenny and Captain Mark Buccigrossi were awarded the Silver Star, the third highest award for valour in the face of the enemy in the US military. Bart Quinn and Ken Hanson would also win Silver Star medals for valour in the face of the enemy for their opening night mission. They flew again on the afternoon of 18 January.

Of that mission, Quinn's clearest memory is of the sight of the late

Wall to wall HARMs. Here the flagship of the 561st TFS recovers after an early morning mission. Note the endcap that normally covers the braking parachute is open, thus it's at the end of a mission. This photo was taken in late 1989 at George AFB, California. Notice the stark surroundings and compare it to the Weasels' environment during the war. (USAF)

afternoon sun shining on towering clouds of the brewing thunderstorms and the armada of big KC-135 tankers ploughing around and through those clouds.

Joining up with the tankers was the strike package of fifty F-16s headed for ground attack missions in Kuwait. Quinn led a four ship of Weasels to protect the package. The sight of all those aircraft in that colourful sky tableau is still vivid to him today.

His next mission was memorable for a different reason, a bandit at his six o'clock.

It was another afternoon 'go'; this time he was leading a four ship that was only numbered three due to one of the jets ground aborting in advance of some RAF Tornado GR1s attacking al Jabar airfield at extremely low level. Formally named Ahmed al Jabar, it was a former Kuwaiti Air Force base that had been occupied by the Iraqis. It lay about thirty-five miles south-west of Kuwait City. Using the JP233 runway denial weapon, the Tornadoes streaked in just above the sandy desert floor at around 600 knots.

At that altitude, they were game for every Iraqi weapon heavier than a slingshot. They counted on surprise and high speed to get in and out of the target. They were very successful in their low-level attacks, but at a heavy cost of five Tornadoes within the first week.

Says Quinn of the British aviators:

Pound for pound, those are some of the ballsiest crews in any Air Force.

We set up our orbit to the south of the airfield with somebody in the orbit always pointing towards the field. Looking down at the target, it looked like the overhead shots at a rock concert where everyone is popping off flashbulbs continuously. Except theses flashes were AAA and the Tornadoes headed directly into it to lay down their loads. That was a very brave thing to see.

During this, AWACS called out two F1s taking off from north of us heading south, then the targets faded.

A minute later or so, AWACS called out a bogey north of us, low. Then my RHAW scope showed the F1's radar, the Cyrano multi-mode radar, in search mode at about seven miles from me.

Our Eagle CAP was up in the 30s, not in a position to intercept in time. Then the APR-47 shows a trackbar from the Cyrano, which means he's looking at me specifically.

Howdy hits the chaff and the F1 bites off on it for a minute, then comes back onto me. He's within two miles and approaching my six o'clock. The -47 is giving us a good bearing and range, then the indications go away. We don't know where he is or where he went.

We'd been flying north during this, and at the airfield turn south as part of the Weasel orbit. Our # 3, who was pointing north, called 'Magnum' at a site he was working. Howdy is still thinking of the F1 and his mindset is still air-to-air. He sees the missile flash and streak from behind us and yells for me to 'Break!' I knew it was # 3's HARM, so I didn't and got Howdy's SA back. But it was a 'sporty' evening.

Joe Healy also saw some RAF Tornadoes in action. Escorting them in their attack on a POL [petroleum/oil/lubricant] dump in southern Iraq, he recalls:

It was pitch black, not a light anywhere. We're offset about five miles south of the target, and nothing's radiating any sort of threat to the Tornadoes.

Right at their TOT, I see the first bomb go off. In that flash, I saw this tall cylindrical tower or storage tank that spewed an incredibly tall column of flame from the top. I'm guessing it was 1,000 feet tall and lit up the desert for probably five miles around. That fire lasted for many minutes and was still burning as we flew out of sight to the south-east.

VQ Quinn and Momar Spaar's first night sortie on 20 January offered moments of comedy and tension in rapid succession. Tasked with protecting a strike over Baghdad, they flew in a nearly straight line. Fuel considerations combined with the need to remain on station to cover the strikers' TOT meant the Weasels had no extra gas to devote

Bart Quinn gets gas from a KC-135 'Stratotanker' in this formation flight. (Gary Rattray)

to any feints or finesse on the Iraqis. Like a gunslinger walking down Main Street in an old western movie, the F-4s had to wade directly into the fight.

As they approached the outskirts of Baghdad, they saw the tremendous light show from the many numbers and calibres of Iraqi AAA guns. VQ recalls telling Momar, 'Those guys are furious.' Not exactly famous last words, but a call from another member of their flight lightened up the mood.

Their wingman, a younger pilot, radioed, 'Lead, they're shooting at us!'

VQ answered, 'Yeah, that's how this works. We shoot at them, they shoot at us.'

The radio went silent after that.

Orbiting near Baghdad, Spaar acquired an SA-3 going active very close to them midway between the city and Baghdad International Airport. So close in fact, that they were almost within the minimum range the HARM needed to launch, acquire and turn to seek out the target.

Spaar designated the SAM site and fed the data to a HARM. However, the SA-3's operator was savvy enough to not transmit continuously and pinpoint his location. Finally, he stayed on the air long enough, around twenty seconds, for the APR-47 to get a good lock on the target. At seven miles, Spaar pickled the HARM.

VQ had a grandstand seat to an amazing duel of missiles. At about the time Spaar launched their HARM, he saw the SA-3 rocket from the ground. He could see the dot from the HARM's motor as well as the smoke trail going downhill and simultaneously saw the pinpoint of light of the SA-3 heading up towards him.

The missiles passed in the air, VQ keeping both in sight. The SA-3 passed by their jet outside lethal range and the HARM tracked like an arrow and exploded at the target on the ground. The site never came back up.

The next day, 'Black' Bart Quinn's third day of multiple sorties on each day, turned into an endurance test of epic proportions. On 21 January he led a two ship of F-4Gs in support of a 'Scud hunt' mission. Saddam's forces lobbed these modified Scud ground-to-ground missiles at targets in Saudi Arabia and Bahrain in the south and especially at Israel to the west of Iraq. By irritating the Israelis enough, Saddam hoped to bring them into the war and thus break the Allied coalition of Western and Arab countries aligned against him. The Scud hunts were designed to spot and kill the Scud launchers before he could launch more.

In this mission, Quinn's role was to hang on the tanker, constantly topping up his fuel, so that in the event any of the hunters found a SAM or AAA site that needed attention, the Weasels could go do their thing. The plan was for Quinn and company to be 'on call' for about two hours then they'd be replaced by another set of F-4s.

The tanker orbit was way in the west of Saudi Arabia with the Scud hunting area being the far west of Iraq. The threats in that area included the Iraqi fighter bases called H2 and H3. Both fields had been heavily pounded in the previous days by RAF Tornadoes and US F-16s, but they still had usable runways and an unknown number of operational fighters housed in thick concrete shelters. And that's before worrying about surviving SA-2 and SA-6 batteries and the AAA.

From 0000 until 0300, Quinn and his wingman hung on the tanker, getting gas periodically and waiting for the call. So tired were they from their previous missions and so confident was Quinn about his refuelling ability that he relates, 'I dozed while on the boom.'

As the time for his relief Weasels drew closer, Sheikh Isa ops called the battle commander aboard the AWACS who then asked Quinn if he could take the next 'vul time' since the weather back in Bahrain was shot due to intense ground fog.

'Affirmative,' came the answer from Quinn and he settled in to catch a sunrise and log three more hours strapped in the Phantom. Quinn explains:

It's not pleasant sitting on the ejection seat after a while and the 'facilities' for the body's needs are primitive to say the least.

I had brought along several 'piddle packs' [plastic packages that contain a funnel for the human equipment to let loose and a highly absorbent lining to hold the 'download'.], but Ken had nothing. I don't know how he held out.

Hanson revealed that he'd had to use one of the boots from his chemical warfare ensemble that each man crammed into his helmet bag.

Quinn continues:

After the sun came up, we turned towards home after Isa said they were still unable to launch anything, but we were cleared to divert to Riyadh.

Approaching there, it, too, was weathered out, as was anything else close by. We headed back to the tanker to get gas since we'd burned most of ours motoring back home to the east.

We sat on the tanker for an hour to an hour and half while we waited on the weather in the east to clear. I saw myself in the canopy bow mirror and thought, 'Man, you look bad.' The effects of stress, lack of sleep and not eating much really took a lot out of you. The cliché about 'ageing overnight' was vividly illustrated by my face that morning.

Then we started hearing chatter about SAMs on the AWACS threat frequency. We asked them what's up and they said there was activity happening around H2/H3 but they couldn't give us anything more specific, so we cleared the tanker and headed to the fight.

By now, we'd been airborne for nearly nine hours, but as soon as we got to the area, we forgot about being tired. We picked up SAM indications, followed quickly by MiGs, so we headed back to the tanker while the air-to-air guys dealt with that.

It sounds much more cut and dried telling it, but it was a confusing picture listening to the radios and trying to figure out all the activity. Turns out there was a CSAR [combat search and rescue] going on after an F-14 went down in the area and, eventually, we found out we weren't needed.

We are just pooped by now, so I call AWACS and ask them what is open anywhere. For some reason, they couldn't give us any info despite repeated calls to them.

Finally, an EF-111 came up and said, 'Go to Tobuk.'

Located in the extreme far west of Saudi Arabia, Tobuk was the temporary home to EF-111s and some F-15s. It was a long flight there, but we finally made it. After shutting down, we logged eleven hours and fifteen minutes in the jet. I had used up all my piddle packs and was a soggy mess when I climbed, slowly, out of the jet. I still don't know how Howdy lasted.

Hanson dumped his 'boot' on the ground after climbing down from his cockpit.

Quinn continues:

Not long after we landed, Sheikh Isa called us and asked us to launch and cover some strikes since they still couldn't get airborne due to weather.

For the first time in my career, I had to tell the boss 'no'. There was just no way we could push anymore.

We were so tired that even though Tobuk came under Scud attack shortly after we landed, I never heard the sirens. I slept through the whole thing.

SCHREINER, 22 JANUARY 1991 D + 159 W + 5

I'm writing this days after the fact because this is the first opportunity I've had to write since the second day. So far, I've flown seven sorties in six days and until today, I was totally exhausted. Normally, eight hours' sleep is enough for me, but I've pumped so much adrenaline in the past few days that my body was rapidly becoming fatigued.

My Baghdad sortie [second sortie on 19 January 1991] was anything but routine. And the target area was actually the least stressful part of the mission.

We started out flying some 400 miles just to get to the tanker. We had two tankers, with the F-111 strikers on one and we four F-4Gs on the trailer.

The first part of the track was clear, but one of the F-111s still managed to hit the lead tanker causing minor damage. Both the lead tanker and the F-111 aborted and went home.

Whoever was flying our tanker must have had his head up his ass because he decided to follow his lead home rather than proceed up track towards the target area like he was supposed to.

Finally, our flight lead, 'Teach' Jenny, convinced him to turn around. That tanker's stupidity cost us about five valuable minutes, which meant we would have to use more fuel to go faster to make our TOT.

As we continued north along 'Olive Track', we entered some

A close up of
F-4G EWO
Capt. Rob
'Peaches'
Pietras (USAF)

pretty thick weather. After flying on the wing for more than two hours, I was pretty fatigued. Flying in and out of the weather was making me disoriented. I couldn't tell if we were turning or straight and level. I had the 'leans' and had to rely on Dan to keep me straight.

Several times, the bonehead tanker flew into some pretty thick cloud, once so thick that I almost lost sight of him. All the tanker had to do was climb a few thousand feet to get out of the goo, but his lack of judgement and flexibility would not allow that.

Again, after much 'gnashing of teeth', Teach managed to convince him to climb above the weather. No wonder these guys finished last in their class in pilot training.

Off to Baghdad! Some sixty miles out the entire area around the city exploded with AAA. The sky was filled with tens of thousands of bullets and shells. Keeping in mind that only one out of every four or five rounds is a tracer, then the bullet density must have been horrendous. There is no way an aircraft can penetrate that wall of lead and hope to survive. It's easy to see why the majority of our aircraft losses have been due to AAA.

Fortunately for us, most of it only goes to the mid-teens, while we 'safely' cruise above it in the mid-twenties. Occasionally, a bright flash explodes overhead, indicating the presence of large calibre (85–100 mm) AAA, so we are not completely safe. None of it seems to be radar guided or we'd throw a HARM at it.

One has to wonder what happens when all this metal falls back to earth, some of it exploding when it does. The thought of the mostly innocent civilians bearing the brunt of that pains me a little. I realise most of them are unwitting and probably ignorant of the real reason we are causing them all this grief.

The radar signals, as usual, seem rather scant, but we manage to find a couple of SA-3 operators and put them out of business.

Our return to the refuelling track is uneventful. It seems we have undisputed control of the skies. Occasionally, AWACS calls out a single hostile, but the closest was 180 miles at our stern. The F-15 Eagles have done an admirable job taking out the few MiGs and Mirages foolish enough to challenge them. As of this writing, we've knocked down twenty to twenty-five of them. While our losses are in the upper teens, none of them have been shot down by enemy fighters, and only one that I know of, to a radar-guided SAM. [A USN F/A-18 was shot down on the opening night of the war, attributed to an Iraqi MiG-25. There is some contention regarding this loss, but the fact remains that no radar-guided SAMs shot down Allied aircraft while Weasels were present.] God knows how many of their aircraft we've destroyed on the ground.

Finding the tanker in the weather is a little sporty, but there were breaks in the cloud that allowed us to find him. Our jet was the first one on the tanker – we RTB separately after Weaselling;

Wall to wall HARMs show that this Weasel is getting gas prior to going into combat over Kuwait. Iraq bound jets needed three external fuel tanks, thus could only carry two of the devastating SAM-killing missiles. (USAF)

it's easier than trying to get back together in the target area.

Again, I am reminded of the calibre of some of the tanker pilots. Our refuelling track is practically split down the middle with thick cloud to the east and clear airspace to the west. Rather than use a little common sense and orbit in the western half of our track, our tankers decided to maintain the track come hell or high water – or shitty weather.

Sure enough, our # 3 and # 4 go lost wingman (lost sight of the formation). It took Teach five minutes to convince the tanker to work west and climb out of the goo. Finally, he does and 3 and 4 rejoin. I should've washed more of these bozos out when I was a UPT [Undergraduate Pilot Training] instructor.

Chapter Twelve

The first three days of the air war had been finely crafted via the Air Tasking Order (ATO). There was a feeling at CENTCOM (Central Command) that Saddam would quit after a couple of days of heavy pounding from the air, so further planning was thought to be superfluous.

A more specific factor regarding the lack of longer range planning was that the ATO was a living document as it progressed from initial plan to final execution. So, strikes launched on the first days might or might not have destroyed the intended targets deemed the highest priority or felt to be the highest threat. If those targets were not destroyed, then subsequent strikes would be necessary to hit them again, thus planning too far into the future might all be for naught and the plan rewritten at the last minute anyway. Better to get some damage results in from the first strikes to plan for follow on attacks.

One of the lighter notes in the ATO process, as related by Jim Keck, the Weasel planner in the Riyadh headquarters, deals with the assignment of mission call signs. During the war, each type of aircraft usually had one of a group of similar names. The tankers were, naturally, variations of oil and gas companies like Exxon or Mobil during the build up to Operation *Desert Shield*. The Weasels usually used some brand of beer like Coors, Miller, or even some regional brews like Lonestar, a Texas brand of suds.

The Iraqis weren't stupid and by listening to the radio frequencies, could often make a determination of what types of forces were in a specific strike package. If they heard a 'beer call sign' after the first couple of days of being HARM catchers, they quickly turned off their radars, trading military effectiveness for survival.

The F-15C air-to-air fighters took on the 'gas' call signs during actual hostilities in an effort to catch the Iraqis unaware. The ruse worked initially and fifteen Iraqi fighers were shot down in the first week of the war, but after several days the trick lost its effectiveness. They then called up the Weasels asking to 'trade' for a day. The trick worked and for that day, the F-15Cs, using 'beer' call signs, never faced a surface-to-air threat, while the Weasels became Exxon, Mobil, and the like and found numerous SAM and AAA radars up, at least until another barrage of HARMs put them down, usually permanently.

Said Keck:

> Jeff Feinstein and I gave the Weasels the 'beer' call signs for the ATO. We also reserved the call sign 'Whiner' to whichever unit was being the most pain in our ass at any given time. Prior to the war's kick-off, Col Walton used to call us up complaining about our defensive ATO – the one we used as a 'just in case' if Saddam attacked south. We stuck him with 'Whiner' for one mission and we never heard from him again.
>
> From then on, 'Whiner' became the theatre joke, given to whichever unit we deemed as committing the latest act of buffoonery. It was dark humour, but it helped keep everyone sane, at least a little bit.

One aspect of the 'canned' ATO wasn't quite so funny, at least to one Weasel crew. The third night of the war, 20 January, saw the only loss of a Weasel ascribed officially to enemy action. Captain Tim Burke, pilot, and EWO Captain Juan Galindez had been part of a strike package against the major airfield complexes in the far west of Iraq, the H2 and H3 sites. Officially, the loss was put down to enemy AAA damage since the post-crash inspection revealed a small hole in one fuel tank. Within the Weasel community, the loss was attributed to bad luck.

Taking off on the third night of the war, Falstaff 01-04, led by VQ Quinn and Momar Spaar, roared into the late night sky heading to Iraq to escort a strike by F-111s going against Al Taqqadum Air Base. Unfortunately, each ATO is based on a twenty-four hour cycle that advances to the next ATO at midnight Zulu or 'Z' time [Greenwich Mean Time – used as a standard reference so that all participants can do the maths to adjust Zulu to local time].

The ATO for the fourth day had not been distributed to the Weasels in time for Falstaff flight to get much of the vital information they needed – items like tanker frequencies and their transponder squawks so the F-4s could find them and get gas. Even more important were the IFF codes to be used by the Weasels as the Zulu day rolled over. If an Allied fighter took a peek at them with its own IFF interrogator and didn't get the correct code, the Weasels were in real danger of getting shot down by a friendly. They'd be just as dead hit by an American missile as they would be by an Iraqi one, hence their concern about not having the ATO frag before take-off.

Not helping the situation was the weather almost everywhere in the theatre. At take-off, Isa had thick fog and a solid cloud deck at 3,000 feet. Their briefed divert field, King Khalid Military City in north-central Saudi Arabia, also had a 3,000 foot ceiling but was clear below.

Falstaff flight flew their mission, encountering nothing stronger than intermittent radar signals so none of the four jets took a HARM shot. As the F-111s left the area, the Weasels also turned to the south, heading in a wide arc back into Saudi airspace and, hopefully, some waiting tankers. In the meantime, midnight Zulu had occurred and now no one in the F-4s had the correct tanker squawks.

Using their radar and APX interrogator, the flight, in a trail formation, saw only a gaggle of radar contacts and ambiguous IFF returns. Quinn, in the lead, saw a collection of radar hits in the area of the expected tanker track, so he flew there. Of course, the widespread bad weather noted at take-off was still around, and the tanker tracks were no exceptions. Thick cloud and no visibility were the standard for the night.

After pulling up into the pre-contact position, instead of the expected flying boom of the KC-135 tanker, the only metal pointing at him was the tail gun of a Boeing B-52 Stratofortress heavy bomber. Not exactly a welcoming sight. Quinn radioed the rest of his flight that he hadn't found the tankers and a small free-for-all developed as each crew hunted for a flying fill-up.

Quinn correctly assumed that the BUFF had to be on a tanker, so if he, Quinn, moved forward, he'd find the tanker. Being nearly out of fuel, he really had no other choice. He broke off from pre-contact and swung wide to the side, keeping the B-52's wing visual, until he cleared the flexing metal. Quinn scooted forward until he was abeam the bomber's nose and found himself behind another BUFF!

It took him three tries to work to the leader of the bomber cell and near the tanker's boom, the latter snugly plugged into a thirsty BUFF. Quinn made a call on Guard and got the B-52 to back off while the F-4 swung into position. (Guard is the UHF frequency used by military aircraft to signal distress. It is monitored by all aircraft at all times for just such an event.] Quinn today gives compliments to both the B-52 driver for backing off in the miserable weather and limited visibility just enough for the F-4 to squeeze in and to the boom operator who swung the refuelling boom to its extreme limits in order to plug the bone dry fighter.

A more few minutes' delay, and Quinn and Spaar would have found themselves as passengers in a very quiet, rapidly descending McDonnell-Douglas-built lawn dart as the engines shut down from lack of fuel.

Such is what happened to Falstaff 03 crewed by Burke and EWO Galindez. Burke radioed the closest AWACS to find him a tanker and provide vectors to get him there ASAP.

AWACS sent him to the correct point, but the tanker had dialled in the wrong latitude and was actually sixty miles away from where he was supposed to be and where Burke needed him to be. They headed to the misplaced tanker, but in the lousy weather drove underneath him, not knowing he had turned northward to expedite the join up. Burke saw the tanker at the last second, but due to the nearly head-on crossing angles, couldn't turn in time to make the hook-up.

By now, Falstaff 03's fuel was so low that they couldn't spare the gas to chase the tanker but had to head directly to the divert field at KKMC. Upon arrival, they found the weather much worse than forecast.

Descending through the heavy clouds, they expected to get into the clear by 3,000 feet AGL (above ground level), but the goo went all the way to the ground. Burke requested a PAR (precision approach radar – technique where an air traffic controller at the field uses a very precise radar lined up with the runway to 'talk' a jet down). He had 2,500 lb of fuel remaining.

Going down the PAR chute, the jet never broke out of the clouds and they had to have at least 100 feet visibility to see the runway. What made the situation worse was that KKMC had not yet been outfitted with highly visible runway approach lights that aid a crew to the correct runway alignment and glide slope to find the pavement.

After several of these missed approaches, Burke and Galindez were in serious trouble regarding their gas. They started their last approach with less than 400 lb and they and the controller knew that a nylon letdown was in the offing unless this approach worked.

Again, they came down but could not see the runway. Burke added power, raised the landing gear and steered the jet about 10 degrees off the runway's orientation. He told Galindez to eject and followed him out of the F-4G a few seconds later. He watched the jet disappear into the fog and then, as his parachute lowered him to the desert, he saw the dim blue taxiway lights of the airfield.

KKMC personnel heard the booms as the two crewmembers ejected, but none when the jet hit the ground. Once the sun came up, they found the Phantom remarkably undamaged. Burke had trimmed the jet up for level flight and it stayed that way as it slowly descended into the desert sand. So empty of flammable fuel was the rugged F-4G that it didn't explode – instead it slid to a stop in the dirt, only a bent nose showing the worse for wear.

Officially, the cause was put down to enemy fire since bullet holes supposedly were found in one of the external wing tanks. The crew involved have their doubts, however. They think if they'd found a tanker or caught a break in the weather, they would have landed safely and had the jet back in action.

Being short on fuel in bad weather was not an isolated occurrence in the Weasel's war.

A brief note should be made of events on the night take-off for the missions flown on 21 January. The unexpected heavy weather that so plagued the Allies and benefited the Iraqis continued on this night. So thick, in fact, was the fog at Sheikh Isa that all the crews expected their missions to be cancelled. With a scheduled take-off of midnight local time, the fog steadily thickened as the night progressed.

All during the intel and weather briefings, they waited for someone in the Weasel leadership to interrupt with a 'Not tonight, guys. Weather's too dogshit'. But the interruption never came.

Riding in the crowded 'bread' truck that conveyed them to their respective jets, they couldn't see ten feet in front of the truck. 'Surely, it'll be cancelled before we start engines,' they thought. Nope, the eight jets fragged for this first 'go' all cranked the two J-79s in each F-4, the rpm and exhaust gas temperature gauges all settling nicely into the green zone on the dial.

Major Tom Gummo, the SOF, repeatedly queried the command post seeking a 'go, no-go' decision. Finally, the abrupt command from the wing commander barked through the VHF radio in the SOF tower. 'This mission is going. Get there!' A string of B-52s, taking off from their base in sunny Diego Garcia, an island in the Indian Ocean hundreds of miles away, were not affected by the weather and depended on the Weasels to keep the Iraqi SAMs in check as the BUFFs pounded Saddam's vaunted Republican Guard units with hundreds of 750-lb bombs. Destroying the Republican Guard was one of *Desert Storm* commander, General Schwarzkopf's prime directives. This mission was important.

Incredulous, each Phantom crept slowly from its revetment, each pilot unable to see past the nose of his jet. Guided onto the taxiway by the crew chief walking backward and signalling 'come ahead' with lighted flashlights, the jets rolled at a snail's pace down the parallel taxiway.

So bad was the visibility for even the simple step of taxiing, each EWO in the following jet used the APX interrogator to monitor where the preceding jet was in relation to him. The EWO then gave instructions to his pilot on how to proceed.

VQ and Momar again were the flight lead for this mission. VQ finally reached the end of the runway and, using his directional gyro, lined up on the runway's heading. Thrusting the two throttles forward, past the minor detent at the limit for military power, he shoved them into full afterburner, using nosewheel steering and then rudder to keep the heading. At no time did he or any of the following pilots see the runway as they clawed for the sky.

Gummo, in his SOF position in the tower, could hear but not see the jets lift off despite the bright, powerful glow usually seen streaking from the tail of the two J-79s like uninterrupted Roman candles. Tonight he saw nothing. He radioed the departing F-4s a nice compliment before the flight switched frequencies from Isa to tactical. 'Gutsiest move I never saw, guys.'

The Weasels kept their *rendezvous* with the BUFFs, watching the Technicolor bursts on the ground as the bombs rained down from nearly six miles up onto the Republican Guards' positions. Following the mission, the flight of Weasels diverted to Doha, Qatar, to sit out the rest of the night. Isa's fog only lifted with the morning sun. The rest of that night's operations were cancelled, small comfort to the eight ship that took off blind.

As a side note, however, post-war interrogations of captured Iraqi army officers and soldiers revealed that the B-52 bombings were the thing they feared the most. So high did the bombers fly that the soldiers did not know there was an airborne threat. The first indication was when a never-ending series of violent explosions and concussions rattled the ones who survived the devastation. Thousands of them did not.

SCHREINER, 23 JANUARY 1991 D + 160 W + 6

Mission # 5 was flown to extreme western Iraq in support of a strike on a Scud emplacement.

'SCUD ALARM, SCUD ALARM, SCUD ALARM! Don mask and take cover!' That statement has been broadcast over Big Voice [basewide PA system], at least several times a night since the war started. So far, every Scud fired at Saudi Arabia has been intercepted and destroyed by our own Patriot SAMs.

When we first arrived, a number of Patriot batteries were set up for the express purpose of shooting down any chemical or otherwise laden Iraqi Scud missiles. Originally, it was thought that the Patriot had only a 10% Pk [probability of kill] against the Scud. So far, every Patriot fired has successfully intercepted its target – a far greater success rate than even the controlled tests set up by Raytheon when the missile first came out. So much for the anti-defence naysayers who said it was a waste of money and wouldn't work

So far, none of the missiles have had anything but a conventional high-explosive warhead. The only Scuds to hit their targets are the ones shot into Israel, in the hope of dragging them into the war. Last night, in their third attack on Israel, several managed to get through a newly emplaced Patriot battery. Sadly, there were three killed and up to ninety wounded in what up to now have been purely nuisance attacks. Still, only three fatalities is surprisingly low for the amount of effort that has gone into those attacks.

Here at Sheikh Isa, the only thing the Scuds have managed is to be a pain in the ass. The other night, after a long sortie, I was looking forward to eating a sloppy joe after the maintenance debrief.

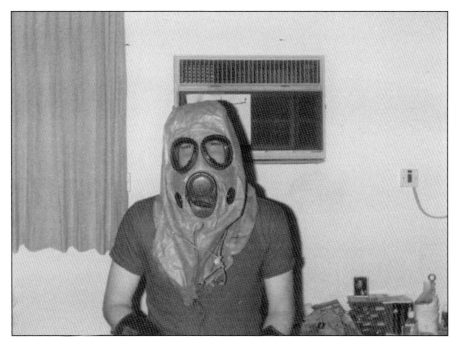

"SCUD ALARM! SCUD ALARM!" The minimum protection needed from a sound sleep in the event of a chemical attack is the gas mask and attached hood from a chemical warfare suit. Here Ed Fisher shows the haute coutre in chem. suits. (Ed Fisher)

After waiting in line for twenty minutes, I was just sitting down in the crew van, ready to enjoy my meal, when 'SCUD ALARM, SCUD ALARM . . .' The command post finally sounded the all clear after a half-hour but, by now, my meal was ruined. On top of that, I managed to knock over a nearly full soda and some of it went in my helmet bag. What a pain in the ass; I'm tired, hungry, and now, pissed off.

The alarms occur with such frequency that if I'm in my room, I no longer respond unless I hear an explosion or see one of the Patriot launch, neither of which has happened.

Back to flying. The mission out to western Iraq, all 1,800 miles and 5.6 hours of it, was fairly routine and unexciting. I don't know if the strikers hit their targets, but there weren't any radars for us to shoot so we brought our missiles home.

The following day's sortie was a little more interesting. Sortie number six, back to Baghdad and, for the first time, a day sortie.

From the very beginning, things were fucked up. The ARN-101 in our first jet would not work, so I had to abort to one that would. Climbing into that one, a maintenance senior master sergeant still hasn't figured out that there's a war on.

He was pissed because I didn't give his trouble shooters enough time to fix the problem and now we were going to take another jet out of phase [all US military aircraft are subject to 'phase inspections' – periodic checks of various systems and components done] and screw up his schedule. Tough shit. We're fighting a war, people are dying and he's worried about a fucking maintenance schedule. Some people just don't get it.

We finally took off about seven minutes late and fifty-six miles behind the rest of our four ship, but thanks to Dan's tanker intercept and my visual rejoin (yes, I can blow my own horn, thank you), we still managed to join up on time.

I stayed on the boom for an inordinate amount of time, but my right (exterior fuel tank) 'FULL' light would not come on. All the other indicators were good so I figured this was just one more example of a jet whose 'FULL' lights don't work properly.

I was almost at Baghdad when I realised my mistaken assumption – the F-4 has no way of indicating how much is in an external tank unless it's full or empty and I thought the 'FULL' light was broken. In any event, I knew I would have to RTB for fuel before we had fired our HARMs so I decided to stick around just long enough to kill an SA-2 and SA-3.

Being a day sortie, I could not see the AAA coming up at us although I knew it was there. The aerial threat I had anticipated never materialised. As a matter of fact, after a week and nine sorties, I haven't seen anything or even heard from AWACS any mention of enemy aircraft. We own the skies over Iraq, no doubt about it.

Even though I much prefer to fly training sorties during the day, the fact that I could not see ground-to-air threats made it unnerving. I think I prefer night sorties in combat.

After we shot our missiles, I elected to RTB without my flight lead. I also decided to climb as high as possible to conserve fuel.

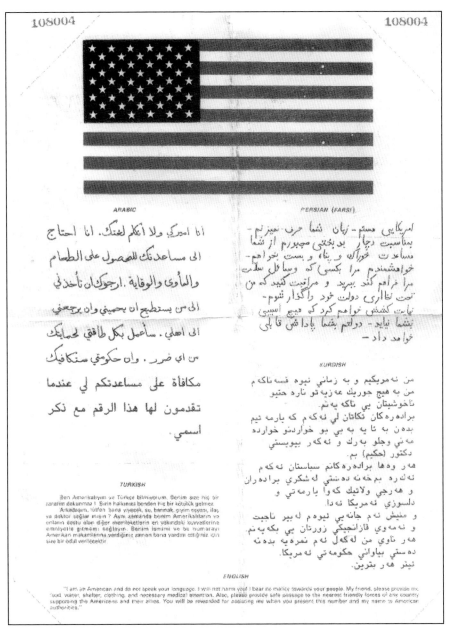

Jim Schreiner's 'blood chit.' Carried by every US aircrew, this message printed on special paper in a variety of local languages promises the finder that he will be rewarded if he helps the downed airman reach safety. (Jim Schreiner)

I was up at 36,000 feet, fat, dumb and happy, when Dan yelled, 'Hey, we're conning!'

I didn't get a good weather brief so I didn't know what the contrail altitude was – another mistake. I immediately began a descent to an altitude where we wouldn't con. Contrails can be seen sometimes for hundreds of miles and are a dead give-away. They're better than radar because bad guys can see you but you don't know they're looking at you or from where.

All along the route to the tanker track, some 200 miles of it, I calculated the fuel to make sure we'd have enough. I figured we'd have enough for about five minutes of search time before we had to divert.

Sure enough, as we got further south towards our track, the clouds began to appear. By the time we arrived at the track, the entire area was socked in. And wouldn't you know it, the tankers weren't squawking the right IFF/SIF [Identification, Friend or Foe/Selective Identification Feature] codes so we had no way of picking them out of the rest of the package. We tried in vain to find them but the weather was just too thick.

Finally, with 3,000 lb of fuel remaining, about twenty-five minutes' flying time at altitude, I made the decision to abort and find a place to land.

King Khalid Military City (KKMC) is an airfield built by the Saudis out in the middle of nowhere, but it was only sixty miles – eight minutes – away. I started a fuel-conserving climb and radioed them to find out their weather conditions.

'Ceiling 100–200 feet, visibility ¼ to ½ mile.' Great! Dog shit weather and no other fields close enough to land at. I thought it never rained in the desert or that they had any weather for that matter. Fortunately, they had a PAR [precision approach radar] but it would still be tight.

By this time, my fuel low level light was on so I declared emergency fuel. I began my descent getting more and more nervous, knowing that I had one or two chances to make it work before we flamed out and had to get a nylon letdown.

There is nothing worse than the feeling of being low on fuel and having no decent place to land. I had to make this work.

The female controller started giving me azimuth (heading) and glideslope (descent) information but something was wrong. Her corrections were coming in too slow. Apparently she was in-experienced because my deviations became pretty large before she would tell me.

I started above glideslope but had worked my way down to below glideslope, i.e., too low, before she would tell me. Now I was also drifting off course.

This was bad. One of the few times I've ever depended on flying an excellent approach and between the two of us, we were fucking it up.

I had set my radar altimeter to 150 feet, so 'Bitching Betty' would remind me of the altitude when we got there. By this time, I was well below glideslope and left of course when I heard 'Altitude! Altitude!'

I couldn't see shit; wait! There it is! I finally saw the runway and, yeah, I was low and to the left, but it was salvageable. But I had gotten fast. I was doing close to 250 mph when I did finally breakout – a good 60 mph too fast. So I pulled the power back to slow us down, but still touched down at close to 200 mph.

I immediately deployed the drag chute and, fortunately, it worked as we gradually began to slow. I still needed all 10,000 feet of the runway to stop but I was glad it was over. I could now remove the seat cushion that I had sucked up in my ass.

My hat's off to Dan because while I was flying, all he could do was sit back there and watch. He told me afterward that he had his hand on the ejection handle – just in case . . .

Down on the ground, we found our way to the hot pits and got refuelled. We had to leave the chute, which meant we'd land back at Isa without one. I've done a number of those and we have 12,000 feet of concrete so no sweat.

Twenty minutes later we were out of there and headed home.

The RTB was uneventful except that the weather was rapidly falling. Great, another precision approach! At least the ceiling and viz were a little better.

This approach went better and we landed on speed but without our chute. I decided to aerobrake to bleed off some of our speed. I raised the nose a little too quickly and we went airborne again momentarily.

One wing dipped, but I managed to catch it and gently settle the aircraft back down. It gave Dan a scare though. Sorry, Dan.

As Schreiner wrote in his journal, he preferred night combat missions because at least then you had an idea of AAA fire coming at you due to the tracers. SAMs were also usually more visible at night due to their fiery rocket motors against the dark sky. To a man, all the Weasels interviewed for this book felt the same.

Kevin Hale, still crewed with pilot Jack Patterson, recounted a night mission where they thought they were out of harm's way but, in fact, were not.

We were up around 30,000 feet, out of range of anything except the bigger SAMs or the really heavy AAA like the 100-mm stuff. We were on an orbit over Baghdad going from the north-east to the south-west, just turning to the right to start heading towards the northern end of our line.

I could see some AAA at our ten o'clock, but no spikes on the APR-47, so had no worries at that moment.

Then it felt like a giant sledgehammer hit the bottom of the jet. The bottom of our jet was illuminated and that explosion was followed rapidly by two more. We were flipped upside down with about 120 degrees of bank and lost about 8,000 feet as we fell out of control.

Jack immediately punched off the [external] tanks while we were still upside down. He yelled at me, 'Grinch, we're out of control.'

I was worried about a couple of tons of metal coming back down on top of us and told him, 'Yeah, Jack, just fly it out,' which of course he was. It actually felt like a simulator practice for out of control conditions.

We'd lost one of our hydraulic systems, the AN/ALQ-184 ECM pod, and, of course, our tanks so we were way short on gas.

We headed directly for the border, calling for AWACS to find us a tanker close by. Of course, for the first time I can remember, there's not one anywhere near us. We finally found one about 150 miles away and convinced him to head toward us.

At the same time, I can hear the rest of the guys in our flight talking, thinking they'd lost us to AAA. We managed to call back to Sheikh Isa to let them know we were still flying and we passed the code word for the damage we knew about.

They didn't believe us at first and we had to confirm the call several times. When we landed, there was a whole parade of folks to look at the jet.

Besides the damage I mentioned, we'd also had our port lights blown off, but amazingly, there wasn't one hole in the jet. All the damage had been caused by the tremendous concussion of a close 100-mm AAA round. The jet was repaired and flew again.

Chapter Thirteen

Turkey, the NATO member and historically strong supporter of the US, lay north of Iraq. The Turkish government agreed to the economic sanctions levied against Iraq in the wake of the Kuwait invasion. Indeed, Turkey shut off two oil pipelines carrying Iraqi oil to terminals on her coast. Turkey's internal political picture, however, made joining in the military part of *Desert Storm* problematic.

With a large, restive Kurdish population in the border region adjoining Iraq, Turkey feared that any military action against Iraq might embolden Kurdish separatists into pushing for an independent Kurdistan, comprising the Kurd areas of northern Iraq and southern Turkey. A civil war was something Turkey wished to avoid at all costs. US planners didn't think they'd be allowed to conduct air strikes from US bases in Turkey, but made contingency plans just in case.

One of those plans involved forming what became Joint Task Force Proven Force. An amalgamation of United States Air Forces in Europe (USAFE) units and a few units deployed from the States, JTF Proven Force operated as one 'super wing', the 7440th Composite Wing from Incirlik Air Base in Turkey. The massive wing consisted of twenty F-111Es, an earlier model of the two-seat medium bomber that did such stellar work in hitting precision targets in the southern air war; two dozen F-16Cs; ten F-15Cs; a half dozen F-4Es; another contingent of RF-4C reconnaissance Phantoms; E-3 AWACS; special operations C-130s; 'vanilla' C-130s; and four elderly KC-135A refuelling tankers. Eventually, the composite wing had nearly eighty aircraft under its control.

To protect this force, USAFE's remaining Weasels, the 23d Tactical Fighter Squadron, The Fighting Hawks, received their orders to join the 7440th in Turkey. The 23d TFS deployed with another dozen F-4Gs, but unlike all the Bahrain-based Weasels, the 23d brought their F-16s with them and flew as hunter/killer teams. The addition of the Incirlik-based squadron brought the number of F-4Gs in theatre to sixty.

Incirlik provided a second, smaller avenue to attack targets in northern Iraq. The bulk of the Allied air forces far to the south of Iraq couldn't reach those targets without a tremendous drain on scarce tanker resources.

Never the main focus of the offensive plan, Incirlik suffered under a shortage of many assets, particularly tankers. Nevertheless, simply by being a threat to the north, never mind the actual damage they would inflict later, the airmen in Turkey kept the Iraqis guessing.

Proven Force warriors began striking targets on 18 January 1991. They first took out Iraqi radar and early warning sites in the north, mimicking the concept being employed in the south by *Desert Storm*. They first wanted to blind the Iraqi air defences before going after other targets.

One item in particular affected the Weasels both in the north and in the south. The 35th Wing (Provisional) at Sheikh Isa flew under the control of the *Desert Storm* ATO while the 7440th Composite Wing's Weasels flew under the Proven Force ATO's control. While there was coordination at the staff level between the two ATO shops, at the tactical level, there was a gap in communications. At first, Baghdad was about as far north as the Bahrain-based F-4Gs flew due to fuel considerations while the 23d's F-4Gs stayed to the north of the Iraqi capital. The possibility of two Weasel missions being targeted on the same IAD target were low, but as the war progressed, the chances increased. The HARM's long range only added to this possibility.

Especially once the ground war kicked off and Allied forces drove deep into Iraq, a demarcation line for any Weasel shooting south had to be drawn. The risk of mis-identifying a friendly air defence unit radiating and being detected by the Weasels was just too great. So although a few Proven Force sorties did fly as far south as Baghdad, most had to be confined to northern Iraq.

Of course, the shortage of tankers available to Proven Force forced the Incirlik crews to keep their leash fairly short as well. Brian 'Basa' Baxley, then a captain piloting the F-4G recalled:

Wednesday 16 January 1991, 0700 Central European Time. I had finished my Mission Ready checkride just before Christmas and was still slowly unpacking boxes at home after my move to Germany in November 1990. My wife Rhonda was a nurse stationed at Bitburg Air Base in the OB/GYN clinic, and was still in-processing the Base after her arrival in Germany two weeks earlier. There had been constant talk over the past five to six months of when the US led coalition would invade Iraq, and how many more troops would deploy to join those already in the Middle East for Operation *Desert Shield*. That morning at breakfast, Rhonda and I listened to the news with growing excitement and apprehension that the US and their allies had in fact invaded Iraq. Shortly before 0700, Rhonda left our village of Dudeldorf, conveniently located halfway between Spangdahlem and Bitburg, for her work at the hospital. Just two to three moments later I was in the shower when the telephone rang, and one of the officers from my 23rd Fighter Squadron told me 'Pack your bags for an indefinite amount of time, I can't tell you where we are going, and we leave in about five hours.' This was on Wednesday 16 January 1991.

I could hardly contain my excitement – I was going to war to do what I had been training for over the past four years – find and kill Surface to Air Missile sites.

I jumped back in the shower and was almost finished when Rhonda came back in the house to pick up her in-processing documents she had accidentally left in the house. I told her the great news that I was deploying today, and was a little surprised that she wasn't excited, in fact, the news definitely made her sad. I gave her a quick kiss good bye, still standing in the shower, and in typical fashion of a young male with an aggressive Type A personality, I thought perhaps Rhonda didn't see the importance of what was about to happen and compartmentalised the entire event so I wouldn't have to think about it. It wasn't until much later I truly understood how right she was.

My chem warfare bag was already packed in the car, and I had most of my deployment bag already packed in the house as well, so I quickly added a few more clothes and toiletries (always pack toilet paper) and loaded it into the car. My parents lived in Wiesbaden, Germany, at the time working as teachers for the military's school system, so I called them too and told them I was leaving and would call again as soon as possible. The typically short five-minute drive took over fifteen minutes due to all the traffic trying to enter the Base and the heightened security checks by the police. A military policeman on foot was walking down the line of stopped cars, and told anyone wearing flight suits to pull over into the lane of on-coming traffic to bypass the waiting traffic. The security police manning the checkpoint to get onto Spangdahlem Air Base simply waved me thorough and wished me good luck. Then I was finally at the 23rd Fighter Squadron, home of the 'Hawks'.

The level of energy and excitement there was incredible, and there was so much work to be done. When the crews and line-up was announced, I found myself flying with Lt Col 'Boy Wonder' Kissel, and we would be # 5 in the first flight to leave for Incirlik, Turkey. While it was certainly great to be in the first group to deploy, especially since our awesome squadron commander, Lt Col 'Mooman' Moody, was leading it, I was slightly less excited when briefed that the # 5 of each formation flight would divert into Sigonella, Sicily, since our tankers coming from England would not have enough gas to offload for all five aircraft to get to Incirlik.

TR Kissel and I finished going through the final mobility line, where shot records were checked and additional shots given, emergency next-of-kin notification data was updated, and we had an opportunity to talk to the chaplain. All the pilots and Electronic Warfare Officers (EWOs) in the squadron were given an intelligence and threat update briefing around 1100, and a short talk on what to expect upon arrival in Incirlik, Turkey. At 1130 Mooman gave a fifteen-minute briefing for our five ship, and we stepped out to pre-flight our aircraft. Mooman was # 1 of the first five ship flying an F-16CJ, numbers 2 and 3 were F-4Gs, # 4 was an F-16CJ, and TR and I were flying an F-4G as # 5. At first I was very excited to be in the first formation to depart Spangdahlem, but the downfall was the fifth aircraft of every flight would divert into Sigonella.

The five ship launched with all the live missiles armed, and we proceeded to the first refuelling orbit in the south-western part of Germany to join our tankers arriving from England. The rejoin of the fighters to the tankers went smoothly, and then it was time to begin flying through France en route to Incirlik, Turkey.

Unfortunately the French were not particularly in favour of the US-led attack against Iraq, and the French controllers were directed to refuse entry of any US fighter into French airspace. After five minutes of negotiations and the French eventually refusing to talk, Mooman said words I had never heard before, 'This is HARM flight, and we are proceeding with Due Regard.' (I don't remember the actual call sign of the flight, but there is actually a DoD [Department of Defense] Instruction 4540.01 that defines proceeding with Due Regard). A French fighter was sent to intercept us, but he maintained a considerable distance from us and took no action.

Diverting into Sigonella, I taxied clear of the runway and was met by a strange sight for this Air Force pilot – Navy personnel standing on the taxiway who issued instructions to shut down the left engine so they could wrap the F-4G drag chute over the left wing! I had never seen or even heard of such an operation, but complied with the request and made it to the parking area with the drag chute draped over the left wing, ending just inches in front of the left tyre.

No rooms were available at Sigonella nor were there any hotel vacancies in the near area, so we were bussed about an hour away to a hotel. Since the armoury was full too, we brought our weapons with us, which made quite the impression as we checked into the mom-and-pop hotel in a small village. Trying to depart Sigonella the next day was quite the chore. The senior Air Force officer was Lt Col 'Mild Bill' Miller, and he spent hours on the phone with USAFE HQ and Incirlik trying to find out the latest on the United States' efforts to negotiate with the Turkish government on the number of aircraft and personnel that would be allowed into Turkey for Operation *Proven Force*. Finally in the late afternoon, the word came to launch. Except the Italians didn't seem to be completely on-board with this decision, and refused to let us take off. And so for the second time in two days, I heard the now very stirring words, 'We are proceeding with Due Regard.'

The flight to Turkey was fairly uneventful, with the highlight being part of a five ship of F-4Gs in a line-abreast two-mile wide wall, leaving contrails as the sunset. Greece of course refused to speak to us since we were landing in Turkey, but finally Mild Bill was able to get in touch with Turkish controllers, and we landed at night in Incirlik. The entire airfield was packed with people, machinery, and aircraft. Parking aprons that normally housed one or maybe two aircraft had five parked nose-to-nose and over-lapping wing tips. Maintenance did a phenomenal job keeping the operation safe and able to delivery combat ready aircraft on time as requested.

The flight operations from Incirlik, Turkey, were similar to the *Red Flag* and *Cope Thunder* type operations that many of has had participated in. A face-to-face mass briefing, launching of all the aircraft from a single airfield, ingress and egress as a package, and mass debrief to assess the plan and execution.

The night mission mass briefing was generally around 1500 and covered the usual items of weather, threat assessment update by intelligence, administrative details such as departure sequence and refuelling plan, then finally the target objective and plan of attack. The mass brief would last sixty to ninety minutes, with one of the pilots or a WSO (Weapon System Officer) from the F-111 squadron out of Lakenheath serving as the Mission Commander. Our first night mission was on 19 January 1991.

The briefing room was in one of the Operations Centres on the north side of the runway, and overflowing with people. The targets were military installations around Mosul and Kirkuk. Intel briefed the surrounding threats and a long list of buildings and areas on the protected site list that we were not to disturb.

Following the mass briefing, we collected our .45 calibre pistol and survival pack from Life Support, and a blood chit and highly detailed map from intel.

By 1700 we began our flight brief, and as an experienced F-4G pilot but new to the squadron, I would fly as # 4 or # 2 in a four ship. The first six missions I flew with Major 'Pappy' Parent, an experienced and very good EWO. We had never flown together before, so we spent a little bit of extra time discussing how we would fly, complete checklists, react to threats, and how close we were willing to get to the Surface-to-Air Missile sites we were attacking.

After dinner we went to our particular hanger and pre-flighted the two HARM missiles, the ALQ jamming pod, and all the other equipment. Taxiing to the runway was actually difficult for two reasons – congestion and reduced lighting. With little to no room to pass other aircraft on the taxiway, it was critical that aircraft depart the parking area in the order they had to take off. A significant portion of the mass brief was spent identifying by tail number who followed who, the exact taxi route to use, and where different formations would fall in trail with each other.

Fortunately my F-16CJ element lead was parked next to me, and I simply followed him out to the taxiway. Reduced lighting was necessary since there were so many aircraft and personnel on the taxiway, and to make it more difficult for those outside the perimeter of the base to estimate what kind and how many aircraft were taking off.

Arming of all the aircraft was actually done on the taxiway, with aircraft lined up behind each other. A 30-degree heading offset from the axis of the taxiway was used so missiles were not pointed at the preceding aircraft when being armed.

One other unique part of the arming process that night was I noticed a couple of pilots had opened their canopies and were leaning over the side. The intensity and stress level was so high some of the pilots threw-up prior to take-off.

Finally the first four ship of F-15Cs took off to provide air cover. Then the AWACS departed, followed by a KC-135 and another four ship of F-15Cs. Our tanker launched next, followed by four more F-15Cs, then our four ship of F-4G – F-16CJ – F-16CJ – and Pappy and I in an F-4G.

In another measure meant to make it more difficult for those opposed to military action against Iraq, we were to turn off all external lighting as soon as we were airborne. While that seemed to make sense during the mass brief, as I watched the KC-135 vanish in front of my eyes even prior to it going into the weather, I suddenly realised the tanker rejoin was going to be more difficult than usual. And it was.

Straight ahead tanker rejoins are usually fairly benign since they progress slowly. However, trying to ensure we had the other seven aircraft on radar and that we joined on the last of them was nerve racking, especially when I couldn't see my F-16 element lead outside of 1,000 feet. We finally rejoined on the blacked out tanker, and we continued our eastward climb towards Lake Van.

Intel has also briefed that Syria would be sympathetic to Iraq, and as predicted, their surveillance radars would light up sequentially along the Syrian border about fifty miles off our right wing as we continued eastwards. Fortunately this had also been considered during the mass brief, and once rejoined on the tanker, we were to turn all equipment that emitted electronic signals to standby, such as our radar and TACAN (TACtical Air Navigation), and only use our encrypted, frequency-hopping radio when absolutely necessary.

Once over Lake Van in the eastern part of Turkey, all the aircraft refuelled for the last time. The F-4Gs always refuelled last since we had the highest fuel burn and shortest time on-station. By this time it was ninety minutes after take-off and the F-111s had joined the package. The Mission Commander in the F-111 and the Air Boss in the AWACS conducted a roll call and status check, and the decision was given to execute the mission as briefed.

Looking south from Lake Van into Iraq, everything was pitch black on the ground. The blackness was absolute and complete; I could have been looking at the ocean or into space. But at as we entered Iraqi airspace, in front of us at some unknown distance and height, there appeared a moving red carpet flapping slowly in the breeze. It was exploding AAA, and finally all those count-less hours I had spent studying made complete sense.

Most of the AAA was barrage fire, the unguided gun shots that exploded at predetermined heights based on the calibre and type of gun. The waving carpet of exploding shells was between 18,000 and 23,000 feet, but although it was easy to see at night, there were no visual references to let me know if I was above, below, or in the band of exploding shells. After a very tense twenty minutes' drive south, Pappy and I were both quite relieved that we were in fact above the unguided AAA.

A four ship of F-15Cs remained to the north along the Iraq–Turkey border as a barrier CAP (Combat Air Patrol) for the AWACS and tankers, with the other F-15Cs setting up CAPs just north of the target area in and around Mosul. The F-4G/F-16CJ mixed pairs set up their CAPs just south of the target area, about 20 NM from briefed locations of the SA-2 sites. As the F-111s came in from multiple axis, some of the SAM sites finally came up. Pappy designated the SA-2 on the APR-47, I selected the right inboard station missile, and Pappy fired the first HARM missile either of us had ever shot. Unlike the smaller AIM-7, AIM-9 and Maverick missiles we had both fired, the HARM was huge and much more powerful.

As Pappy hit the fire button and called 'Magnum' on the radio, several things happened. First, nothing seemed to happen, and I thought I had not properly set the switches and armed the missile.

Second, when the missile did fire, the intensity of the missile motor seemed to pull the right side of the aircraft forward in a slip, and I considered whether or not we and the aircraft could survive a hung missile at full power. That thought abruptly ended when the missile left the aircraft and I looked up, only to be blinded by the brightest light I had ever seen and at a very close range. I quickly closed my eyes and looked back down in the cockpit, but it took a couple of minutes to be able to read the cockpit instruments again.

Those couple of minutes were quite exciting because I was absolutely convinced that we had been hit by something, probably by the waving red carpet of AAA. The aircraft shook violently and the very pungent smell of burning cordient filled the cockpit. I did my best to squint my still blinded eyes to turn the Phantom back to the north and start heading home without over-flying the SA-2 site we had just shot at.

After about five seconds though the shaking seemed to stop, and in another half minute all the burning smell was gone. I was almost ready to call my element lead and let him know we needed to continue heading north to go home and declare an emergency for battle damage, when Pappy and I came to the real-isation the exhaust of the 2,000-pound missile had gone down of right intake! The disturbed airflow had shaken the jet, and the rocket exhaust had been the source of the burning smell.

Thirty minutes later when Pappy and I were ready to take our second shot, I selected the left inboard station, pitched up about 10 degrees, and as soon as Pappy fired I rolled the aircraft to the right. Sure enough, we didn't suffer any 'battle damage' on that shot.

The flight home was fairly uneventful, and the adrenaline was very high. Pappy and I had flown well together as a team, our element lead had done a great job hanging on our wing in the target area at night with us almost completely blacked out, and no one in the entire package had been lost or damaged.

The F-4Gs went back to the tanker for a little more gas, which was a wise decision. When forty-five to fifty aircraft launch within forty-five minutes as a large package, they generally want to land as a group of forty-five to fifty within twenty minutes of each other (patience is not normally an attribute of aviators).

Landing at Incirlik after my first combat mission for Operation *Proven Force* was absolutely amazing. Since we needed to go [to] the tanker for gas, the F-4Gs and the F-16CJs were at the end of the arrival flow of the 35+ fighters. As we approached Incirlik from the east, we descended to about 5,000 feet as we passed to the north of the base (Runway 09 was the active for take-off and landing that night).

Looking down at the base, we could see moving aircraft on the taxiways, about four aircraft on the runway rolling out from their landing, and another eight aircraft inside of 5 NM from the runway threshold with their gear down and landing light on. We were landing an aircraft every thirty seconds, at night, with live ordnance, and behind different kinds of aircraft from different squadrons we had never flown with before. It was an incredible sight!

The level of energy and intensity during debrief was as high as the brief. It appeared the targets had been hit, shots taken against the SAM sites, and none of the aircraft suffered damage.

After about ten days into the war, the concept eventually known as 'Weasel Police' was born. So effective were the F-4Gs in keeping the Iraqi air defence forces out of the air, that strike package leaders were refusing to fly without dedicated Weasel support.

Due to the non-stop nature of the air war, there just weren't enough F-4Gs to go around. Indeed, the situation became so contentious, that the CENTAF commander, Gen Horner, put out the word, 'I'll decide if you fly or not without Weasel support. You go unless otherwise directed.'

In order to cover as many strike packages as possible, the planners at Riyadh, in conjunction with Ballanco and Uken and the Weasel leadership at Sheikh Isa, came up with a Weasel CAP mission dubbed Weasel Police due to the similarity of a street cop walking a beat. So too would the Weasels 'walk' the KTO beat.

Particularly in the small KTO, Weasels would be on hand to cover all the Allied aircraft that struck targets during a specific time period. To do that, typically, a six ship of F-4Gs would launch to cover a window of time. Two jets would actually be on station while two were going to a tanker for gas and another two were coming off the tanker to relieve the 'on patrol' Weasels. Using such a tactic, six jets could cover a six-hour or more window of time in the compact KTO.

Often, the Weasels wouldn't know much more than a call sign and a time for each strike package, but usually that was enough. If the Weasels knew that 'Claw 41' had a TOT at X time at X point, they'd ensured they were in position to detect and schwack any Iraqi ground threat. Once Claw was off target, the Weasels proceeded on to the next strike package, often hitting a target in the same area due to careful planning done by the ATO shop in Riyadh. 'Weasels on Patrol' was an instant success and continued for the remainder of the war.

Weasel Police were not as effective in Iraq due to the much larger and more dispersed nature of the country and its military infra-structure. For targets in Iraq, Weasels continued to fly direct support missions until the last day of the war.

Chapter Fourteen

On 23 January, Iraqi forces destroyed the Sea Island pumping station in Kuwait's harbour that filled the supertankers in times of peace. In addition, those forces emptied several tankers still in port and the storage tanks surrounding the facility. The spill of 1.1 million barrels of oil was the worst in history. Saddam's rationale for ordering the dumping was, apparently, two-fold.

First, the heavy sludge would interfere with any Allied amphibious assault on Kuwait. Since a division of US Marines was on transports near Kuwait to give the impression of just such an assault, Saddam's reasoning made sense. However, the amphibious option was mainly a bluff as the ground war would subsequently show.

Second, many of the Gulf States depended on desalinisation of sea water for their fresh water needs. The dumped oil could clog up those plants and put them out of commission. No water for the civilians, never mind the Allied troops, would soon force the Arab nations arrayed against Iraq to change their minds.

A hastily mounted, but superbly executed F-111 strike on the oil terminal soon put a halt to the dumping. The desalinisation plants were protected by floating booms that deflected the oil on the surface and time and the tide eventually dispersed the massive oil slick. It was another failed gambit by an increasingly desperate Saddam.

SCHREINER, 27 JANUARY 1991 D + 164 W + 10

> Last night's mission was in support of B-52 and GR-1 strikes near Rumalaya oilfields – part of the disputed oilfield in north-west Kuwait.

On our way out, I could see several large fires burning out of control in eastern Kuwait. Apparently the oil that shithead Saddam is dumping in the Gulf is on fire. What does he hope to accomplish by trashing the upper Gulf? Does he really think that dumping thousands of barrels of oil into the Gulf will stop us? Aside from turning the area into an ecological wasteland, he is accomplishing nothing.

The sortie was a milk run. There were hardly radar emissions to speak of. Certainly nothing threatening us or the strikers. But, unfortunately, nothing up long enough for us to shoot. Not even a garage door opener . . .

What has struck me about my last few missions in particular is the almost complete lack of resistance I've seen in the form of AAA, SAMs or enemy fighters. So far, the F-15s have shot down most everything the Iraqis have sent up. I'm sure the Iraqi pilots are scared, some have even flown to Iran for sanctuary. We don't know yet what their real purpose for doing that is.

I have not fired any HARMs in the past three sorties because there haven't been any signals up to shoot. Where are Saddam's vaunted air defences? Sure, the AAA is there, but it is largely ineffective and gradually diminishing in density.

What are they holding back for? I don't think we have destroyed that many of their aircraft on the ground and I know we haven't blown up all their SAMs.

It is too quiet up there. He must have something up his sleeve, but what? Only time will tell.

In fact, after losing nearly forty aircraft in the first week of the war, the Iraqi Air Force did fly many of its surviving aircraft to airfields in Iran. For several days, the Allied High Command was unsure if Iran was a willing participant in this mass exodus and if those newly based jets would become a threat from Iran. Accurate figures are unknown, but over 120 Iraqi aircraft are thought to have fled.

Eventually, a virtual wall of F-15s and US Navy F-14s sealed off the escape route and the remainder of Saddam's Air Force was destroyed, for the most part, in its hangars. The Iraqis may have thought that after the war, Iran would give the aircraft back and Saddam would have his air force back, but such was not the case. Left to moulder as they were found, the abandoned jets became so much junk. Even the Iraqi aircrews were held for several years by the Iranians before being handed back to Saddam. Another poor strategic choice by the 'Butcher of Baghdad'. But it did add another element of worry for both the strategy shapers in Washington and Riyadh as well as the guy in the cockpit who now had to watch for threats from yet another direction. Iran's eventual shooting down of two of the escaping Iraqis and damaging several more helped reassure the Coalition that Iran was an unwilling participant in the exodus.

Also on the night of the 27th, but far to the west, EWO Paul Gregory put another of Saddam's SAMs out of commission for good as well as one of his AAA radars. He was flying another night sortie in support of three B-52s, but this time nearly on the Syrian border. The BUFFs were bombing Scud sites that Saddam's rocket forces continued to lob at Israel in futile attempts to break the Coalition.

> We were number two in the Weasel two ship – Michelob 53 was Capts Lou Shogry and Shaun Copelin, Vince Cooper and I were Michelob 54 – supporting Patty 35 flight, three B-52s bombing suspected SCUD sites. It was a very dark night with no moon. Initially, there wasn't any AAA, but I started getting indications of an SA-3 target tracking radar coming up and down.
>
> We set up south of the target area while Patty came in from south-east. Once they dropped their bombs, they had to make a hard right turn to keep from flying into Syria.
>
> Just prior to the TOT, the SA-3 came up again – on for ten to fifteen seconds, then off. When he was radiating, I had perfect SA-3 'Cricket' audio on the APR-47. He came back up again and I heard the radar go into high PRF just as I looked into the darkness and saw him launch.
>
> I called 'SAM launch, two o'clock' and told Vince to come right to shoot this guy. I hit the Handoff button and got an immediate 'ready' light.
>
> I pickled the HARM off and told Vince 'Hard right turn.' The turn took about twenty seconds and as soon as we rolled out of the turn, I looked left into the darkness and had a perfect 'flash-bulb' picture of the HARM exploding over the SA-3 site. A true 'Kodak moment'.
>
> The range at launch was about eight miles. After the war, my wife hired Ronald Wong, a noted aviation artist, to paint a picture

of the moment of the HARM detonation. It hangs in our living room today.

The BUFFs called off target and started their egress. We continued out to the north-east abeam Al Qaim, which was now illuminated by tons of AAA coming up after the SAM launch, the HARM detonation, and the tons of bombs dropped by the B-52s. A Flap Wheel AAA radar came up. I designated it, quickly got good range information, and launched our last HARM. The Flap Wheel signal went down at the end of the HARM's TOF [Time of Flight]. We claimed it as destroyed.

That was a long 6.0-hour mission.

Schreiner, 30 January 1991 D + 167 W + 13

Last night's mission flown to just north of Kuwait. We had a full moon and very little cloud cover. A scattered deck at 8,000 [feet] prevented complete viewing of the ground but most of it was visible. Numerous ground fires indicated that our side continues to inflict damage and casualties on the enemy but with little reciprocity.

One fire was particularly interesting. One lucky bomber managed to find what was apparently a Republican Guard ammo dump. For the entire thirty minutes we were in the area, the fire burned with a steady orange glow, punctuated every minute or so with large white explosions indicating more rounds cooking off.

Sitting in my cockpit at 27,000 feet, I felt quite insulated from what must have been a horrendous experience for those unfortunate enough to have been caught when the bomber originally found his mark.

Daily, it seems, Iraqi fighters, bombers, and transports continue to seek 'safe haven' in Iran. To date, estimates run at around 100 aircraft. Iran steadfastly maintains that these aircraft will be detained until the war is over, as is required of a 'neutral' country by international law.

What is really going on? Are they defecting as our generals are speculating or are they massing for a surprise attack against our

The "WW" tailcode was made famous during Vietnam. Here the tailcode carried by the George AFB jets is highlighted in this photo taken in Bahrain. (USAF)

fleet in the Gulf? Were they to do that, Iran would no longer be considered neutral. Personally, I think we can defeat Iraq in about two months' time. However, with Iran in the picture, all bets are off.

Tonight, our target is a chemical storage facility about sixty miles west of Baghdad.

SCHREINER, 1 FEBRUARY 1991 D + 169 W + 15

Last night, actually this morning, we flew in support of RAF Tornadoes. Their target was listed in the frag as a 'Pet Store'.

Tent complex of the 'recce' RF-4Cs of the Nevada Air National Guard that formed part of the 35th TFW (P). (Ed Fisher)

Apparently, someone in Riyadh has a sense of humour, thinking of the alleged 'Baby Milk' factory that was bombed last week.

For the first time since the war began, I could actually see the ground in Iraq for the entire mission. There was absolutely no visible light emanating from the ground save one minor fire, possibly a bon-fire right along the Euphrates River just west of our target.

The first TOT was at 0153 and [at] precisely that time a string of six Mk 82 500-lb bombs impacted near the target. Apparently they missed, but these bombs woke up the Iraqis because the sky around the impact exploded with AAA. Up to this point, there hadn't been so much as a peep.

At about the same time, a 'One Eye' early warning radar came up longer than the usual few seconds Iraqi radars have been emitting. After seeing him for about ten seconds, Dan and I decided that this radar was all we were going to see tonight, so we decided to poke out that One Eye.

The signal stayed up for the predicted HARM time of flight and then ceased transmitting. It's apparent that Dan and I scored again. Too bad it wasn't a SAM radar.

Two minutes later, another Tornado made his target run and this time made his presence known. The entire area erupted with a huge fireball several thousand feet high. The second string of Mk 82s had found the 'Pet Store'. Cats and dogs were flying everywhere. Numerous secondary explosions added to the already raging inferno. Scratch one Iraqi petroleum storage area ('PET STORE'). This is what we call a 'shack'.

GI humor (Fisher)

After we landed, I was greeted with congratulations from the Tornado flight. It seems that our HARM didn't get the One Eye but instead 'flexed' to an SA-3 that was engaging one of the Tornadoes. That pilot apparently saw the site explode after we called our shot. Whether we in fact actually scored a hit, I may never know. I have to review the CONRAC to see if it was possible, but since we were the only ones to shoot anything, it is very likely that we also scored a shack.

Chapter Fifteen

T o borrow a line from the movie Star Wars, at the end of January, the 'circle was now complete' regarding every Wild Weasel unit in the Air Force. A contingent of six additional aircrews, originally destined to be combat loss replacements – remember the '20–30 per cent loss rate' briefed on opening night – arrived in Bahrain. These crews were from the 90th TFS, 'the Pair o' Dice' stationed at Clark Air

Shot of the Phillipine-based 'Pair o' Dice' 90th TFS F-4Gs. Although none of their jets flew in DESERT STORM, the six relief crews provided a much needed addition to the crew line-up. (USAF)

Captains Bob Dupuis (r) and Ed 'Tuna' Fisher (sitting on HARM) before climbing into the massive F-4G 'Wild Weasel.' (Ed Fisher)

Base in the Philippines. Now, every base with the F-4G Wild Weasel mission was represented in *Desert Storm*.

Thankfully, these new crews weren't needed to make up for dead Weasels, but they did help significantly in giving the dead-tired Weasels a break from the daily grind. Since the war began, nearly every crew had flown at least one mission per day, sometimes two or three. Their mission times varied from day to night and back again with no time to adjust internal body clocks. Normally, aircrews are afforded twelve hours from their last mission until reporting for the brief for the next. However, so great was the need for Weasel support for the thousands of Allied sorties every day, that this time was shortened to eight hours, sometimes less. The pace was just brutal and couldn't be kept up forever. The six crews from Clark were given a day or two to spin up – that is, get smart on the ROE, the tactics being employed and the way the missions were being conducted and then fed into the daily line-up.

One of the twelve airmen, EWO Captain Ed 'Tuna' Fisher, says of his first impression of Sheikh Isa:

Everyone walks around carrying a pistol and gas mask on their waist. The atmosphere is very relaxed though. All the crews have been flying hard and telling war stories. Most of the people here have been here six months and are sick of it.

In a scene reminiscent of Tom Gummo's frustrating experience with the new 9-mm semi-auto pistols at Lajes Air Base during the initial deployment to the Gulf, so too did the Philippine-based flyers find their sidearms problematic.

Fisher continues:

Farrell and Fisher taxiing out, note proximity of the taxi way to the Persian Gulf, seen as dark line in distance. (Ed Fisher)

The quaint character of a 'tent city' street. (Fisher)

We haven't found any clips or ammo for our 9 mm pistols.
Everyone else here carries .38 Specials. Our ammo got accidentally diverted to Diego Garcia. It's hard to believe you can't find
bullets in a war zone!

A couple of days later, they did find some ammunition for the guns:

We found clips and ammo today. The Marines were the only
folks with a big enough grip to give it to us. All the other ground
support 'warriors' refused to give up theirs. They must think the
Iraqis are about to attack Bahrain, and therefore they needed
their clips more than aircrews who might have to eject over
enemy territory. Pretty ridiculous!

The new crews were folded into the flying line-up, which continued
without let-up. Ed Fisher flew his first mission on 2 February. His pilot

was fellow squadronmate Captain Vinnie Farrell. Fisher recounts his first combat experience:

We were part of Coors 71 flight. We took off at 1905 on a 2.9-hour mission in support of three B-52s and four Saudi Tornadoes on strikes against the Republican Guard. About ten miles south of the target, the AAA started getting close, to within a mile and at our altitude, about 25,000 to 30,000 feet. We said the hell with this and turned the jet away. No use in flying straight and level in the bullets!

We worked around the area of the heaviest fire. We saw a lot of lighter flak at about 15,000 feet and intermittently some heavier stuff up there with us. I picked up several signals but was unable to get enough data to shoot. The signals went up and down, and stayed mostly down.

We wandered through southern Iraq and northern Kuwait hoping to bait somebody, but had no luck. But good on the Saudis. We saw secondary explosions and a large fire in

Farrell (front cockpit) and Fisher (rear) in their 'office' prior to starting engines for a mission. Ed (Fisher)

At the 'arm-de-arm' point. Here weapons are made live and 'last chance' inspections for anything wrong with the jet are made. Next stop is the runway and take-off. (Ed Fisher)

the target area during their TOT. Shit hot! All in all, the adrenaline pumped out and we did pretty good for a couple of 'cherry boys.' We go back for more tomorrow night."

SCHREINER, 4 FEBRUARY 1991 D + 172 W + 18

WOPs – Weasels On Patrol. That's what our mission has been referred to in the past few days. The mission: take off, hit a tanker, go orbit in Kuwait looking for any type of radar threat until low on fuel, hit a tanker, repeat.

These missions last over five hours and most of the time nothing comes up. Not even AAA, with one exception. Yesterday, I could see three large contrails coming from the

A flight of F-4Gs waiting their turn for gas, taken from the fourth jet in the four-ship flight. (Ed Fisher)

direction of Iraq, i.e., the west and headed towards Kuwait. A three ship of B-52s were on their way to make a couple of hundred Iraqi soldiers' day a little noisy.

At altitude, even daylight precision bombing in this high tech era is anything but precise. Carpet bombing as it is also referred to does little more than keep the troops awake and their morale low. That may be good enough.

I didn't know where their particular target was located that day until they dropped their load. From 37,000 feet bombs, even 'dumb' ones, travel a long way. Somewhere in the neighbourhood of five to six miles from the point of release. As soon as a large group of bombs fell on what looked like a group of warehouses, the Iraqis responded with six or seven futile bursts of 57-mm AAA. It came nowhere near the BUFFs, only getting as high as 27,000 feet.

F-4s at sunset (USAF)

They had long since turned south and may not have even been aware of its presence. However, we were orbiting only a few miles away at 26,000, so it added a little excitement to an otherwise 'slow' day.

To date, I've flown some eighteen sorties for a total of fifty-five hours. I have never flown this much in such a short amount of time and I thought I'd never say this, but I'm tired of flying.

Actually, I'm tired of getting up before 3 a.m. after not getting enough sleep. I haven't been able to adjust to the early hours and so have not been able to get the rest I need. I am tired before I climb into the jet and exhausted once I land. I've begun to fly by rote and I have to force myself to stay in position off lead and provide good mutual support, i.e., check six.

Fortunately, the threat is very low and though long, the missions aren't particularly demanding. Were either the case, I may well be a danger to the flight. Hopefully, these early hours will end and I'll get a much needed day of rest.

One side note, one of those three B-52s crashed on returning to

Diego Garcia. Apparently, some sort of mechanical malfunction occurred because I seriously doubt any type of AAA fire hit them. At this point, three crewmembers have been found while the other three remain missing. I hope they find them, but it's looking pretty grim.

Other Weasels remember the chronic fatigue and the lethargy induced by it. Kevin Hale recalled a string of night Weasel Police missions that all ran together:

We were on a night KTO mission supporting B-52s doing their thing on the Republican Guard. We saw the carpet bombing rolling out underneath us and it took a few seconds to realise that if the bombs were going off directly underneath us, then the BUFFs must be dropping directly overhead! We moved out of the way right smartly!

Another night, we were in a two ship with our number two spread out to the side and behind us by a couple of miles. Everything was quiet and no emitters were up. We were way too exhausted and way too relaxed by this time so even when we saw an SA-2 launched ballistically and move aft in relation to our canopy, we knew it wasn't guiding on us. We finally figured out that it could guide on our wingman and we finally called it out. But they'd seen it too and avoided it. Both of us were just too tired and too complacent.

We also thought we saw a nuke explosion one night. We were patrolling in the north-west of Kuwait when the underside of our jet lit up. We rolled to one side and didn't see anything and rolled the other way. Still nothing. Finally, Jack Patterson, my pilot, rolled the wings through 90 degrees so we could look straight down and we saw a mushroom cloud! Turns out it was a fuel-air mixture explosive, but for a second there, we thought things had really escalated!

In fact, the 'fuel-air mixture' weapon was actually the BLU-82 bomb. The world's largest conventional weapon, the BLU-82 had first been used during the Vietnam War as a quick method to blast helicopter landing zones in the thick jungle of that country. Nicknamed the 'Daisy Cutter' in a macabre reference to its use as a foliage clearer, Air

Force and Army planners hoped that the 15,000-pound bomb would be useful in breaching the 'Saddam Line' of mines, anti-tank traps, and trenches the Iraqis had built on the border between Kuwait and Saudi Arabia.

The bomb was dropped at altitude from MC-130 Combat Talon special operations versions of the venerable Lockheed C-130 Hercules cargo hauler. The bomb was mounted on a pallet and pushed out of the lowered ramp of the MC-130. After clearing the aircraft, a massive parachute deployed and slowed the bomb's descent. A six-foot long nose fuse detonated the bomb just above the surface of the desert in what could easily be misconstrued as a small nuclear explosion.

The BLU-82's mix of ammonium nitrate and aluminium powder produced a shock wave, called 'overpressure', on the order of 1,000 lb/psi. The human eardrum ruptures at around 5 lb/psi. A 50 lb/psi shock wave will kill half the people hit. Anyone in the large effects area of the BLU-82 stood no chance.

Besides the blast effect, the force of the shock wave killed by making objects lying around – rifles, shovels, canned rations – into lethal projectiles, killing and maiming the soft, squishy mechanisms of the human body. Besides, these gory methods of killing, any Iraqis who managed to survive the blast by being inside a strong bunker or other shelter literally had the air sucked from their lungs, and sometimes the lungs themselves from their chest, by the explosion sucking all the air from the surrounding area for a micro-second.

Although the BLU-82 did not perform as well as the planners had expected since the softer desert soil absorbed much of the blast and left many of the mines in place, the four drops of the big bomb certainly got both the Iraqis' attention as well as anyone flying overhead who saw the faux nuke.

Even if the originally deployed Weasels had gotten used to the routine of war, 'new guy' Ed Fisher hadn't had time to become blasé about the mission yet. His second mission was to assist another B-52 pounding of the Iraqis dug into southern Iraq and northern Kuwait. His third mission, however, was away from the Weasel Police over Kuwait and deeper into the more wild and woolly Iraqi airspace:

Last night, we were Oly 77, the number three in a four ship supporting B-52s bombing the Shahiyat fuel depot twenty miles south-west of Baghdad. The strike package had us, the BUFFS, two EF-111s to do the jamming and two F-15s keeping the skies clear.

I had the job of taking a PET [pre-emptive target] shot against a known SA-2 site if nothing else was active in the target area. As we approached the time to take my shot, my adrenaline started pumping. I took my shot about 30 degrees off the nose and the HARM roared towards the target, a bright flame shooting off into the distance.

Right after I took my shot, an SA-2 came up at my GRP (geographic reference point – the spot on the ground where I programmed the missile to hit), so we may have ended up with a kill, but I was too busy to watch and confirm the shot.

My APR-47 lit up with multiple indications of SA-2s, -3s, -6s, -8s, Rolands, Flapwheels, etc. All of the signals were up and down, using EMCON [emission control] to keep from being shot. A number of -8s came up right underneath us, so we frantically looked for SAM launches and moved away from them. We were tracked momentarily by one site, but saw no launch. We got -47 indications of optical launches, but saw none of them.

Then I saw a launch at our five o'clock several miles away, and although it appeared to not to be targeted on us, we rolled and pulled anyway, putting out chaff and using our ECM pod. The sustainer [motor] on the SAM burned bright until the missile was above us and then extinguished. I could still see the heated missile though.

All this time I was working an SA-3 that was exactly where intel said it was. The SAM's radar kept going up and down, not giving me good information. He stayed 'dotted' most of the time, but I could still hear his radar signal, although very weak. The characteristic high-pitched rattlesnake sound was there.

Since he was close to my GRP, and I felt his position was accurate, we took our second shot with less information from the APR-47 than is optimum. Once again a HARM roared off our jet, but since he was dotted at the TOT, I'll never know if we killed him or not. He did not come back up while we were on station that night, however.

Vinnie Quinn and Ken Spaar were a little more jaded at this stage, having flown dozens of sorties by now. On 7 February 1991, they flew a day mission with some excitement that shook them out of their boredom:

> We were a three ship after we had one guy abort with a bad jet, supporting Brit Tornadoes dropping a bridge over the Euphrates River east of Baghdad.
>
> They had a unique method of dropping the precision weapons needed to drop the bridge. Each Tornado carried two LGMs [laser guided munitions] that needed to 'see' the laser designator to hit the point of impact. They used a [Blackburn] Buccaneer to lase the target; the nav in the back seat would aim his hand-held laser designator at the target, call that he was radiating and then a Tornado would roll in and drop. The seeker head on the LGM acquired the laser and using the fins on its body would adjust its falling flightpath to intersect the point where the laser touched the bridge.
>
> We'd been briefed about an SA-2 in the area and after the one F-4 aborted, we flew a spread out 'vic' formation, with me in the lead, # 2 and # 3 on each wing. We were in the target area, heading north, when the SA-2 came up, but with some 'ambiguity' to the signal. The -47 couldn't decide whether it was a -2 or a -6.
>
> We made a left turn, heading west, to get a few more 'cuts' on the signal to pinpoint what and where he was. When we made the turn, the SAM launched, but we couldn't see it since it was behind us. Our # 2 did see the launch and called it out and I turned back north.
>
> Momar picked up the missile, 'Eleven o'clock, high, tracking.' Which told me to look slightly left of the nose, up, and that the SAM was targeting us. We watched it head towards us, then kind of 'burble' as it tried to decide whether to turn on us or into our wingman. In the end, it split the difference and passed between us as I manoeuvred around it.
>
> During all this, we got split up from the flight and were now [a] single ship. Momar picked up an SA-3 radar tracking us while we were dancing with the -2, thinking he could sneak one in on us while we were busy.
>
> Instead, we put the -3 on the nose, pickled a HARM, and killed him. My attitude by this point was we ruled the sky over the

AOR. How dare anybody actually have the balls to track us with a full system lock on? For that crime, he had to die.

Joe Healy was the EWO in a Weasel four minutes behind Vinnie Quinn's flight. His view of that mission follows.

I got a -6 at about ten miles in front of us, off to the left (west) side, for a few seconds, but he never stayed up or came back up. It may

The crew chief not only cared for the jet, but the crew as well. Here a crew is helped to strap in prior to a flight. (USAF)

have been a reflection, I just don't know. At the same time that the -2 shot at them, we picked up -3 indications and shot at them.

One of the Tornadoes, in a rather excited British tone called, 'SAM three! Weasels!' He fairly screamed the last words and his voice went up several octaves. It so happened that I had launched my second HARM about twenty to thirty seconds prior to his call on a -3 that had stayed on the air for quite a while. If either of my shots killed something, it was probably that one.

At the same time, three SA-8s came up during the SA-3 duels and with several Weasel flights in the area, it became something of a feeding frenzy! There were numerous white HARM smoke trails arcing up into the clear blue sky. This was especially rewarding after the boring Weasel Police missions in Kuwait.

Not all the Iraqi SAM operators were inefficient. Weasel EWO Gary Rattray remembered a mission flown over Kuwait's International Airport in mid-February where three separate flights of Weasels worked an SA-6 site.

He'd continuously go 'on', then 'off'. Our two ship relieved the flight before us who shot at this guy but he kept coming up. During our station time, we shot at him, and the flight that relieved us all had him come up. They launched at him as well. Between the three flights, this guy had something like seven or eight HARMs sent to him and he's up the next day, ready to play. Good on him for knowing his stuff, I guess . . .

On the same day, on a different mission, Schreiner had a completely different experience in the western Iraqi skies.

Schreiner, 10 February 1991, D + 187 W + 24

All's quiet on the Iraqi front (with apologies to Erich M. Remarque). The last HARM shot I fired was a PET shot at an SA-2 at Al Qom in western Iraq. We were supporting an RF-4 recce run in the area and were given the coordinates of a suspected SA-2 site.

At two minutes before their TOT, we fired our missile at those coordinates, hoping something, preferably that SA-2, would be radiating when our missile got there. One minute, fifteen seconds after we launched we received the missile guidance frequency of the SA-2 right at our GRP! Could we have lucked out again?!

When we landed, one of the recce pilots came up to us and told us he saw something burning right at our GRP, so there's a good chance we got him. Unfortunately, he wasn't able to get a picture of it so, as always, we're not sure.

SCHREINER, 15 FEBRUARY 1991 D + 183 W + 29

I had planned to write about several things today but peace was not one of them.

Baghdad announced that they were now willing to withdraw their forces from Kuwait! Could this be? After all this bullshit and a war, could there finally be light at the end of the tunnel?

To date, our forces have destroyed about ⅓ of the Iraqi army with the loss of fewer than 100 of our own people. Admittedly these figures are our own as announced by the Pentagon, but I can see little advantage in falsifying this type of information. Additionally, we have controlled the skies from day one, flying anywhere in Iraq or Kuwait we wished with virtual impunity. We can bomb anything we want and there is very little the Iraqis can do about it.

We are slowly but systematically destroying Iraq's armed forces and their ability to wage war. It is only a matter of time and Saddam has to realise that he cannot win. Based on his past actions, I didn't believe he'd give up so soon. I fully believed we would be forced to invade and destroy his army and physically eject him from Kuwait.

There's a lot of negotiating to be done and who knows how long it will take. It's also possible this is a ploy to give Saddam time to regroup, although I'm sure if there was any inkling of that, we would 'remind' him of our capabilities.

Regardless, at least today, everyone is in a jubilant mood and glad that the war may be over and, more importantly, we will be going home soon. God, I hope so!

Today our mission took us on an airfield tour of central Iraq. Actually, our flight was escorting a two ship of recces while they took pictures of five or six airfields, all sixty miles or closer to Baghdad.

As usual, we encountered very little opposition and being a day sortie, I couldn't see any AAA anyway, so ignorance is bliss.

We did manage to get decent ranging on an SA-3 in the vicinity of Baghdad. Naturally, we shot it, although after reviewing the tape, I can't tell if we hit it. It did stop emitting though.

This was the first time in five or six sorties that I had actually shot something. Wouldn't it be great if it was the last?

This brief moment of hope was caused by Saddam Hussein telling the world that he'd leave his '19th' Province if the Allies stopped pounding his forces and in his own time frame. Naturally, this attempt at saving his forces through diplomacy on his own terms failed and the relentless grinding of his forces into the Mesopotamian dust continued.

Plainly, peace was not at hand.

Chapter Sixteen

SCHREINER 22 FEBRUARY 1991 D + 190 W + 36

Not so fast! As expected or at least suspected Saddam attached several conditions to his pull-out proposal, which turned out to be nothing more than a rehash of his original proposal back in August: Israel must pull out of its occupied territories; the Palestinian issue must be settled, etc., etc.

The US response was predictable. Bombing will continue as before. The only countries that supported Saddam's 'peace proposal' were the same ones that have supported him all along – Jordan, Yemen, Libya, Cuba, and the Palestinians.

For days now, intel has been telling us that our ground assault is imminent. On several occasions, I've stepped to fly believing that the ground war would be going by the time I returned.

Obviously, that hasn't happened yet. Several occurrences may have contributed to the delay. One, the weather has been pretty shitty. A lot of rain fell in south-eastern Iraq and Kuwait making any ground movement more difficult. We even cancelled a mission because of it.

More significantly, the Soviets proposed a new peace plan, which today was outlined in public. Initially, a copy was sent to Bush although he was asked not to publicise it, which he honoured. He did, however, indicate that the proposal fell 'far short' of the UN Resolutions although he did not reject it outright.

The proposal does call for a complete Iraqi pull out although we must stop our bombing for two days prior and there is no mention for when the Iraqi pull out must be completed. There are other provisions as well.

Saddam finally agreed to it today although the fact that Bush doesn't like it may have something to do with that. In any event, the UN Security Council is scheduled to meet to discuss it. Stay tuned.

Yesterday, our mission took us to Baghdad. Actually, our tasking was to escort a couple of RF-4s on a recce run of several airfields in and around the Baghdad area. The weather over Baghdad was perfect and it seems the reported smoke screen set up by some Baghdad citizens did not exist or at least had little effect. The almost complete lack of opposition was amazing if not a little eerie. Our radar receiver scopes were almost completely blank except for some friendly signals. Where are the Iraqi SAMs and AAA?

Other missions flown in the past week include a 6.5-hour marathon Weasel Police mission to western Iraq. We watched three B-52s pummel an Iraqi ammo storage facility. No missiles [were] fired. Another mission had us support four Saudi F-5s while they bombed a minor Iraqi position just across the border. Again no signals came up.

Apparently, the Saudis lost an F-5 the day prior in the area and so probably as a political gesture, we tasked four Weasels and two F-15s to protect them. I had heard the F-5 go down and I suspect he flew into the ground because of his own stupidity not because of any Iraqi ground fire. What a waste.

Last night was a little interesting. I was lying in bed half-asleep when I heard the characteristic double-bang of a sonic boom. Some jarhead going a little fast over the base or so I thought.

About a minute later, I heard two other lesser explosions that I couldn't explain. Another minute passed and 'SCUD ALARM! SCUD ALARM! SCUD ALARM! Don mask . . . '

There was no doubt what had happened! A first for this base and Bahrain itself. Whether the Scuds were specifically targeted at Dharan or Bahrain is unclear but apparently two missiles found their way to our area.

Once again, the Scuds intercepted our outgoing Patriots and brought them down. Some of the pieces fell near the chow hall and the Weasel Dome but happily, no one was hurt. A few lucky individuals got some souvenirs to take home. Again, the Scuds contained conventional warheads.

Just as different Weasels had different perceptions to the same mission, so too did several of them remember the Scud attack differently. Said Joe Healy:

I was up writing a letter and watching a movie in the dorm 'lounge' with a couple of other guys when at about 0215, we heard a sonic boom.

One guy said, 'The Bahrainis just "boomed" us again.' I replied, 'It might have been a Patriot launch.'

Turns out, I was right because about thirty seconds later, the loudspeakers boomed out 'SCUD ALERT!' This was the first one in over a month.

This morning, after breakfast, I ran into one of our intel NCOs who said a Scud or two was fired at Dharan but due to winds and/or bad aim, it came towards us, and apparently pieces landed a mile or so north of the main gate and another hit the water offshore to the east.

Ed Fisher, having arrived within the period since the last Scud alarm, was woken from a sound sleep by a loud bang.

I immediately looked out the window at the Patriot site, but didn't see anything. As I lay back down, the PA system squealed to life, 'SCUD ALARM! SCUD ALARM!'

Everyone scrambled to put on their [chemical] mask and gloves. I lay in bed with my mask on for about forty-five minutes until the all-clear was sounded. Then I went out to investigate.

It turns out our Patriot site shot down a Scud targeted against the base. I didn't hear the Patriot launch or transition through the Mach, but woke up when I heard the warhead explode. Another Scud or Scuds fell short or flew long and were not intercepted. The intercept was several miles away, yet there was some widely scattered debris near our dormitory. I now have a piece as a souvenir.

90th TFS pilot Dennis Malfer, then a captain, and another of the recently arrived Philippine-based crews, recalled scrambling into his

APR-47 CONTROLS AND INDICATORS

REAR COCKPIT

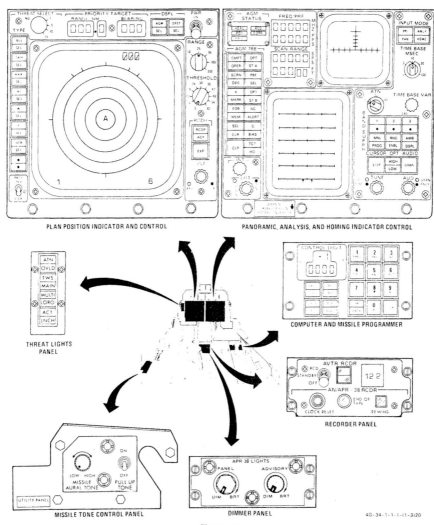

PLAN POSITION INDICATOR AND CONTROL

PANORAMIC, ANALYSIS, AND HOMING INDICATOR CONTROL

THREAT LIGHTS PANEL

COMPUTER AND MISSILE PROGRAMMER

RECORDER PANEL

MISSILE TONE CONTROL PANEL

DIMMER PANEL

4G-34-1-1-(1-3)20

Figure 1-40

1-107

The 'brain' of the Weasel's unique radar hunting system, the AN/APR-47. This is a page from the technical order about the system showing the major components of the EWO's display panels. The left hand scope was the plan position indicator console (PPIC) which displayed threats in relation to the jet. The right hand scopes could help discriminate between specific received signals. The various switches, knobs, etc. operated the -47. (USAF)

chemical protective gear, looking around and seeing his EWO similarly garbed with his pistol out, ready to defend the place! A good
laugh was had by all . . .

EWO Steve Johns had a slightly different view of this attack:

> I was sitting in the arming area. The Patriot battery was off our
> right wing as we were arming the aircraft for departure. We had
> just finished arming the final aircraft when the 'Scud Alarm'
> came across the radio.
>
> About the same time, I see two Patriot missiles launch from the
> battery. I watched as the Patriot headed north after the Scud, and
> we were told by the tower to hold our position in the arming area.
> We had closed our canopies and wanted to get out of the area.
> Scott and I figured that if the Scud contained chemicals, we
> would be better off airborne and be available to launch from

Line of F-4Gs in their Shaikh Isa revetments. Not all the jets around the
world had been painted in the lower-visibility grey paint by the start of the
war. (USAF)

another base if needed. Unfortunately, the tower did not see it that way.

As Scott asked for clearance for immediate take-off, tower tells us to hold position, we were under attack . . . *No kidding*, that is why we want to get out of here.

We switched over to the SOF (Gummi I think) and asked him to talk with tower folks and let us go… launch for survival. After a couple of minutes, we were cleared for take-off… at our own risk. (Scott and I laughed about that; we always launch at our own risk.) Patriot batteries were engaging incoming Scuds, so be aware you may be targeted. We figured we had a better chance airborne, talking with AWACS than sitting on the ground with possible Scuds with chemicals landing our way.

We launched and headed north, keeping a good eye on the APR-47, adhering to prescribed departure procedures and making sure we were squawking our assigned IFF codes. We definitely did not want some trigger happy Patriot battery to mistake us for a Scud.

While this excitement was happening at Sheikh Isa, the grim business of methodically destroying the Iraqi armed forces continued. Victor Ballanco was the number three in a four ship flight covering strikes on Taji Airfield, which lay to the north of Baghdad:

As we went by Baghdad International Airport, we saw an SA-3 come up for a few seconds. We shot at him, but missed, but he did stay off the air for the rest of our time in the area.

Another site shot at us, but our first indication was the launch. I believe they tracked us optically, using NVGs [night vision goggles]. Then their radar came up to guide the SAMs onto us.

We got a solution and shot, but then had to go defensive to defeat the two SAMs guiding on us. It all seemed to me to be happening in relative slow motion. We popped chaff, I went back inside the cockpit to check our speed when my EWO called out one of the SAMs was going ballistic [no longer guiding on them] and the other detonated too far away.

Meanwhile, our HARM timed out and the radar went down so we got him. Checking the CONRAC afterwards confirmed that kill.

The next night, Schreiner would tangle with the airport SA-3 as well.

SCHREINER, 23 FEBRUARY 1991 D + 191 W + 37

He who hesitates is lost. Last mission took us back to Baghdad in support of a nine ship B-52 raid just north of the city. As we approached our working area the long absent AAA was once again active. It may be that being at night, we could see it. I hadn't flown at night in over two weeks so the AAA may have been there the whole time; I just never saw it.

SAMs were also in evidence last night. On our second trip around the Weasel orbit, an SA-3 came up and stayed up a lot longer than usual. Normally, they only do that when they intend to fire and sure enough, just as we ourselves were about to shoot, I saw two missiles climb out of the murk.

At first, the missiles climbed straight up but gradually they began to arc over towards us. Dan was in the back working the signal, trying to get better ranging. It had just gone dotted, which meant it was no longer transmitting. Therefore, shooting now would probably result in a miss.

All Iraqi (the Soviet-supplied ones anyway) SAMs can fire visually if they know where their target is. Apparently they did and it was us!

Those missiles that were going straight up were now holding steady as two orange dots, not moving in the windscreen. Anything you can see moving is good – it's not on a collision course, it's not going to hit. Anything on a collision course does not move; it just gets bigger.

I could no longer wait for Dan to get better ranging. I immediately rolled inverted and pulled down. I called for chaff and for Dan to turn on our ECM pod. I also made the mistake of hitting my ECM switch, which I had left set to dispense flares.

Now they knew where we were, since I had just lit the way. Fortunately, my SAM defensive manoeuvre had worked and the SA-3s missed. The first thing I did after recovering from the dive was deselect the flares.

We had successfully defeated the SA-3 but missed what would be our only chance to shoot back. In hindsight, had we shot earlier, when the signal was first up, we probably would have gotten a good shot off. At least we kept the Iraqis' attention on us and off the B-52s, which had no trouble getting through to their target.

In other news, President Bush put forth the conditions for the Iraqi pull out. He gave them until noon eastern or 8 p.m. local to respond and begin their pull out of Kuwait. They have two days to be out of Kuwait City, and seven to be out of Kuwait altogether. There are other conditions as well.

I'm sceptical about the rumours saying Saddam might accept this proposal based on his past performance. Kuwait itself is now ablaze with some 150–200 oil wells set on fire. The thick black smoke is now covering the eastern half of Kuwait and is also overhead here. It looks like LA on a bad smog day outside.

On the other hand, I just watched CNN live footage taken by Peter Arnett, aka 'Baghdad Pete', of our latest raid on Baghdad. Light to medium AAA was in abundance although not nearly as dense as the early part of the war.

Our bombers apparently scored a direct hit on another baby milk factory as it was burning furiously with numerous secondary explosions. It's amazing how flammable Iraqi baby milk is.

Chapter Seventeen

On 24 February, the long anticipated Allied ground offensive began. For a month, the Allies played to the Iraqi suspicion that the war would begin as a breach of the Saddam Line, probably at the Wadi al-Batin, a natural canyon running north into Iraq. Located at the extreme western end of Kuwait, the US 1st Armored Calvary Division made elaborate preparations and presented convincing presentations of an armoured force preparing to assault a fixed position. Small probing attacks, armed ground reconnaissance and sustained artillery barrages all added to the Iraqis' certainty of the predicted attack point.

This preparation was all a charade, however. General Schwarzkopf and his staff devised a simple, yet devastatingly effective, plan to drive the Iraqis out of Kuwait and destroy as much of both their conventional armoured forces and the Republican Guard divisions as possible.

On a grand scale the plan was for two US Marine divisions and the Joint Forces Command (JFC) North and East (the Arab coalition forces) to drive into Kuwait, capturing the Iraqis' attention and keeping the enemy's forces busy. Meanwhile, the main thrust of the offensive, a massive 'left hook', would launch from far out to the west of Saudi Arabia and into Iraq, rolling forward and destroying everything in its path.

Each Allied division had its own part in the grand plan. To the east of Kuwait, the US 1st Marine Division with the Arab Joint Forces Command East (JFC-E) on its eastern flank penetrated the Saddam Line with stunning success, achieved with ingenuity and incredible bravery. They drove due north for Kuwait City pushing the Iraqis ever northward. As part of that push, the Marines would beat back the only significant Iraqi counter-effort in Kuwait by winning decisively the largest tank battle in Marine Corps' history.

Also assaulting Kuwait was the US 2d Marine Division with JFC-N to its immediate west. Augmenting the 2d Marines was the Tiger Brigade, a US Army armoured unit deployed from Ft Hood, Texas, to augment the Marines with more heavy, mobile firepower.

The main effort of this second Marine advance was to cut the major road junction of al-Jahra, west of Kuwait City. By cutting that junction, the Iraqi forces inside Kuwait would be trapped and easy pickings as they waited to be slaughtered.

Politically necessary but thought to be of little tactical use, the Arab forces in the two JFC units, North and East, performed very well. In the east, JFC-E, primarily comprising Saudi forces, rolled steadily up the coast of Kuwait, taking on Iraqi beach defence forces and capturing thousands of demoralised enemy troops.

JFC-N was a much larger organisation. In addition to Saudi and Kuwait troops, by far the Egyptian II Corps had the biggest presence with nearly 34,000 men. Divided into an armoured division, one mechanised division and an additional regiment, the Egyptians were actually the most experienced in desert warfare of all the Coalition troops.

While a powerful attack in its own right, the action against Kuwait proper was but a secondary effort compared with the main offensive. In a masterful strategic stroke, this offensive began far in the west of Iraq as several American and Allied divisions of armour and mechanised personnel carriers rolled nearly unopposed into Iraq.

Starting to the far west of the western offensive since dubbed the 'Hail Mary', the French Daguet Division, placed under the command of the US XVIII Airborne Corps, set out to capture the airfield at As Salmon, over 100 miles inside Iraq. The Allies wanted the airfield to serve as a FOB (forward operating base) for the hard-hitting attack helicopters of the US 82d Airborne. The 82d, in turn, would guard the western and northern flank of the main offensive.

Directly east of the 82d, the US 101st Airborne (Air Assault) Division also plunged deeply into Iraq, nearly seventy miles, to capture another FOB. Using that, the 'Screaming Eagles' would use their 100+ helicopters to resupply the heavier, armoured forces rolling to their east. Additionally, the 101st assaulted trouble spots and continued manning the ever-lengthening flank of the progressing ground offensive.

The heaviest element of the XVIII Airborne Corps was the attached US 24th Mechanized Infantry Division. Equipped with hundreds of heavy, M1A1 Abrams tanks and Bradley infantry fighting vehicles, the 24th gave substantial punch to the normally lightly armed, but fast-moving Airborne forces.

The main punch of the Hail Mary came in the form of the US VII Corps, moved to the desert far from its envisioned Cold War battle-ground of central Europe. VII Corps consisted of the US 1st Infantry (actually mechanised infantry), the British 1st Armoured Division, the US 1st Calvary Division (Armored), and the US 1st and 3d Armored Divisions, as well as substantial supporting units.

While XVIII Airborne Corps moved swiftly into southern central Iraq, the heavy VII Corps went north into Iraq and then made a sharp right directly to Iraq's eastern border with Kuwait. It was here that Saddam had repositioned his Republican Guard divisions with their better equipment and training compared with the line Iraqi Army units. Although sharp fights did occur, nothing like the massive battles expected materialised. Without making light of the efforts of the ground forces, they rolled through the Iraqis like a tidal wave, over-running positions and taking entire units captive. Hundreds of thousands of Iraqi troops surrendered wholesale.

So numerous were the captives, that often times a patch of desert would be marked with a single line of wire. The Iraqis would be herded into the temporary detention and the advancing Allied units pressed forward, leaving only a couple of soldiers to guard the exhausted, but relieved to be out of the fight, Iraqi captives.

The expected frontal assault into Kuwait and into the fixed Iraqi positions was revealed as a diversion. With the bulk of his remaining forces pinned down there, Saddam was caught completely by surprise by the massive armoured steamroller driving east. He was caught in a vice. If he tried to turn and face the oncoming threat from the west, the northward pushing Marines and Arab forces would simply press that much faster into Kuwait and destroy his forces from behind. If he kept his forces fighting the Marines, the approaching juggernaut out of the west would do the same thing. Saddam therefore attempted to fight in both directions and lost in both directions.

The main reason for going into any detail regarding the ground war in a book on the airborne Wild Weasels, is to bring attention to the fact that the incredible speed of the Allied offensive had tactical repercussions on how the Weasels, in fact all Allied air operations, evolved and on weapons employment.

The advancing good guys carried their own built-in short-range air defence weapons like mobile SAMs and tracked AAA guns, and these weapons usually used radar to track a target. The Weasels therefore had to be extra-careful in weeding out friendly signals from any Iraqi ones.

Since there was such a mix of purchased and stolen systems on the Iraqi side (HAWK surface-to-air missiles, the German–French 'Super Fledermaus' AAA radar, etc.), the Weasels had to be kept informed of the advancing line of Allied gains to ensure they didn't shoot a friendly with a HARM by mistake.

So concerned was the Weasel leadership about such a 'blue on blue' incident, that within hours of the start of the ground war, the order to not shoot anything while the F-4G was pointed south was issued. Even then, due to the HARM's remarkable ability to manoeuvre to find a target, specific ranges and much higher quality of data had to be met for a HARM to come off an F-4G's rail.

SCHREINER, 24 FEBRUARY 1991 D + 192 W + 38

Being a leader of a country does not necessarily mean that person is smart, at least in the case of Saddam Hussein. He was dumb enough to challenge the world and even dumber still to not get out while he could, with his country and army intact. Now he has to pay for that stupidity. Sadly, many innocent civilians and fine soldiers on both sides will also have to pay.

Our grand operations to liberate Kuwait began at 0400 local as I was preparing for another sortie to Baghdad. Up until that time, I had not known when or even if the invasion would take place. I had always believed it would though.

Once again, the 'experts' have been wrong in their predictions. I don't know about the tides, but last night was a half moon, although it had set before H-Hour. The predicted seaborne invasion to take place just south of Kuwait City did not happen nor did the massive pre-invasion airstrikes. We even dropped the 101st Airborne Division deep into Iraq with their apparent objective an Iraqi airfield, As Salmon, presumably to be used later as a FARP – forward air refuelling point – for helicopters. I don't recall any of the 'experts' mention this type of operation as a possibility. It hasn't even been mentioned in the press yet as it's still classified.

As of the time of this writing, 2100 local, our forces are smashing their way through Kuwait with incredible speed. Iraqi forces are surrendering by the thousands and we are encountering only token resistance so far. We are twice as far as originally planned and still going.

Reports indicate that we may be at the outskirts of Kuwait City although I haven't seen our own intel since noon so I don't know. I'm told that no sooner does our intel shop plot the latest front lines than it is already out of date.

Obviously, we have a lot of work to do, but if things continue like this, the war will be over before anyone would have predicted. One can only hope.

EWO Joe Healy flew that night and recalled:

A short 2.7-hour mission to escort RAF Tornadoes and Buccaneers to Talil Airfield in south-east Iraq. Lots of restrictions on when we can fire HARMs went into effect today because the ground offensive has begun! Finally!

The target was completely obscured by black oil smoke and the Brits didn't drop. No signals up at all. We all think our days of shooting HARMs may be over and we're flying our last combat sorties.

With the fast moving ground offensive radically changing the nature of the war, the Weasels did have a change to their operations. With friendly ground forces containing their own air defence forces – mobile radars, mechanised AAA and point-defence SAMs – the risk of fratricide or 'blue on blue' clashes increased dramatically. Weasels could no longer fire missiles heading south or west without authorisation. Instead, some of their combat loads contained the shorter-ranged AGM-45 Shrike and the AGM-65 Maverick.

Proven Force veteran Sid Mayeux said of the edict to carry Shrikes:

'We all decided to get them out of the inventory once and for all. If we took off with one, we made very certain that we didn't return with it. It was not a good weapon at all.'

Ed Fisher noted at the time, 'The ground war is really moving along fast. Everyone is kicking butt. The only areas Weasels are cleared to shoot without specific clearance is H2/H3 and Baghdad.'

SCHREINER, 26 FEBRUARY 1991 D + 194 W + 40

It's not over till it's over. It's not over till the fat lady sings – and she's in a former Iraqi bunker warming up.

Incredible! Never in my wildest dreams did I ever think our forces would be as successful as they have been. The ground war is a mere two days old and we are kicking the shit out of the Iraqi Army. Even the vaunted Republican Guard appears to be no match for our troops.

American mechanised infantry along with the French Foreign Legion (ballsy bastards!) have pushed all the way to the Euphrates River, almost halfway between Baghdad and Basra. The Iraqi withdrawal/retreat is effectively cut-off. The only way out now is through our forces.

Kuwait City is almost completely surrounded and it should be in our hands shortly. The feared house to house fighting may not even be necessary. Those enemy forces able to get out are jamming up the northerly Kuwait–Basra road, crawling along at about 3 mph. Our ground attack units (A-10s, A-6s, Harriers) are having a field day picking them off, destroying huge numbers of vehicles. God, how I wish I was with my old A-10 unit!

Our mission today was flown to Al Taqaddum Airfield about forty miles west of Baghdad in support of British Tornadoes. Unfortunately, there was a solid overcast over the target, preventing them from delivering their ordinance. We ended up droning around for twenty minutes looking for targets of opportunity.

Our APR-47 system didn't seem to be working properly so we didn't get very many signals up and took no shots. Lead, on the other hand, got excellent range quality on an SA-3 and shot it.

Captain Joe Healy and his pilot Captain Jim Hartle also flew this day to the same target area. Says Healy of that mission:

> Got up there and the weather was lousy. Nothing came up. Jim and I made a pass going from west to east about eight nautical miles south of the target and turned around back to the west and drove past it again.
>
> The Tornadoes and Buccaneers couldn't see the target and aborted their attack. Still no signals and it looked like just another dry run of a sortie. We turned back to a heading of north-east for one last pass with the target airfield on the nose.
>
> I was casually leaning against one corner of the cockpit suggesting to Jim that we launch a pre-briefed shot and call 'Magnum Arnett'. (The CNN reporter was not one of our favourite people!)
>
> Suddenly up pops an SA-3 at about eight to nine miles. I designated it and got a RQ-2 [range quality -2, a 'fair' target position quality indication] in about five seconds or so. We turned north

Nothing sweeter than homecoming. Here a crowd of well-wishers greets a flight of returning F-4s on a fuel stop in Indiana. (Jim Schreiner)

Brian 'Basa' Baxley, an F-4G pilot during DESERT STORM. After the Weasel was retired, he transitioned to the F-15 'Eagle.' Here he is in the cockpit of that jet, but once again in the desert during the long years of quasi-peace between the first Gulf War and Operation IRAQI FREEDOM. (Brian Baxley)

to put the site at our three o'clock and dispensed some chaff since we were now in the heart of his envelope at about seven nautical miles. I told Jim to be ready to go defensive if he launches.

I continued to work the signal and we got about twelve to fifteen miles north-west of the site when we turned away towards west, put out some chaff, continued the turn and came back to a heading of south, putting him at about 9:30 or ten o'clock to us. I was so excited and tired that I forgot to hand it off [select a specific HARM hanging from the jet] and only hit the pickle button.

Nothing happened! I yelled at Jim, 'Master arm?!' thinking his annoying habit of acting as a QC [quality control check] of my shots was screwing up this shot.

Another quick check of my own situation revealed my mistake to me. I handed off, fired and just watched the missile dive into the clouds to our left front. The site was on and off – mostly on – a couple of times throughout the time of flight for the missile, then he went off the air about the end of the TOF and never came up again!

Just when I thought I'd taken my last shot a week ago, this beautiful opportunity came up!

The tape review showed a kill and it was scored as our last one of the war.

SCHREINER, 26 FEBRUARY 1991 D + 194 W + 40

The weather the past few days has been as shitty as I've seen since we've been here. Yesterday, we 'weaselled' in the weather in [a] 3–6 NM trail of our leader. We did take two shots against an SA-2 and an SA-3 though they were marginal.

Today, most of our time on the tanker was spent in and out of

Line-up of F-4Gs return to George AFB following the war. (Jim Schreiner)

Running to homecoming. (Schreiner)

the weather. That extra workload only exacerbated my already fatigued state. I'm glad I'm not flying tomorrow as I don't think I can stay alert. I will say that the tanker pilot did an admirable job keeping out of the worst of the weather, a performance far better than what I have noted in the past.

At the risk of being wrong once again, today's sortie might be my last combat mission for a while. I guess I won't make fifty missions after all.

SCHREINER, 28 FEBRUARY D + 196 W + 42

Fifty sorties! Hah! I got up this morning at my usual 2 a.m. for our usual 6 a.m. take-off. I didn't really think I was going to fly. Hell, what's left to bomb?

At 0500, President Bush came on CNN to announce at midnight eastern (three hours hence), our troops would cease offensive combat operations, i.e., a cease-fire.

We won! Hallelujah!

We have beaten, almost totally destroyed, the world's fourth largest army in only 100 hours of ground fighting. I can't begin to describe the sense of jubilation that I'm feeling right now.

Complete and undisputed victory. We have destroyed over 4,000 tanks, thousands more artillery pieces and armoured troop carriers. Rendered combat ineffective forty-two infantry, mechanised infantry, and armoured divisions including the 'vaunted' Republican Guards. Their casualties are estimated to be close to 100,000 killed, countless more wounded or taken prisoner.

We have achieved all of our goals quickly and effectively with fewer than 100 of our own killed and Iraq has agreed to all of the conditions for cease-fire.

I have survived combat! Thirty-three missions and 125 hours in forty-three days of the most intense aerial bombardment since World War II, maybe ever!

Is this how Americans felt on V-E or V-J day? What a sense of accomplishment. I have never felt so satisfied in my life. How

The families await the return of their warriors. (Jim Schreiner)

Jim and his sister at the welcome home ceremony at George AFB. (Jim Schreiner)

incredibly lucky we were. Our unit didn't lose a single aircraft to combat and all of our aircrew are alive.

I don't even know how many people I've killed; this was such an antiseptic war. I can fly above the battlefield and witness the destruction in a detached way. This was a most peculiar and unlikely war.

No doubt countless historians and armchair generals will study the 'Gulf War' for decades to come. All kinds of people will go over it with a fine toothcomb and pick it apart. Describe what went right and what went wrong.

But I was here! I know what this beast looks like from the inside. I have faced the most challenging forty-three days of my life and I succeeded in staring down my worst fears. I know what it's like to have AAA and SAMs fired at *me*! I know what it's like to have someone try to kill *me*! I know that I can survive!

Finally, I can get some rest. I am exhausted. I never got used to these early get-ups and [there] were times when I didn't think I could go on. Thank God for backseaters – having Dan fly, even for a few minutes, allowed me to recoup my strength.

Now I can sleep as long as I want, get up when I want, get drunk if I want. I just can't wait to get out of this shithole and get home. I don't know if I'll be able to hold back the tears when I see my family and friends. I never realised how much they cared. Or how much they mean to me. And the complete strangers who took the time to write and send care packages.

They say a war changes a person. I'll leave that judgement to someone else although I don't think I'll ever look at life the same way again.

On 22 March 1991, Jim Schreiner flew an F-4G Wild Weasel home to California.

Operational Wild Weasel Platforms

NORTH AMERICAN F-100F SUPER SABRE

The North American F-100F Super Sabre was first flown in 1956. A two-seat version of the F-100 single-seat fighter, it served at first as a trainer. Upon the initiation of the 'Wild Weasel 1' project, the F-100F was chosen as the first version of the Weasel.

It was modified to carry the AN/APR-25 radar homing and warning receiver, the AN/APR-26 missile guidance launch signal detector and, later, the IR-133 radar homing and warning receiver that detected the 'S' band radar of the SA-2.

SPECIFICATIONS

Wingspan:	38 ft 9 in
Length:	50 ft 0 in
Height:	16 ft 3 in
Empty weight :	21,712 lb
Max weight:	39,122 lb

Engine:	One Pratt & Whitney J-57-P-21/21A after-burning turbojet, producing 16,000 lb of thrust with afterburner
Max speed:	852 mph
Max range:	1,294 nautical miles (NM) without aerial refuelling
Combat radius:	358 NM without refuelling
Armament:	Two 20-mm M-39 cannon; 5000 lb of under-wing stores, including rocket pods, cluster bomb units, conventional bombs, Shrike anti-radiation missiles

A total of seven F-100F Wild Weasels were produced. Three were lost in combat operations. The last F-100 Weasel mission occurred in 1966.

Republic F-105F/G Thunderchief

The Republic F-105F/G Thunderchief was designed to replace the F-100s that proved to be too slow in the field when operating with bomb-dropping F-105s. The two-seat F and G model of the renowned 'Thud' served until 1984.

In addition to the F-100F's electronics, the Thud Weasel carried the QRC-317 Sense, Exploit and Evade SAMs device. This sensor detected when a SAM fire control radar switched to high PRF. In other words, it could tell when a SAM was about to come off the launcher. The AE-100 sensor detected radar signals ahead of the aircraft and put a green light on the pilot's gunsight in the general vicinity of the SAM site, thus aiding greatly in the pilot acquiring the SAM site more quickly.

The ATI ER-142 expanded frequency detection bands and used a second display scope in the EWO's cockpit to display S and C bands, the latter being used by AAA radar sites.

SPECIFICATIONS

Wingspan:	34 ft 9 in
Length:	69 ft 6 in
Height:	20 ft 2 in
Empty weight:	28,393 lb
Max weight:	54,000 lb
Engine:	One Pratt & Whitney J75-19W afterburning turbojet, producing 24,500 lb of thrust with afterburner
Max speed:	1,390 mph
Max range:	2,210 NM without aerial refuelling
Combat radius:	780 NM without refuelling
Armament:	One 20-mm M-61A1 cannon; 14,000 lb of bomb bay and underwing stores, including rocket pods, cluster bomb units, conventional bombs, Shrike anti-radiation missiles, AGM-78 anti-radiation missile, AIM-9 Sidewinder air-to-air missiles

A total of eighty-six F-105F Wild Weasels were produced. Sixty-one one of these were later converted into the F-105G. A total of forty-five F-105 Weasel jets were lost in combat operations. The last F-105 Weasel flight occurred in 1984.

McDONNELL F-4C PHANTOM II

The McDonnell F-4C Phantom II was an attempt to use the more modern F-4 fighter-bomber to replace the F-105. The F-4C Weasel initially used the same electronics as the F-105G, but later added upgraded RHAW gear, including the AN/ALR-46 and ALR-53. The IR-133 was replaced with the ER-142, which displayed threats as an alphanumeric character on a scope with range rings instead of simple strobe lines

Unusually, the F-4C was not wired to accommodate the AGM-78 missile with its thirty-five-mile range, which was replacing the short-ranged Shrike. Also, the F-4 was designed without an internal gun. Later, the F-4E model did have an internal M-61 cannon. The thirty-six F-4C Wild Weasel aircraft were converted back to stock F-4C configuration upon the entry of the F-4G into service.

SPECIFICATIONS

Wingspan:	38 ft 5 in
Length:	58 ft 3.75 in
Height:	16 ft 3 in
Empty weight:	28,496 lb
Max weight:	51,441 lb
Engines:	Two General Electric J79GE-15 turbojets, each producing 17,000 lb thrust with afterburner
Max speed:	1,433 mph
Max range:	1,926 NM without refuelling
Combat radius:	538 NM unrefuelled
Armament:	16,000 lb of external ordnance, including AGM-45, CBU, iron bombs, rocket pods, pod-mounted 20-mm cannon, four AIM-7 Sparrow radar-guided missiles, four AIM-9 Sidewinders

McDonnell Douglas F-4G Phantom II

The final variant of the US F-4 series, the G model took a clean slate approach to designing the ultimate Weasel aircraft. Although based on the cannon-armed F-4E, the space requirements for the AN/APR-38 HAWC's (Homing and Warning Computer) 64 K digital 'brain' meant that the cannon was deleted and the space filled with the black boxes used by the HAWC. A spider-like array of fifty-four antennas fed highly accurate data to the processor, giving the EWO very precise information about the type, bearing, and range of threats in the area. With the AN/APR-38, the F-4G also acquired the ability to use the new AGM-88 HARM (High speed Anti-Radiation Missile). A 'smart' missile, the HARM can be retargeted during flight to look for different threat emitters, unlike the Shrike, which was programmed on the ground to look for a specific system. The HARM could kill almost anything it could find and at much longer ranges than the Shrike.

Later, AN/APR-47 using the upgraded WASP (Weasel Attack Signal Processor) with 256 K of memory replaced the APR-38 system.

Specifications

Wingspan:	38 ft 11 in
Length:	62 ft 11 in
Height:	16 ft 5 in
Empty weight:	30,328 lb
Max weight:	62,000 lb
Engines:	Two General Electric J79-GE-17 turbojets
Max speed:	1,432 mph at altitude
Max range:	1,300 NM without aerial refuelling
Combat radius:	540 NM without aerial refuelling

Armament: AIM-7 Sparrow, AIM-9 Sidewinder, AGM-88A HARM, AGM-45 Shrike, AGM-65 Maverick, Mk 80 series conventional bombs, CBU

LOCKHEED-MARTIN F-16CJ 'FIGHTING FALCON' BLOCK 50/52

The newest models of the F-16 in USAF service, blocks 50 and 52 differ only in the engine. 'CJ' designates the jet as carrying the HTS HARM Targeting System. A single-seat, multi-role fighter, the F-16CJ is the primary SEAD asset for the USAF. Replacing the F-4G, the F-16CJ has a much more capable multi-mode radar, the ability to employ many more weapons, and shares commonality with the other USAF F-16 models, thus easing maintenance and logistics issues.

A single-seat jet, the HTS and SEAD mission makes for an extremely high pilot workload. The HTS does not offer 360-degree coverage as did the F-4G's AN/APR-47. However, since at the time of writing it is operational, its limitations will not be further discussed.

SPECIFICATIONS

Wingspan: 32 ft 8 in

Length: 49 ft 5 in

Height: 16 ft

Empty weight: 18,238 lb

Max weight: 42,300 lb

Engine, block 50: General Electric F110-GE-129 turbofan producing 28,984 lb of thrust with afterburner

Engine, block 52: Pratt & Whitney F100-PW-229 turbofan producing 28,500 lb of thrust with afterburner

Max speed:	1,321 mph at altitude
Max range:	864 NM without aerial refuelling
Combat radius:	340 NM without aerial refuelling
Armament:	1 x 20-mm gun, AIM-9 Sidewinder, AIM-120 AMRAAM, Mk 80 series of conventional bombs, AGM-88 HARM, AGM-65 Maverick, CBU, JDAM, GBU-10/12 guided munitions

HTS – AN/ASQ 213 HARM TARGETING SYSTEM – is an external pod dubbed 'Weasel in a can'. It detects radar signals, then feeds the data to the HARM, whereupon the pilot determines whether to shoot or not. The newest version of HTS incorporates GPS and other technology to use other weapons as well as HARMs to destroy radars.

Iraqi Integrated Air Defence Order of Battle

Surface-to-Air Missiles (SAMs) (NATO designations)

SA-2 'Guideline'

- The Soviet (now Russian) SA-2 was designed to defend both fixed emplacements and to move with mobile field forces. Although the arrangement of the missile launchers can vary according to the terrain, the classic 'Star of David' pattern is the standard emplacement first encountered in Vietnam. A battery consists of six launching positions, usually revetted, deployed around a guidance radar. The sites are permanent, however the launchers, radars, and control vans are usually mounted on wheeled vehicles and capable of movement within several hours.
- The missile is a two-stage unit with a large solid propellant booster characterised by a bright flash and orange smoke at launch. The core stage is liquid-fuelled and accelerates the weapon up to Mach 4.0. The maximum range of the missile is 35 kilometres.
- Associated radars with the SA-2 are the Spoon Rest warning and target acquisition unit with a maximum detection range of 275 kilometres and the Fan Song fire control set with a maximum range of around 65 kilometres.

Length: 10.6 m

Launch weight: 2,300 kg

Max altitude: 25,000 m

Warhead: 188 kg of high explosive

Iraq had an estimated 160 SA-2 sites at the start of *Desert Storm*.

SA-3 'Goa'

- Used for both fixed and mobile target protection, each component is fully mobile but normally operates from prepared sites.
- Two-stage solid fuel missile with booster and sustainer stages. Maximum range of the missile is 25 kilometres.
- Associated radars include the Flat Face surveillance and target acquisition unit, the Squat Eye surveillance and target acquisition unit, and the Low Blow fire control radar unit. Target acquisition ranges can be as much as 200 kilometres with an effective firing solution capable of being reached at 40–80 kilometres. The Low Blow also has a TV camera for visual guiding of the SA-3 missile in the presence of electronic countermeasures.

Length: 6.7 m

Launch weight: 400 kg

Max altitude: 25,000 m

Warhead: High explosive

Iraq had an estimated 140 SA-3s at the start of *Desert Storm*.

SA-6 'Gainful'

- A highly mobile SAM, the SA-6 first gained prominence during the 1973 Arab–Israeli War when it nearly brought the Israeli Air Force to its knees. Designed to be as mobile as the armoured and mechanised infantry forces for which it provides protection, the SA-6 battery consists of two or three tracked missile-launching TELs (transporter erector launchers) and a fire control vehicle.

- A two-stage solid fuel, low to medium altitude SAM, its maximum range is 24 kilometres and is effective from 100 metres up to about 11,000 metres.
- Associated radars include the Straight Flush fire control unit with a maximum detection range of 75 kilometres anda targeting solution range of 28 kilometres as well as an optical tracking system with a range of 25 kilometres.

Length: 5.7 m

Launch weight: 599 kg

Max altitude: 11,000 m

Warhead: 59 kg of high explosive

Iraq had an estimated 140–150 SA-6s at the start of *Desert Storm*.

SA-7 'Grail'
- A man portable, shoulder-fired, infrared SAM, the SA-7 was produced and fielded by the thousands. It provides a deadly, undetectable low-level SAM defence against both fixed and mobile targets. It is a 'fire and forget' weapon in that after the operator visually acquires the target and shoots the missile, the missile then uses its infrared seeker head to detect the exhaust of the attacking aircraft and homes in on that heat source.
- Its disadvantages are its small warhead and its limited range both horizontally and vertically. Its advantages are its portability and ease of use by anyone.

Length: 1.47 m

Launch weight: 9.97 kg

Max altitude: 4,500 m

Warhead: 1.15 kg of high explosive

Iraq had several thousand SA-7s at the start of *Desert Storm*.

SA-8 'Gecko'
- Highly mobile, short-range, point defence SAM system. It consists of several six-wheeled TELARS (transporter erector launcher and radar) carrying four ready-to-fire missiles along with a very quick reload capability and several resupply vehicles carrying up to eighteen additional rounds in each.
- Associated radars include the Land Roll system, capable of detection out to 35 kilometres and tracking at 30. The SA-8 also has an optical tracking system to defeat jamming and anti-radiation missile detection.

Length: 3.2 m

Launch weight: 130 kg

Max altitude: 12,000 m

Warhead: 19 kg of high explosive

Iraq had an estimated 170–190 SA-8s at the start of *Desert Storm*.

SA-14 'Gremlin'
- Improved SA-7 that features a much more sensitive infrared seeker head that can detect the difference between countermeasures like flares and the actual target aircraft

Length: 1.4 m

Launch weight: 10.3 kg

Max altitude: 6,000 m

Warhead: 1.0 kg of high explosive

Iraq had several thousand SA-14s at the start of *Desert Storm*.

Roland
- A Franco-German short-range SAM, the Roland is a two-stage, highly mobile, effective point defence system capable of operating in a heavy jamming environment.
- Associated radars include the Siemans/Thomson D-band Doppler search radar and the Thomson-CSF J-band target acquisition and tracking radar.
- Capable of firing two rounds at a time, it is a very fast system to reload and shoot again.

Length: 2.4 m

Launch weight: 67 kg

Max altitude: 5,500 m

Warhead: 6.5 kg pre-fragmented high explosive

Iraq had an estimated 90–100 Rolands at the start of *Desert Storm*.

I-HAWK
- A low to medium altitude, medium-range US-designed SAM system, the HAWK (Homing All the Way Killer) system first became operational in 1960. Improvements in the various radar systems led to the I-HAWK (Improved HAWK) by the 1980s. Exported to several friendly countries including Kuwait, Iraq captured several batteries during its invasion of Kuwait.
- The system consists of several components: the HAWK firing unit; a towed launcher with three missiles per launcher; a continuous wave acquisition radar; a high power illuminator radar for target tracking; and an IFF (Identification Friend or Foe) interrogator set.

Length 3.81 m

Launch weight: 635 kg

Max altitude: 90,000 m

Warhead: 136.2 kg of high explosive

Iraq claimed to have three captured but operational I-HAWK batteries at the start of *Desert Storm*

Anti-aircraft Artillery (AAA)

23 mm
The ZSU-23-4 'Shilka' is a Soviet-designed tracked, self-propelled anti-aircraft gun. Using its Gun Dish tracking radar to guide the fire of its four rapid-firing 23 mm cannon, the ZSU-23 can put out 800 to 1,000 rounds per minute each although a lower rate of fire is more typical.

Capable of moving with armoured and mechanised forces, the ZSU-23-4 is a fearsome weapon against low-flying aircraft. Its maximum effective altitude range is 3,000 metres. It is a very easily dispersed system and can appear anywhere on the battlefield, although it normally advances with the leading edge of its parent force.

37 mm
The M1939 37 mm towed automatic anti-aircraft gun is based on the highly successful Bofors 40 mm AA gun of World War II fame. It fires up to 160 rounds per minute using drop-in clips. It is sighted entirely by visual means and is not associated with any fire control radar. Its maximum effective height is 2,500 metres.

57 mm
The ZSU-57-2 anti-aircraft self-propelled gun mounted two 57 mm cannon used for visual tracking of low-flying aircraft. There is no fire control radar associated with this lightly armoured vehicle but due to is mobility, it could be encountered nearly anywhere. Its drawbacks included a slow rate of fire and the difficulty of tracking and hitting fast-moving jets at low altitude. Its maximum effective altitude is 4,000 metres.

85 mm
KS-12A towed 85 mm anti-aircraft artillery. The Iraqis used larger calibre AAA to fire barrages. They would attempt to put as much metal as possible in a contained area of airspace in the hope of hitting Coalition aircraft. They tied the weapons to various fire control control radars like the Fire Can. The maximum altitude of the 85 mm AAA was about 11,000 metres. It could fire up to ten rounds per minute.

100 mm
The KS-19 100 mm towed AAA had a maximum altitude into the 12,600 metres range and was a threat to most Coalition aircraft. Its slow rate of fire (ten rounds per minute) was a big factor in avoiding being hit by this weapon.

130 mm
The KS-30 towed 130 mm AAA piece was the 'big daddy' of Iraq's AAA weapons. It used the Fire Wheel radar to track targets and could reach altitudes of 13,720 metres.

Iraq had in excess of 6,000 pieces of AAA at the start of *Desert Storm*.

FIGHTERS

Mirage F1
A very capable air defence and air superiority fighter, the F1 manu-factured by Dassault-Breguet first flew in 1966. Besides serving as France's frontline fighter for nearly twenty years, the F1 was exported to numerous countries, including ninety-four to Iraq. The F1 also has a limited ground attack capability.

Length:	49 ft
Wingspan:	27 ft 7 in
Max weight:	30,340 lb
Engine:	One SNECMA Atar 9K50 turbojet with after-burner

Max speed:	Mach 2.2
Ceiling:	52,000 ft
Radar:	Cyrano IVM
Weapons:	Two 30-mm DEFA 553 cannon; two Matra Magic R550 heat-seeking infrared air-to-air missiles; various bombs and rockets for ground attack

MiG-19/J-6 – NATO code name 'Farmer'

The Soviet Union's first supersonic capable fighter, the MiG-19 entered production in 1955. Given the NATO code name 'Farmer', nearly 10,000 were produced including ones produced by the People's Republic of China (PRC). This variant is labelled the J-6. Iraq bought both versions and had an estimated thirty in service at the start of *Desert Storm.*

Length:	42 ft 11 in
Wingspan:	29 ft 6 in
Max weight:	19,888 lb
Engine:	Two Tumansky turbojets with afterburner
Max speed:	Mach 1.35
Ceiling:	53,700 ft
Radar:	IZM gunlaying radar
Weapons:	Two or three NR-30 mm cannon; various bombs and rockets for ground attack

MiG-21/J-7 'Fishbed'

Another 1950s Soviet design, the MiG-21 'Fishbed' and its many variants, including the PRC-produced J-7, offered superb performance in a relatively simple airframe. North Vietnam flew MiG-21s against US aircraft throughout that conflict. Many countries including China still fly upgraded versions to this day. Iraq was thought to have around 190 MiG-21/J-7s at the start of *Desert Storm*.

Length:	51 ft 9 in
Wingspan:	23 ft 6 in
Max weight:	18,080 lb
Engine:	One Tumansky R-11F-300 with afterburner
Max speed:	Mach 1.5
Ceiling:	50,000 ft
Radar:	Spin Scan/Jay Bird radar
Weapons:	One NR-30 mm cannon; two AA-2 'Atoll' or two AA-8 'Aphid' heat-seeking infrared missiles; various bombs and rockets for ground attack

MiG-23 'Flogger'

The 'Flogger' was the first Soviet fighter to offer such complexities as an advanced air-to-air radar, a variable sweep wing and high performance in large numbers. Designed as a successor to the MiG-21, the –23 became operational in 1971.

It is a highly capable point defence interceptor with a limited ground attack mission. A variant, the MiG-27, reversed this role and specialised in low-level ground attack but at the cost of an air-to-air radar. Widely exported, Iraq had an estimated ninety of these potent fighters at the start of *Desert Storm*.

Length:	55 ft
Wingspan:	46 ft 9 in (swept fully forward)
Max weight:	45,474 lb

Engine:	One Khachaturov R-35-300 turbojet with afterburner
Max speed:	Mach 2.35
Ceiling:	60,700 ft
Radar:	High Lark
Weapons:	One GSh-23L 23mm cannon; AA-8 'Aphid'; AA-7 'Apex'; a radar-guided air-to-air-missile

MiG-25 'Foxbat'

A world-class interceptor, the MiG-25 'Foxbat' entered service in 1970 and was the epitome of the Soviet 'bogeyman' fighter. Rumours of this fighter's capabilities directly influenced the design and development of its US adversary, the McDonnell-Douglas F-15 Eagle. A Mach 2+ fighter with an advanced 'look down, shoot down' digital radar, the MiG-25 was a closely guarded Soviet design until being exported to client states in the late 1970s. Iraq had thirty-two MiG-25s at the start of *Desert Storm* and, reportedly, a MiG-25 made the only air-to-air kill on the opening night of the war against a USN F/A-18.

Length:	64 ft 10 in
Wingspan:	45 ft 11.5 in
Max weight:	80,952 lb
Engine:	Two Tumansky R-15B-300 turbojets
Max speed:	Mach 2.8+
Ceiling:	67,915 ft
Radar:	RP-25 Smerch
Weapons:	Four AA-8 'Aphids' heat-seeking infrared

missiles; four AA-6 'Acrid' radar-guided
missiles

MiG-29 'Fulcrum'
The Soviet Union's 'fourth generation' fighter, the MiG-29 'Fulcrum'
was designed to go head to head with its Western adversaries like the
Lockheed F-16 and the Northrop F/A-18. In operation since 1983, Iraq
purchased some thirty of these advanced fighters prior to the start of
Desert Storm and reportedly assigned its best pilots to the aircraft.
However, US pilots downed five MiG-29s with no losses to themselves. It is a highly manoeuvrable, highly advanced aircraft and was
thought to pose the most serious threat to Coalition aircraft at the start
of the war.

Length:	57 ft
Wingspan:	37 ft 3 in
Max weight:	46,300 lb
Engine:	Two Klimov RD-33 turbofans with after-burner
Max speed:	Mach 2.4
Ceiling:	59,100 ft
Radar:	Phazotron N-019 pulse Doppler radar
Weapons:	One GSh-30-1 30 mm cannon; up to six air-to-air missiles – various combinations of AA-8 'Aphid' heat seekers and AA-10 'Alamo' radar-guided missiles

In addition to the primarily air-to-air fighters listed above, Iraq had
nearly two hundred ground attack aircraft that had a limited air-to-air
capability. These jets included the Su-7/20/22 line of jet fighter-
bombers and the Su-25 'tank killer' attack jet.

CENTAF Weasel HARM 'Shot Log'

CENTAF planners and intelligence officers kept a Weasel HARM 'shot log' to track which targets were hit successfully and which ones were unsuccessful and thus needed a re-attack mission planned, as well as identifying trends in both friendly and enemy tactics during the SEAD campaign. The shot log reproduced here is as the original, including inconsistencies in names and place names.

Log Legend, reading from left to right:

MSN:	ATO mission number	A:	AAA
CALLSIGN:	Self-explanatory	E:	'E' band unknown radar
CREW:	Last names of F-4G crew	W:	Early warning radar
TGTAREA:	Self-explanatory	GD:	Gun Dish radar
DATE:	US style (month/day/year)	FW:	Flap Wheel
TAIL NUMBER:	Last digits of the jet firing the HARM	HF:	Height finder radar
TYPESHOT:	HARM mode	RASIT:	Artillery tracking radar
	RK: Range known	SUCCESS:	Assessment of HARM shot taken
	RU: Range unknown	T:	True or successful HARM shot
	PET: Pre-emptive targeting	F:	False or unsuccessful HARM shot
TGT TYPE:	ID of radar HARM shot taken against	U:	Unknown results of HARM shot
D:	'D' band unknown radar	QUALITY:	Quality of APR-47 data at time of HARM shot, 1 being the best
X:	Allied associated radar (a friendly emitter)		
M:	HAWK radar	THEATRE:	Location of combat, BAG – Iraq, KTO – Kuwait

MSN	CALLSIGN	CREW	TGTAREA	DATE	TAIL-NUMBER	TYPE-SHOT	TGT-TYPE	SUCCESS	QUALITY	THEATER
2331W	LOWENBRA31	ALFIERI/VIGLUCCI	BAGHDAD	1/19/1991	0	RK	SA-2	F	1	BAG
2331W	LOWENBRA31	ALFIERI/VIGLUCCI	BAGHDAD	1/19/1991	0	RK	SA-2	F	1	BAG
0311W	MICH 13	ALFIERI/VIGLUCCI	AL TAQADDUM	2/7/1991	0	RK	SA-3	F	3	BAG
0751W	COORS 51	ALFIERI/VIGLUCCI	AL TAQADDUM	2/25/1991	0	RK	SA-3	U	3	BAG
0461W	LONESTAR63	ALFIERI/VIGLUCCI	AL TAQADDUM	2/14/1991	202	RK	SA-3	F	1	BAG
1125W	MILLER 27	ALFIERI/VIGLUCCI	SALMAN PAK	1/17/1991	241	RU	SA-8	F	2	BAG
1125W	MILLER 27	ALFIERI/VIGLUCCI	SALMAN PAK	1/17/1991	241	RU	SA-8	F	2	BAG
0245W	COORS 47	ALFIERI/VIGLUCCI	S. BAGHDAD	1/26/1991	250	RK	FW	F	1	BAG
0245W	COORS 47	ALFIERI/VIGLUCCI	S. BAGHDAD	1/26/1991	250	RK	FW	F	1	BAG
5401W	COORS 05	ALFIERI/VIGLUCCI	KTO	2/10/1991	256	RK	SA-3	U	3	KTO
1261W	OLY 64	ATENCIO/JONES	KTO	1/21/1991	0	RU	SA-2	F	2	KTO
0431W	COORS 34	ATENCIO/JONES	BAGHDAD	1/17/1991	0	RK	SA-8	T	1	BAG
0431W	COORS 34	ATENCIO/JONES	BAGHDAD	1/17/1991	0	RK	SA-8	T	1	BAG
1261W	OLY 64	ATENCIO/JONES	KTO	1/21/1991	0	RU	D	T	2	KTO
5441W	MILLER 44	ATENCIO/JONES	KTO	1/30/1991	0	RU	X	T	1	KTO
1361W	OLY 64	ATENCIO/JONES	KTO	1/20/1991	0	M		U	3	KTO
1361W	OLY 64	ATENCIO/JONES	KTO	1/20/1991	0	SA-2		U	3	KTO
2361W	BLATZ 64	ATENCIO/JONES	KTO	1/24/1991	250	RU	A	F	2	KTO
1761W	PABST 64	ATENCIO/JONES	AL JAHRA	1/23/1991	251	RU	E	U	1	BAG
5471W	MICHELOB72	ATENCIO/JONES	AL JARRAH	2/27/1991	300	PET	ROLAN	F	2	KTO
1165W	LONESTAR68	ATENCIO/JONES	BAGHDAD	1/18/1991	7201	RK	SA-2	T	2	BAG
1165W	LONESTAR68	ATENCIO/JONES	BAGHDAD	1/18/1991	7201	RU	SA-8	U	3	BAG
0561W	STROHS 64	ATENCIO/JONES	BAGHDAD	2/3/1991	7207	RU	SA-2	U	1	BAG
0561W	STROHS 64	ATENCIO/JONES	BAGHDAD	2/3/1991	7207	RK	SA-2	U	1	BAG

MAGNUM! THE WILD WEASELS IN DESERT STORM

MSN	CALLSIGN	CREW	TGTAREA	DATE	TAIL-NUMBER	TYPE-SHOT	TGT-TYPE	SUCCESS	QUALITY	THEATER
5461W	COORS 63	BALLANCO/CHELALES	BAGHDAD	2/22/1991	210	RK	SA-3	F	1	BAG
5461W	COORS 63	BALLANCO/CHELALES	BAGHDAD	2/22/1991	210	RK	SA-3	T	1	BAG
5451W	FALSTAFF54	BALLANCO/CHELALES	TAJI	2/19/1991	248	RK	SA-3	F	1	BAG
5451W	SCHLITZ 51	BALLANCO/CHELALES	KTO	2/1/1991	250	RU	D	F	1	KTO
2261W	MICH65	BALLANCO/CHELALES	BAGHDAD	2/6/1991	286	RK	SA-3	T	1	BAG
2261W	MICH 65	BALLANCO/CHELALES	BAGHDAD	2/6/1991	286	RK	SA-8	T	1	BAG
1361W	STROHS 61	BALLANCO/CHELALES	KTO	2/5/1991	558	RU	FC	T	1	KTO
5435W	BUD 35	BALLANCO/DORSEY	KTO	2/2/1991	241	RU	D	F	2	KTO
1451W	SCHLITZ251	BALLANCO/DORSEY	KTO	1/29/1991	278	RU	D	T	1	KTO
1271W	PEARL 73	BALLANCO/GARLAND	SAMARRA	1/20/1991	234	RK	SA-2	T	2	BAG
1271W	PEARL 73	BALLANCO/GARLAND	SAMARRA	1/20/1991	234	RK	SA-3	T	2	BAG
1651W	MICH 53	BALLANCO/GARLAND	KTO	1/21/1991	242	RK	SA-3	F	2	KTO
1651W	MICH 53	BALLANCO/GARLAND	KTO	1/21/1991	242	RK	SA-2	T	2	KTO
1231W	COORS 36	BALLANCO/WHITTLER	S KTO	1/17/1991	250	RK	SA-6	T	1	KTO
1231W	COORS 36	BALLANCO/WHITTLER	S KTO	1/17/1991	250	RK	SA-6	T	2	KTO
1231W	COORS 36	BALLANCO/WHITTLER	S KTO	1/17/1991	250	RK	SA-2	T	2	KTO
1231W	COORS 36	BALLANCO/WHITTLER	S KTO	1/17/1991	250	RU	SA-6	U	2	KTO
0161W	MICHELOB62	BALLANCO/WHITTLER	JALIBAH	1/24/1991	286	RU	F	F	1	KTO
0455W	FALSTAFF58	BELLINGER/THOMPSON	AL TAQADDUM	1/21/1991	243	RK	SA-3	T	1	BAG
2261W	PABST 64	BELLINGER/THOMPSON	H-2	1/22/1991	265	PET	SA-2	F	2	H2/3
2251W	PEARL 54	BELLINGER/THOMPSON	AL TAQADDUM	1/17/1991	273	RK	SA-2	F	3	BAG
2251W	PEARL 54	BELLINGER/THOMPSON	AL TAQADDUM	1/17/1991	273	RK	SA-2	T	3	BAG
5441W	STROHS 44	BELLINGER/THOMPSON	BAGHDAD	2/6/1991	288	RK	SA-2	F	1	BAG
5441W	STROHS 44	BELLINGER/THOMPSON	BAGHDAD	2/6/1991	288	RK	SA-2	U	1	BAG

0605W	FALSTAFF06	BELLINGER/THOMPSON	KTO	2/15/1991	7257	RK	SA-6	F	1	KTO
0605W	FALSTAFF06	BELLINGER/THOMPSON	KTO	2/15/1991	7257	RK	SA-6	F	1	KTO
1271W	PEARL 72	BENYSHEK/ALLEN	SAMARRA	1/20/1991	0	RK	SA-3	T	2	BAG
1651W	MICH 52	BENYSHEK/ALLEN	KTO	1/21/1991	0	RK	SA-2	U	2	KTO
1651W	MICH 52	BENYSHEK/ALLEN	KTO	1/21/1991	0	RK	SA-2	U	2	KTO
0211W	LONE 12	BENYSHEK/ALLEN	AL TAQADDUM	2/7/1991	232	RK	SA-2	T	1	BAG
0565W	BUD 70	BENYSHEK/ALLEN	AL TAQADDUM	2/4/1991	250	RU	SA-3	T	3	BAG
0565W	BUD 70	BENYSHEK/ALLEN	AL TAQADDUM	2/4/1991	250	PET	SA-3	U	3	BAG
1071W	LONESTAR72	BENYSHEK/ALLEN	KTO	1/19/1991	253	RU	SA-2	F	1	KTO
1071W	LONESTAR72	BENYSHEK/ALLEN		1/19/1991	253	RU	W	F	1	KTO
1071W	LONESTAR72	BENYSHEK/ALLEN	KTO	1/19/1991	253	RK	SA-2	F	1	KTO
2401W	PARK 02	BENYSHEK/ALLEN	KTO	1/28/1991	579	RU	FW	F	2	KTO
1241W	BLATZ 42	BENYSHEK/ALLEN	BASRAH	1/17/1991	587	RU	SA-2	F	2	BAG
1241W	BLATZ 42	BENYSHEK/ALLEN	BASRAH	1/17/1991	587	RU	SA-2	F	2	KTO
1341W	BLATZ 43	BRYAN/CHAMBERS	LATIFYA	1/18/1991	0	RK	SA-6	F	1	BAG
1765W	PABST 65	BRYAN/CHAMBERS	H-2/H-3	1/19/1991	0	PET	ROLAN	F	3	H2/3
2251W	PEARL 53	BRYAN/CHAMBERS	AL TAQADUM	1/17/1991	0	RK	SA-3	T	3	BAG
2251W	PEARL 53	BRYAN/CHAMBERS	AL TAQADDUM	1/17/1991	0	RK	SA-2	T	3	BAG
1341W	BLATZ 43	BRYAN/CHAMBERS	LATIFAYA	1/18/1991	0	RK	SA-8	U	3	BAG
1431W	PABST 33	BRYAN/CHAMBERS	LATIFAYA	1/26/1991	0	RU	SA-3	U	2	BAG
1431W	PABST 33	BRYAN/CHAMBERS	LATIFAYA	1/26/1991	0	RK	FW	U	2	BAG
0151W	COORS 53	BRYAN/CHAMBERS	BAGHDAD	2/3/1991	0	RK	SA-2	U	3	BAG
0171W	BUD 03	BRYAN/CHAMBERS	BAGHDAD	2/6/1991	0	RK	SA-8	U	3	BAG
2061W	BUD 63	BRYAN/CHAMBERS	BAGHDAD	2/13/1991	0	RU	ROLAN	U	3	BAG
1761W	SCHLITZ 63	BRYAN/CHAMBERS	BAGHDAD	1/24/1991	246	RK	SA-3	F	1	BAG
2161W	LONESTAR63	BRYAN/CHAMBERS	KTO	1/20/1991	304	PET		U	3	KTO

Magnum! The Wild Weasels in Desert Storm

MSN	CALLSIGN	CREW	TGTAREA	DATE	TAIL-NUMBER	TYPE-SHOT	TGT-TYPE	SUCCESS	QUALITY	THEATER
2161W	LONESTAR 3	BRYAN/CHAMBERS	KTO	1/20/1991	304	PET		U	3	KTO
0451W	OLY 53	BRYAN/CHAMBERS	BAGHDAD	1/21/1991	331	RK	FW	U	3	BAG
0451W	OLY 53	BRYAN/CHAMBERS	BAGHDAD	1/21/1991	331	RU	FF	U	3	BAG
1361W	MILLER 631	BRYAN/CHAMBERS	LATIFAYA	1/25/1991	572	RU	ROLAN	U	2	BAG
0263W	COORS 63	BRYAN/CHAMBERS	ALI AL SALEM	1/23/1991	7233	RU	ROLAN	F	1	KTO
0263W	COORS 63	BRYAN/CHAMBERS	ALI AL SALEM	1/23/1991	7233	RU	ROLAN	F	1	KTO
1611W	LOWENBRA11	BURKE/GALINDEZ	KTO	1/28/1991	241	RK	RASIT	U	3	KTO
1561W	STROHS 63	BURKE/GALINDEZ	KTO	2/2/1991	253	RK	RASIT	U	3	KTO
1551W	STROHS 63	BURKE/GALINDEZ	KTO	2/2/1991	253	RK	RASIT	U	3	KTO
0565W	BUD 67	BURKE/GALINDEZ	AL TAQADDUM	2/4/1991	256	RK	SA-3	U	3	BAG
0565W	BUD 67	BURKE/GALINDEZ	AL TAQADDUM	2/4/1991	256	RK	SA-3	U	3	BAG
0731W	OLY 31	BURKE/GALINDEZ	KTO	1/29/1991	267	RU	FF	U	3	KTO
1241W	BLATZ 43	BURKE/GALINDEZ	SHAIBAH	1/17/1991	286	RK	SA-2	F	1	KTO
1241W	BLATZ 43	BURKE/GALINDEZ	SHAIBAH	1/17/1991	286	RU	FF	F	1	KTO
1241W	BLATZ 43	BURKE/GALINDEZ	SHAIBAH	1/17/1991	286	RK	SA-2	T	1	KTO
1661W	HAMMS 63	BURKE/GALINDEZ	AL TAQADDUM	1/18/1991	293	RU	SA-3	T	2	BAG
5465W	BLATZ65	BURKE/GALINDEZ	KTO	2/14/1991	293	RK	GD	U	1	KTO
0411W	PEARL 13	BYRNE/MATTINGLY	AL TAQADDUM	2/7/1991	243	RK	SA-8	F	1	BAG
2361W	HAMMS 64	BYRNE/SMITH	KTO	1/20/1991	216	PET	SA-6	F	3	KTO
1561W	LOWENBRA64	CARMICHAEL/ONEAL	BAGHDAD	1/24/1991	267	RK	SA-2	F	2	BAG
1551W	COORS 54	CARMICHAEL/ONEAL	H-2/H-3	1/18/1991	267	RU	ROLAN	T	2	H2/3
1561W	LOWENBRA64	CARMICHAEL/ONEAL	BAGHDAD	1/24/1991	267	RK	SA-2	T	2	BAG
1551W	COORS 54	CARMICHAEL/ONEAL	H-2/H-3	1/18/1991	267	RK	SA-8	U	3	H2/3
0561W	PEARL 62	CARMICHAEL/ONEAL	ALI AL SALEM	1/17/1991	558	PET	SA-6	F	2	KTO

ID	Callsign	Crew	Location	Date	Num	Svc	Type	Res	N	Area
1271W	PEARL 74	CARRIER/GRAJSKI	SAMARRA	1/20/1991	0	RK	SA-3	T	1	BAG
1271W	PEARL 74	CARRIER/GRAJSKI	SAMARRA	1/20/1991	0	RK	SA-8	T	1	BAG
1241W	BLATZ 41	CARRIER/GRAJSKI	BASRAH	1/17/1991	253	RK	SA-2	U	1	KTO
1241W	BLATZ 41	CARRIER/GRAJSKI	BASRAH	1/17/1991	253	RK	SA-2	U	1	KTO
5401W	COORS 02	CARRIER/GRAJSKI	KTO	2/8/1991	587	RK	HF	F	1	KTO
2561W	CEDAR 64	CARRIER/GRAJSKI	ALI AL SALEM	1/25/1991	7262	RK	RASIT	U	2	KTO
0261W	COORS 61	CHAVEZ/MATTINGLY	KTO	2/4/1991	243	RU	C	F	3	KTO
5401W	COORS 01	CHAVEZ/MATTINGLY	KTO	2/10/1991	263	RK	X	F	2	KTO
1031W	OLY 31	CHAVEZ/MATTINGLY	AL AMARAH	2/14/1991	263	RK		U	3	KTO
5421W	OLY 21	CHAVEZ/MATTINGLY	KTO	1/31/1991	7231	RU	I	T	2	KTO
0361W	MICH 61	CONNOR/SCHWARTZ	BAGHDAD	1/23/1991	7201	RU	D	F	2	BAG
0361W	MICH 61	CONNOR/SCHWARTZ	BAGHDAD	1/23/1991	7201	RK	SA-3	T	2	BAG
0441W	LONESTAR	CONNOR/SCHWARZE	BAGHDAD	1/17/1991	0	RK	SA-2	F	1	BAG
0441W	LONESTAR	CONNOR/SCHWARZE	BAGHDAD	1/17/1991	0	RU	M	F	1	BAG
5421W	FALSTAFF21	CONNOR/SCHWARZE	ALI AL SALEM	1/29/1991	265	PET	TROPO	U	1	KTO
2461W	COORS61	CONNOR/SCHWARZE	BAGHDAD	2/13/1991	300	RU	SA-3	F	1	BAG
1161W	PEARL 61	CONNOR/SCHWARZE	BAGHDAD	1/18/1991	7201	RK	FW	F	1	BAG
0761W	PLOPLAR 61	CONNOR/SCHWARZE	BAGHDAD	1/25/1991	7201	RK	SA-2	F	1	BAG
2361W	LOWENBRA61	CONNOR/SCHWARZE	ALI AL SALEM	1/31/1991	7201	RU	D	F	1	KTO
5431W	STROHS 31	CONNOR/SCHWARZE	E IRAQ	1/24/1991	7201	RU	D	T	1	KTO
0761W	POPLAR 61	CONNOR/SCHWARZE	BAGHDAD	1/25/1991	7201	RU	D	T	1	BAG
1311W	COORS 11	CONNOR/SCHWARZE	BAGHDAD	2/1/1991	7201	RK	SA-2	T	1	BAG
0161W	PEARL 61	CONNOR/SCHWARZE	BAGHDAD	2/8/1991	7201	RK	SA-2	T	1	BAG
0161W	PEARL 61	CONNOR/SCHWARZE	BAGHDAD	2/8/1991	7201	RK	SA-8	T	1	BAG
1161W	PEARL 61	CONNOR/SCHWARZE	BAGHDAD	1/18/1991	7201	RK	SA-2	U	3	BAG
0531W	MILLER 31	CONNOR/SCHWARZE	BAGHDAD	1/26/1991	7201	RK	SA-2	U	3	BAG

MSN	CALLSIGN	CREW	TGTAREA	DATE	TAIL-NUMBER	TYPE-SHOT	TGT-TYPE	SUCCESS	QUALITY	THEATER
0531W	MILLER 31	CONNOR/SCHWARZE	BAGHDAD	1/26/1991	7201	RK	SA-2	U	3	BAG
5423W	LOWENBRA23	CONNOR/SCHWARZE	AL ASAD	2/25/1991	7201	RU	ROLAN	U	2	BAG
0651W	STROHS 54	COOPER/GREGORY	KTO	1/17/1991	0	RK	SA-3	T	2	KTO
2261W	MICH 62	COOPER/GREGORY	BAGHDAD	2/6/1991	210	RU	SA-8	F	1	BAG
2261W	MICH 62	COOPER/GREGORY	BAGHDAD	2/6/1991	210	RU	SA-3	F	1	BAG
5461W	OLY 61	COOPER/GREGORY	AL QAIM	2/4/1991	234	RK	FW	T	3	H2/3
2761W	FALSTAFF61	COOPER/GREGORY	KTO	2/3/1991	241	RU	SA-3	U	3	KTO
2761W	FALSTAFF61	COOPER/GREGORY	KTO	2/3/1991	241	RU	FF	U	3	KTO
1651W	OLY 54	COOPER/GREGORY	RPG	1/18/1991	245	RK	SA-3	U	3	KTO
1431W	LOWENBRA34	COOPER/GREGORY	TAJI	2/19/1991	248	RK	SA-2	F	1	BAG
2561W	LONESTAR64	COOPER/GREGORY	KTO	1/24/1991	253	RK	RASIT	F	1	KTO
5461W	COORS 64	COOPER/GREGORY	TAJI	2/22/1991	253	RU	SA-3	F	1	BAG
2465W	LONESTAR68	COOPER/GREGORY	BAGHDAD	2/13/1991	278	RK	SA-3	F	1	BAG
2465W	LONESTAR68	COOPER/GREGORY	BAGHDAD	2/13/1991	278	RK	SA-3	F	1	BAG
5445W	COORS 46	COOPER/GREGORY	KTO	2/12/1991	293	RK	RASIT	F	1	KTO
5445W	COORS 46	COOPER/GREGORY	KTO	2/12/1991	293	RK	RASIT	T	1	KTO
2111W	COORS 14	COOPER/GREGORY	TAJI	2/27/1991	293	RK	SA-3	U	3	BAG
5443W	MICHELOB43	COOPER/GREGORY	BAGHDAD	1/27/1991	556	RK	FW	F	1	BAG
5443W	MICHELOB43	COOPER/GREGORY	BAGHDAD	1/27/1991	556	RK	SA-3	T	1	BAG
1161W	MICHELOB64	COOPER/GREGORY	KTO	1/19/1991	579	RK	I	F	2	KTO
0561W	STROHS 54	COOPER/GREGORY	KTO	1/19/1991	579	RU	D	F	2	KTO
0561W	STROHS 54	COOPER/GREGORY	KTO	1/19/1991	579	RU	D	F	2	KTO
1161W	MICHELOB64	COOPER/GREGORY	KTO	1/19/1991	579	RK	SA-6	T	2	KTO
5461W	COORS 64	COOPER/GREGORY	TAJI	2/22/1991	753	RK	SA-3	F	1	BAG

ID	Name	Analyst	Target	Date	No.	Code	Type	Cat	No.	Region
1363W	SCHLITZ 64	CORLEY/DEBREE	KTO	2/6/1991	0	PET	SA-3	U	3	KTO
0311W	MILLER 13	CORLEY/DEBREE	JALIBAH	1/18/1991	303	RU	SA-2	U	2	KTO
5415W	FALSTAF 18	CORLEY/DEBREE	KTO	1/20/1991	0	RU	D	F	2	KTO
2661W	HAMMS 64	CORLEY/DEBREE	AL ASAD	1/22/1991	0	PET	SA-2	F	2	BAG
2661W	HAMMS 64	CORLEY/DEBREE	AL ASAD	1/22/1991	0	PET	SA-2	F	2	BAG
5415W	FALSTAF 18	CORLEY/DEBREE	KTO	1/20/1991	0	RK	SA-3	T	2	KTO
2761W	STROHS 64	CORLEY/DEBREE	BASRAH	2/4/1991	0	RK	X	U	3	KTO
5401W	PEARL 05	CORLEY/DEBREE	KTO	2/11/1991	0	RU	D	U	2	KTO
0311W	MILLER 14	CORLEY/DEBREE	JALIBAH	1/18/1991	303	PET	ROLAN	F	2	KTO
0311W	MILLER 14	CORLEY/DEBREE	JALIBAH	1/18/1991	303	RK	SA-2	U	2	KTO
1371W	LOWNBRAU72	DAHL/SHORB	KTO	1/29/1991	202	RK	A	U	2	KTO
0213W	STROHS 13	DEAS/RATTRAY	KTO	2/5/1991	0	PET	SA-3	F	3	KTO
1261W	MILLER 63	DEAS/RATTRAY	H-2	1/22/1991	0	PET	SA-6	U	3	H2/3
1261W	MILLER 63	DEAS/RATTRAY	H-2	1/22/1991	0	PET	SA-6	U	3	H2/3
0461W	PEARL 63	DEAS/RATTRAY	KTO	1/23/1991	245	RK	FW	T	2	KTO
5421W	PEARL 21	DEAS/RATTRAY	KTO	1/24/1991	253	RK	RASIT	T	1	KTO
5401W	PEARL 01	DEAS/RATTRAY	KTO	2/13/1991	256	RK	SA-2	F	2	KTO
5401W	PEARL 01	DEAS/RATTRAY	KTO	2/13/1991	256	RK	SA-2	F	2	KTO
0611W	MICHELOB13	DEAS/RATTRAY	BAGHDAD	2/27/1991	268	PET	SA-3	F	3	BAG
5411W	OLY 11	DEAS/RATTRAY	KTO	2/15/1991	286	RK	SA-6	T	2	KTO
1261W	OLY 63	DEAS/RATTRAY	RPG	1/19/1991	286	RU	D	U	3	KTO
2361W	HAMMS 63	DEAS/RATTRAY	AL JAHRA	1/17/1991	293	RU	FF	F	2	KTO
2361W	HAMMS 63	DEAS/RATTRAY	AL JAHRA	1/17/1991	293	RU	FF	F	2	KTO
5407W	OLY 07	DEAS/RATTRAY	KTO	2/1/1991	293	RU	D	F	3	KTO
1121W	BUD 23	DEAS/RATTRAY	SALMAN PAK	1/17/1991	293	RK	SA-8	T	1	BAG
1121W	BUD 23	DEAS/RATTRAY	SALMAN PAK	1/17/1991	293	RK	SA-8	T	1	BAG

MAGNUM! THE WILD WEASELS IN DESERT STORM

MSN	CALLSIGN	CREW	TGTAREA	DATE	TAIL-NUMBER	TYPE-SHOT	TGT-TYPE	SUCCESS	QUALITY	THEATER
5401W	MICHELOB3	DEAS/RATTRAY	KTO	1/31/1991	556	RK	X	F	2	KTO
5401W	MICHELOB3	DEAS/RATTRAY	KTO	1/31/1991	556	RK	W	T	2	KTO
0461W	PEARL 64	DREW/SCOTTO	KTO	1/23/1991	0	RU	ROLAN	U	3	KTO
5411W	OLY 12	DREW/SCOTTO	KTO	2/15/1991	202	RK	SA-6	T	3	BAG
5407W	OLY 08	DREW/SCOTTO	KTO	2/1/1991	256	RU	D	F	2	KTO
5401W	PEARL 02	DREW/SCOTTO	KTO	2/13/1991	256	RU	SA-6	F	2	KTO
5401W	PEARL 02	DREW/SCOTTO	KTO	2/13/1991	256	RK	SA-6	F	2	KTO
5421W	PEARL 22	DREW/SCOTTO	KTO	1/24/1991	286	RK	SA-2	T	2	KTO
5421W	PEARL 22	DREW/SCOTTO	KTO	1/24/1991	286	RK	SA-3	T	2	KTO
0611W	MICHELOB14	DREW/SCOTTO	SHAIK AMAZAR	2/27/1991	293	RK	SA-2	U	3	BAG
0611W	MICHELOB14	DREW/SCOTTO	SHAIK AMAZAR	2/27/1991	293	RU	SA-8	U	3	BAG
0621W	HAMMS 23	DUPUIS/DOWDEN	BAGHDAD	2/11/1991	0	RK	SA-3	F	1	BAG
0621W	HAMMS 23	DUPUIS/DOWDEN	BAGHDAD	2/11/1991	0	RK	SA-3	T	1	BAG
1675W	OLY 78	DUPUIS/DOWDEN	AL TAQADDUM	2/4/1991	248	RK	FW	F	1	BAG
1675W	OLY 78	DUPUIS/DOWDEN	AL TAQADDUM	2/4/1991	248	RK	SA-2	T	1	BAG
0151W	SCHLITZ 53	DUPUIS/DOWDEN	TAJI	2/10/1991	250	PET	SA-3	F	2	BAG
0531W	BUD 31	DURHAM/ELLICO	KTO	2/8/1991	0	RU	ROLAN	U	2	KTO
5431W	LOWENBRA33	DURHAM/EUKER	TAJI	2/27/1991	0	RK	SA-8	F	1	BAG
5421W	OLY 25	DURHAM/EUKER	AL TAQADDUM	2/19/1991	216	RU	SUPER	F	2	BAG
5401W	MICHELOB02	DURHAM/EUKER	KTO	2/2/1991	263	RU	FW	F	2	KTO
0335W	OLY 36	DURHAM/EUKER	KTO	2/11/1991	263	RK	X	F	1	KTO
0335W	OLY 36	DURHAM/EUKER	KTO	2/11/1991	263	RK	W	F	1	KTO
0261W	COORS 62	DURHAM/EUKER	KTO	2/4/1991	263	RK	W	T	1	KTO
C261W	COORS 62	DURHAM/EUKER	KTO	2/4/1991	263	RK	X	T	1	KTO

0421W	PABST 21	DURTSCHI/CRUMLEY	KTO	1/17/1991	0	RK	RASIT	F	2	KTO
0421W	PABST 21	DURTSCHI/CRUMLEY	KTO	1/17/1991	0	RK	RASIT	F	2	KTO
2331W	LOWENBRA31	DURTSCHI/CRUMLEY	BAGHDAD	1/19/1991	0	RK	SA-2	T	2	BAG
2331W	LOWENBRA31	DURTSCHI/CRUMLEY	BAGHDAD	1/19/1991	0	RK	SA-2	T	2	BAG
2261W	COORS 61	DURTSCHI/CRUMLEY	KTO	1/18/1991	232	RU	D	F	1	KTO
2261W	COORS 61	DURTSCHI/CRUMLEY	KTO	1/18/1991	232	RU	D	F	2	KTO
2261W	COORS 61	DURTSCHI/CRUMLEY	KTO	1/18/1991	232	RU	D	F	2	KTO
2261W	COORS 61	DURTSCHI/CRUMLEY	KTO	1/18/1991	232	RU	D	F	2	KTO
5411W	SCHLITZ 11	DURTSCHI/CRUMLEY	KTO	1/20/1991	232	RK	SA-3	F	2	KTO
5411W	SCHLITZ 11	DURTSCHI/CRUMLEY	KTO	1/20/1991	232	RK	SA-3	F	2	KTO
5411W	SCHLITZ 11	DURTSCHI/CRUMLEY	KTO	1/20/1991	232	RK	SA-3	T	2	KTO
1125W	MILLER 25	DURTSCHI/CRUMLEY	SALMAN PAK	1/17/1991	270	RU	SA-8	F	1	BAG
0311W	MICH 11	DURTSCHI/CRUMLEY	AL TAQADDUM	2/7/1991	278	RU	SA-8	F	1	BAG
0311W	MICH 11	DURTSCHI/CRUMLEY	AL TAQADDUM	2/7/1991	278	RK	SA-3	T	1	BAG
0311W	LONESTAR11	DURTSCHI/CRUMLEY	KTO	2/10/1991	556	RK	SUPER	F	2	KTO
0363W	HAMMS 64	ELAM/PFLIEGER	BAGHDAD	2/3/1991	258	RK	SA-3	U	1	BAG
1431W	COORS 33	ELAM/PFLIEGER	BAGHDAD	2/5/1991	7286	RK	SA-2	F	3	BAG
1431W	COORS 33	ELAM/PFLIEGER	BAGHDAD	2/5/1991	7286	RK	SA-8	F	3	BAG
2261W	MICH 66	ELAM/SHERMAN	BAGHDAD	2/6/1991	556	RK	SA-8	F	1	BAG
2261W	MICH 66	ELAM/SHERMAN	BAGHDAD	2/6/1991	556	RK	SA-3	F	1	BAG
5471W	HAMMS 75	ELAM/SHERMAN	AL TAQADDUM	2/19/1991	579	RK	FW	T	3	BAG
0431W	STROHS 32	ELWELL/MCCARTHY	ALI AL SALEM	1/18/1991	0	RK	SA-2	F	1	KTO
2531W	LONESTAR32	ELWELL/MCCARTHY	TALLIL	1/18/1991	234	RU	FW	U	3	KTO
1431W	COORS 32	ELWELL/MCCARTHY	BAGHDAD	1/27/1991	250	RK	SA-3	U	3	BAG
1431W	COORS 32	ELWELL/MCCARTHY	BAGHDAD	1/27/1991	250	RK	SA-3	U	3	BAG
0661W	HAMMS 62	ELWELL/MCCARTHY	BAGHDAD	1/21/1991	253	RK	SA-6	U	3	BAG

MAGNUM! THE WILD WEASELS IN DESERT STORM

MSN	CALLSIGN	CREW	TGTAREA	DATE	TAIL-NUMBER	TYPE-SHOT	TGT-TYPE	SUCCESS	QUALITY	THEATER
0661W	HAMMS 62	ELWELL/MCCARTHY	BAGHDAD	1/21/1991	253	RK	SA-6	U	3	BAG
1521W	BLATZ 22	ELWELL/MCCARTHY	AL TAQADDUM	2/26/1991	587	RK	SA-3	F	2	BAG
2661W	BLATZ 62	ELWELL/MCCARTHY	BAGHDAD	1/20/1991	7286	RU	SA-3	F	1	BAG
1675W	OLY 77	FARRELL/FISHER	AL TAQADDUM	2/4/1991	202	PET	SA-2	F	2	BAG
1675W	OLY 77	FARRELL/FISHER	AL TAQADDUM	2/4/1991	202	RU	SA-3	T	2	BAG
0261W	COORS 68	FARRELL/FISHER	BAGHDAD	2/15/1991	248	RU	SA-2	T	2	BAG
0165W	OLY 08	FARRELL/FISHER	BAGHDAD	2/8/1991	267	RK	SA-2	F	1	BAG
0165W	OLY 08	FARRELL/FISHER	BAGHDAD	2/8/1991	267	RK	SA-2	F	1	BAG
2261W	MICHELOB64	FARRELL/FISHER	BAGHDAD	2/6/1991	587	RK	SA-2	F	1	BAG
0613W	PABST 13	FIEBIG/MOORE	AL KHIR	2/5/1991	0	RK	SA-3	T	2	BAG
2661W	HAMMS 61	FIEBIG/MOORE	AL ASAD	1/22/1991	0	PET	SA-3	U	2	BAG
2661W	HAMMS 61	FIEBIG/MOORE	AL ASAD	1/22/1991	0	PET	SA-3	U	2	BAG
2561W	HAMMS 61	FIEBIG/MOORE	KTO	1/23/1991	0	PET	ROLAN	U	3	KTO
2561W	HAMMS 61	FIEBIG/MOORE	KTO	1/23/1991	0	RK	ROLAN	U	3	KTO
1363W	SCHLITZ263	FIEBIG/MOORE	KTO	2/6/1991	246	RU	SA-6	F	1	KTO
2365W	STROHS 65	FIEBIG/MOORE	AL TAQADDUM	2/20/1991	281	RK	SA-3	T	1	BAG
1671W	SCHLITZ 71	FIEBIG/MOORE	BAGHDAD	2/12/1991	300	RU	SA-3	F	1	BAG
1671W	SCHLITZ 71	FIEBIG/MOORE	BAGHDAD	2/12/1991	300	RK	SA-3	F	1	BAG
2755W	HAMMS 55	FIEBIG/MOORE	BAGHDAD	2/14/1991	300	RK	SA-3	F	1	BAG
2755W	HAMMS 55	FIEBIG/MOORE	BAGHDAD	2/14/1991	300	RU	SA-3	F	1	BAG
5441W	MILLER 41	FIEBIG/MOORE	ALI AL SALEM	2/4/1991	572	RU	ROLAN	F	2	KTO
0311W	MILLER 11	FIEBIG/MOORE	JALIBAH	1/18/1991	7260	PET	ROLAN	F	1	KTO
5415W	FALSTAFF11	FIEBIG/MOORE	JALIBAH	1/20/1991	7260	RU	SA-3	F	2	KTO
5415W	FALSTAFF11	FIEBIG/MOORE	JALIBAH	1/20/1991	7260	PET	SA-2	F	2	KTO

0761W	MICHELOB65	FIEBIG/MOORE	BAGHDAD	1/28/1991	7260	RK	SA-8	F	2	BAG
0311W	MILLER 11	FIEBIG/MOORE	JALIBAH	1/18/1991	7260	RU	D	T	2	KTO
0761W	MICHELOB65	FIEBIG/MOORE	BAGHDAD	1/28/1991	7260	RU	SA-8	T	2	BAG
5401W	PEARL 01	FIEBIG/MOORE	AL QAIM	2/1/1991	7550	RK	SA-3	T	1	H2/3
5401W	PEARL 01	FIEBIG/MOORE	AL QAIM	2/1/1991	7550	RK	FW	T	1	H2/3
5425V	MICHELOB27	FOLWER/RICH	KTO	1/26/1991	251	RU	M ACQ	F	1	KTO
5431W	PABST 31	FOWLER/RICH	KTO	1/27/1991	0		FW	U	3	KTO
1331W	BUD 33	FOWLER/RICH	BAGHDAD	1/18/1991	7207	RK	SA-8	F	2	BAG
0163W	PEARL63	FOWLER/RICH	NASSIRYA	2/6/1991	7207	PET	FW	F	3	H2/3
0451W	MICHELOB53	FOWLER/RICH	BAGHDAD	1/17/1991	7207	RK	SA-6	T	2	BAG
1331W	BUD 33	FOWLER/RICH	BAGHDAD	1/18/1991	7207	RK	SA-3	T	2	BAG
5431W	FALSTAFF33	FOWLER/RICH	WADI AL BATIN	2/4/1991	7207	RK	SUPER	U	3	KTO
1061W	PEARL 63	FOWLER/RICH	KTO	1/22/1991	7550	RK	SA-2	T	2	KTO
1061W	PEARL 63	FOWLER/RICH	KTO	1/22/1991	7550	RU	M ACQ	T	2	KTO
5455W	OLY 53	FRALEY/BLACKBURN	KTO	1/26/1991	0	RU	D	F	2	KTO
5455W	OLY 53	FRALEY/BLACKBURN	KTO	1/26/1991	0	RK	SA-2	T	2	KTO
2751W	STROHS 54	FRALEY/BLACKBURN	KTO	1/18/1991	0	RU	D	U	1	KTO
1361W	STROHS 64	FRALEY/BLACKBURN	KTO	1/22/1991	243	RK	SA-3	T	1	KTO
0661W	FALSTAF 64	FRALEY/BLACKBURN	AL JAHRA	1/23/1991	246	RU	ROLAN	F	3	BAG
0565W	MILLER 68	FRALEY/BLACKBURN	BAGHDAD	2/5/1991	246	RK	SA-8	F	1	BAG
0565W	MILLER 68	FRALEY/BLACKBURN	BAGHDAD	2/5/1991	246	RK	SA-2	T	1	BAG
0661W	FALSTAF 64	FRALEY/BLACKBURN	AL JAHRA	1/23/1991	246	RU	ROLAN	U	3	BAG
0261W	COORS 64	FRALEY/BLACKBURN	BAGHDAD	2/14/1991	263	RU	SA-2	U	2	BAG
5451W	BLATZ 56	FRALEY/BLACKBURN	KTO	2/22/1991	7233	RU	D	F	1	KTO
2335W	SCHLITZ 33	FRALEY/BLACKBURN	BAGHDAD	1/19/1991	7550	RK	SA-8	F	2	BAG
2335W	SCHLITZ 33	FRALEY/BLACKBURN	BAGHDAD	1/19/1991	7550	RK	SA-2	T	2	BAG

MSN	CALLSIGN	CREW	TGTAREA	DATE	TAIL-NUMBER	TYPE-SHOT	TGT-TYPE	SUCCESS	QUALITY	THEATER
5451W	BUD 52	FRALEY/CARTER	KTO	2/1/1991	7260	RU	FW	F	2	KTO
0431W	STROHS 31	GARDNER/HOLLAND	ALI AL SALEM	1/18/1991	212	RK	SA-2	U	3	KTO
1431W	COORS 31	GARDNER/HOLLAND	BAGHDAD	2/5/1991	234	RK	SA-3	T	2	BAG
1431W	COORS 31	GARDNER/HOLLAND	BAGHDAD	1/27/1991	245	RK	SA-3	F	1	BAG
1521W	BLATZ 21	GARDNER/HOLLAND	AL TAQADDUM	2/26/1991	267	RK	SA-3	T	2	BAG
2531W	LONESTAR31	GARDNER/HOLLAND	ALI AL SALEM	1/18/1991	278	RK	SUPER	U	3	KTO
2661W	BLATZ 61	GARDNER/HOLLAND	BAGHDAD	1/20/1991	278	RK	SA-3	U	3	BAG
2661W	BLATZ 61	GARDNER/HOLLAND	BAGHDAD	1/20/1991	278	RK	SA-2	U	3	BAG
0661W	HAMMS 61	GARDNER/HOLLAND	BAGHDAD	1/21/1991	587	RK	SA-6	T	2	BAG
0661W	HAMMS 61	GARDNER/HOLLAND	BAGHDAD	1/21/1991	587	RK	SA-8	T	2	BAG
1621W	MICH 13	GARNEAU/HARBOTT	TALLIL	1/18/1991	0	PET	ROLAN	U	3	KTO
0455W	FALSTAFF57	GARNEAU/HARBOTT	AL TAQADDUM	1/21/1991	0	RK	FW	U	3	BAG
0605W	FALSTAFF05	GARNEAU/HARBOTT	KTO	2/15/1991	0	RK	SA-3	U	3	KTO
2221W	SCHLITZ 23	GARNEAU/HARBOTT	LATIFAYA	2/19/1991	216	RK	SDNET	F	1	BAG
0731W	MILLER 33	GARNEAU/HARBOTT	AL TAQADDUM	2/27/1991	251	PET	SA-3	F	3	BAG
0751W	BUD 51	GARNEAU/HARBOTT	JALIBAH	2/24/1991	281	RK	SA-3	U	2	KTO
0461W	SCHLITZ 63	GARNEAU/HARBOTT	LATIFAYA	2/11/1991	572	RK	SA-3	F	1	BAG
0461W	SCHLITZ 63	GARNEAU/HARBOTT	LATIFAYA	2/11/1991	572	RK	SA-3	T	1	BAG
5405W	MICHELOB7	GARNEAU/HARBOTT	KTO	2/5/1991	572	RU	MACQ	U	2	KTO
1341W	BUD 43	GARNEAU/HARBOTT	AL TAQADDUM	1/26/1991	7233	RK	SA-3	T	2	BAG
0265W	BUD 67	GEBHARD/SHORB	KTO	1/19/1991	0	RU	D	F	2	KTO
0561W	PEARL 63	GEBHARD/SHORB	ALI ASALEM	1/17/1991	212	RU	SA-6	F	1	KTO
0561W	PEARL 63	GEBHARD/SHORB	ALI ASALEM	1/17/1991	212	RU	SA-6	F	1	KTO
0561W	PEARL 63	GEBHARD/SHORB	ALI ASALEM	1/17/1991	212	RU	SA-2	F	2	KTO

0561W	PEARL 63	GEBHARD/SHORB	ALI ASALEM	1/17/1991	212	RU	SA-8	T	1	KTO
5431W	PABST 31	GEBHARD/SHORB	KTO	2/13/1991	268	RK	SA-6	F	1	KTO
1561W	LOWENBRA63	GEBHART/SHORB	KARBALA	1/24/1991	232	RK	SA-2	U	3	BAG
1561W	LOWENBRA63	GEBHART/SHORB	KARBALA	1/24/1991	232	RK	SA-2	U	3	BAG
0565W	BUD 69	GEDDES/LIN	AL TAQADDUM	2/4/1991	556	RK	SA-3	F	1	BAG
0565W	BUD 69	GEDDES/LIN	AL TAQADDUM	2/4/1991	556	RK	SA-3	F	1	BAG
5411W	MILLER 13	GEDDES/ONEAL	KTO	2/10/1991	579	RU	D	F	2	KTO
1261W	MILLER 64	GEDDES/SCOTTO	H-2	1/22/1991	293	PET	SA-2	F	2	H2/3
1261W	MILLER 64	GEDDES/SCOTTO	H-2	1/22/1991	293	RU	ROLAN	T	2	H2/3
2761W	FALSTAFF64	GEDDES/SEABAUGH	BASRAH	1/24/1991	556	RU	D	U	3	KTO
0561W	PEARL 64	GELWIX/UKEN	ALI ASALEM	1/17/1991	0	RK	SA-6	T	2	KTO
0561W	PEARL 64	GELWIX/UKEN	ALI ASALEM	1/17/1991	0	RK	SA-6	T	2	KTO
0561W	PEARL 61	GELWIX/UKEN	ALI ASALEM	1/17/1991	0	RU	SA-6	T	2	KTO
1551W	COORS 51	GELWIX/UKEN	H-2/H-3	1/18/1991	248	RU	ROLAN	T	2	H2/3
	MICH 61	GELWIX/UKEN	KTO	1/20/1991	270	RK	SA-6	T	2	KTO
5413w	PEARL 13	GELWIX/UKEN	KTO	2/3/1991	556	RK	FW	T	1	KTO
2465W	PABST 65	GELWIX/UKEN	KTO	1/28/1991	587	RU	ROLAN	F	1	KTO
1165W	LONESTAR66	GOUNAUD/CRABBE	BAGHDAD	1/18/1991	0	RK	SA-3	F	2	BAG
1165W	LONESTAR66	GOUNAUD/CRABBE	BAGHDAD	1/18/1991	0	RU	SA-8	F	1	BAG
0321W	LONESTAR22	GOUNAUD/CRABBE	SHIAK AMAZAR	2/26/1991	0	PET	SA-3	F	3	BAG
1261W	OLY 62	GOUNAUD/CRABBE	KTO	1/21/1991	0	RU	M	U	3	KTO
5421W	OLY 22	GOUNAUD/CRABBE	AL TAQADDUM	2/19/1991	0	PET	SA-3	U	3	BAG
1361W	OLY 62	GOUNAUD/CRABBE	KTO	1/20/1991	243	RU	D	F	2	KTO
1361W	OLY 62	GOUNAUD/CRABBE	KTO	1/20/1991	243	RU	D	T	2	KTO
5421W	STROHS 24	GOUNAUD/CRABBE	KTO	1/27/1991	254	RU	D	F	1	KTO
5421W	STROHS 24	GOUNAUD/CRABBE	KTO	1/27/1991	254	RU	D	F	1	KTO

MSN	CALLSIGN	CREW	TGTAREA	DATE	TAIL-NUMBER	TYPE-SHOT	TGT-TYPE	SUCCESS	QUALITY	THEATER
0431W	COORS 32	GOUNAUD/CRABBE	BAGHDAD	1/17/1991	265	RK	SA-8	F	2	BAG
0431W	COORS 32	GOUNAUD/CRABBE	BAGHDAD	1/17/1991	265	RK	SA-8	T	2	BAG
0431W	COORS 32	GOUNAUD/CRABBE	BAGHDAD	1/17/1991	265	RK	SA-6	T	2	BAG
0431W	COORS 32	GOUNAUD/CRABBE	BAGHDAD	1/17/1991	265	RK	SA-6	T	2	BAG
0561W	STROHS 62	GOUNAUD/CRABBE	BAGHDAD	2/3/1991	281	RK	SA-2	F	2	BAG
0561W	STROHS 62	GOUNAUD/CRABBE	BAGHDAD	2/3/1991	281	RK	SA-2	T	2	BAG
5441W	MILLER42	GOUNAUD/CRABBE	KTO	1/30/1991	7233	RU	BL	F	1	KTO
5421W	HAMMS 22	GOUNAUD/CRABBE	KTO	2/9/1991	7233	RU	D	F	2	KTO
5421W	HAMMS 22	GOUNAUD/CRABBE	KTO	2/9/1991	7233	RU	D	F	2	KTO
0321W	LONESTAR22	GOUNAUD/CRABBE	BAGHDAD	2/27/1991	7260	RK		F	3	BAG
2271W	BLATZ 72	GOUNAUD/KIMM	BAGHDAD	2/15/1991	263	PET	SA-3	F	3	BAG
2161W	LOWEN 64	GRAY/LIN	H-2	1/22/1991	202	RU	EW	F	3	H2/3
5441W	COORS 42	GRAY/LIN	KTO	2/9/1991	210	RK	BL	F	1	KTO
1431W	COORS 34	GRAY/LIN	BAGHDAD	1/27/1991	232	RK	SA-3	F	1	BAG
1431W	COORS 34	GRAY/LIN	BAGHDAD	1/27/1991	232	RK	SA-3	F	1	BAG
0431W	STROHS 34	GRAY/LIN	ALI AL SALEM	1/18/1991	250	RK	SA-2	F	1	KTO
0431W	STROHS 34	GRAY/LIN	ALI AL SALEM	1/18/1991	250	RK	SA-2	T	1	KTO
0661W	HAMMS 64	GRAY/LIN	BAGHDAD	1/21/1991	556	RK	SA-6	F	2	BAG
1231W	COORS 34	GRAY/LIN	S KTO	1/17/1991	579	RU	SA-6	F	2	KTO
1231W	COORS 34	GRAY/LIN	S KTO	1/17/1991	579	RU	SA-6	F	2	KTO
1231W	COORS 34	GRAY/LIN	S KTO	1/17/1991	579	RU	SA-2	F	2	KTO
2065W	PABST 66	GRAY/LIN	AL JAHRA	1/31/1991	587	RK	SA-3	U	1	BAG
0565W	BUD 66	GRIFFIN/SLIGAR	AL TAQADDUM	2/4/1991	202	PET	SA-3	F	2	BAG
0565W	BUD 66	GRIFFIN/SLIGAR	AL TAQADDUM	2/4/1991	202	RK	ROLAN	F	2	BAG

5451W	MICH 51	GRIFFIN/SLIGAR	H-3	2/9/1991	212	RU	D	F	1	H2/3
5431W	COORS 33	GRIFFIN/SLIGAR	BAGHDAD	2/15/1991	250	RU	ROLAN	F	3	BAG
5451W	BLATZ 51	GRIFFIN/SLIGAR	KTO	2/22/1991	270	RU	D	T	2	KTO
5432W	LOWENBRA32	GUZOWSKI/BEDGOOD	TAJI	2/27/1991	216	RK	SA-8	F	2	BAG
5451W	COORS 51	GUZOWSKI/BEDGOOD	KTO	2/23/1991	288	RU	FW	F	1	KTO
2145W	BUD 43	GUZOWSKI/BLACKBURN	TALLIL	1/17/1991	303	RK	ROLAN	F	2	KTO
2145W	BUD 43	GUZOWSKI/BLACKBURN	TALLIL	1/17/1991	303	PET	ROLAN	F	2	KTO
2145W	BUD 43	GUZOWSKI/BLACKBURN	TALLIL	1/17/1991	303	RU	FF	F	2	KTO
1765W	BLATZ 68	GUZOWSKI/BLACKBURN	BAGHDAD	2/21/1991	7231	RK	M	U	1	BAG
1765W	BLATZ 68	GUZOWSKI/BLACKBURN	BAGHDAD	2/21/1991	7231	RK	M	U	1	BAG
2335W	SCHLITZ 35	GUZOWSKI/BOWERS	BAGHDAD	1/19/1991	216	RK	SA-2	U	1	BAG
2335W	SCHLITZ 35	GUZOWSKI/BOWERS	BAGHDAD	1/19/1991	216	RK	SA-8	U	1	BAG
5401W	PEARL 03	GUZOWSKI/EUKER	KTO	2/13/1991	288	RK	SA-6	F	1	KTO
1341W	BLATZ 44	HARGARTEN/BEDGOOD	LATIFAYA	1/18/1991	300	RK	SA-8	T	2	BAG
2251W	PEARL 54	HARGARTEN/FERRARA	AL TAQADDUM	1/17/1991	0	PET	SA-2	U	3	BAG
0451W	OLY 54	HARGARTEN/FERRARA	BAGHDAD	1/21/1991	0	RK	FW	U	3	BAG
0451W	OLY 54	HARGARTEN/FERRARA	BAGHDAD	1/21/1991	0	RU	ROLAN	U	3	BAG
0171W	BUD 04	HARGARTEN/FERRARA	BAGHDAD	2/6/1991	0	RK	SA-3	U	3	BAG
0151W	COORS 54	HARGARTEN/FERRARA	BAGHDAD	2/3/1991	254	RU	SA-2	U	3	BAG
1431W	PABST 34	HARGARTEN/FERRARA	LATIFAYA	1/26/1991	263	PET		U	3	BAG
1431W	PABST 34	HARGARTEN/FERRARA	LATIFAYA	1/26/1991	263	RU	FW	U	3	BAG
1765W	PABST 66	HARGARTEN/FERRARA	H-2/H-3	1/19/1991	265	PET	SA-6	F	3	H2/3
2461W	PEARL 62	HARGARTEN/FERRARA	BAGHDAD	2/21/1991	273	RU	ROLAN	U	3	BAG
2061W	BUD 64	HARGARTEN/FERRARA	H-2	1/22/1991	284	PET		U	1	H2/3
0171W	BUD 04	HARGARTEN/FERRARA	BAGHDAD	2/8/1991	304	RK	SA-3	F	3	BAG
2161W	LOWENBRA64	HARGARTEN/FERRARA	KTO	1/20/1991	7260	SA-6		U	3	KTO

MSN	CALLSIGN	CREW	TGTAREA	DATE	TAIL-NUMBER	TYPE-SHOT	TGT-TYPE	SUCCESS	QUALITY	THEATER
0263W	COORS 64	HARGARTEN/KAD	ALI AL SALEM	1/23/1991	7257	RU	SA-3	F	1	KTO
0263W	COORS 64	HARGARTEN/KAD	ALI AL SALEM	1/23/1991	7257	RK	SA-3	T	1	KTO
2261W	COORS 62	HARTLE/HEALY	KTO	1/18/1991	0	RU	M ACQ	F	2	KTO
0311W	MICH 12	HARTLE/HEALY	AL TAQADDUM	2/7/1991	0	RK	SA-3	F	1	BAG
2261W	COORS 62	HARTLE/HEALY	KTO	1/18/1991	0	RK	SA-2	T	2	KTO
0311W	MICH 12	HARTLE/HEALY	AL TAQADDUM	2/7/1991	0	RK	SA-3	T	1	BAG
5401W	LONESTAR12	HARTLE/HEALY	KTO	2/3/1991	212	RK	SUPER	F	1	KTO
0251W	COORS 52	HARTLE/HEALY	AL TAQADDUM	2/25/1991	242	RK	SA-3	T	2	BAG
0261W	PINE 61	HARTLE/HEALY	KTO	1/25/1991	242	RK	FW	U	2	KTO
1125V	MILLER 26	HARTLE/HEALY	SALMAN PAK	1/17/1991	248	RU	SA-8	F	2	BAG
1125V	MILLER 26	HARTLE/HEALY	SALMAN PAK	1/17/1991	248	RU	SA-8	F	2	BAG
0461W	LONESTAR62	HARTLE/HEALY	BAGHDAD	2/14/1991	262	RK	SA-3	F	1	BAG
2331W	LOWENBRA32	HARTLE/HEALY	BAGHDAD	1/19/1991	267	RK	SA-6	U	3	BAG
2331W	LOWENBRA32	HARTLE/HEALY	BAGHDAD	1/19/1991	267	RK	SA-6	U	3	BAG
5455W	OLY 55	HILLER/BEDGOOD	KTO	1/26/1991	267	RK	SA-2	F	2	KTO
0565W	COORS 63	HILLER/STROUD	KTO	1/17/1991	0	PET	SA-6	F	2	KTO
2751V	STROHS 51	HILLER/STROUD	KTO	1/18/1991	0	RK	RASIT	F	2	KTO
0565V	COORS 63	HILLER/STROUD	KTO	1/17/1991	0	RK	RASIT	T	2	KTO
2751V	STROHS 51	HILLER/STROUD	KTO	1/18/1991	0	RK	RASIT	T	2	KTO
2411V	BLATZ 11	HILLER/STROUD	TALLIL	1/31/1991	0	RU	ROLAN	T	2	KTO
5411W	MICH 11	HILLER/STROUD	KTO	1/30/1991	0	RU	D	U	3	KTO
5411W	MICH 11	HILLER/STROUD	KTO	1/30/1991	0	RU	D	U	3	KTO
2411W	BLATZ 11	HILLER/STROUD	TALLIL	2/10/1991	0	RU	ROLAN	U	3	KTO
0565W	MILLER 65	HILLER/STROUD	BAGHDAD	2/5/1991	238	RK	SA-2	F	1	BAG

ID	Name	Crew	Location	Date	No.	Code	Type	TFU	No.	Sector
0565W	MILLER 65	HILLER/STROUD	BAGHDAD	2/5/1991	238	RK	SA-8	T	1	BAG
2715W	BLATZ 15	HILLER/STROUD	AL QAIM	2/11/1991	267	RU	FF	F	1	BAG
1361W	STROHS 61	HILLER/STROUD	KTO	1/22/1991	267	RU	FF	T	1	KTO
5441W	HAMMS 43	HILLER/STROUD	TAJI	2/25/1991	284	RK	SA-3	F	1	BAG
5441W	HAMMS43	HILLER/STROUD	TAJI	2/25/1991	284	RK	SA-3	T	1	BAG
0661W	FALSTAF 61	HILLER/STROUD	AL JAHRA	1/23/1991	284	RU	EW	U	3	BAG
2361W	HAMMS 61	HILLER/STROUD	KTO	1/20/1991	303	RU	D	F	1	KTO
2361W	HAMMS 61	HILLER/STROUD	KTO	1/20/1991	303	RU	D	F	1	KTO
5401W	COORS 01	HILLER/STROUD	KTO	2/7/1991	304	RK	I	F	1	KTO
5431W	LOWENBRA31	HILLER/STROUD	TAJI	2/27/1991	7233	RK	SA-8	F	1	BAG
5431W	LOWENBRA31	HILLER/STROUD	TAJI	2/27/1991	7233	RK	SA-8	T	1	BAG
2145W	BUD 45	HILLER/STROUD	TALLIL	1/17/1991	9298	PET	ROLAN	F	2	KTO
2145W	BUD 45	HILLER/STROUD	TALLIL	1/17/1991	9298	RU	ROLAN	T	2	KTO
2145W	BUD 45	HILLER/STROUD	TALLIL	1/17/1991	9298	RK	FW	T	2	KTO
2145W	BUD 45	HILLER/STROUD	TALLIL	1/17/1991	9298	RU	ROLAN	T	2	KTO
1565W	MICHELOB66	HOBDAY/KLAPPAUF	BAGHDAD	1/20/1991	0	RU	D	U	3	BAG
5435W	MICHELOB36	HOBDAY/KLAPPAUF	KTO	1/28/1991	202	RK		U	3	KTO
2561W	LONESTAR63	HOBDAY/KLAPPAUF	KTO	1/24/1991	234	RU	FW	T	1	KTO
0561W	COORS 61	HOBDAY/KLAPPAUF	KTO	1/19/1991	286	RK	SA-2	F	1	KTO
2223W	LONESTAR24	HOBDAY/KLAPPAUF	KTO	1/30/1991	7268	RU	SA-3	F	2	KTO
2223W	LONESTAR24	HOBDAY/KLAPPAUF	KTO	1/30/1991	7268	RU	SA-3	F	2	KTO
0741W	OLY 44	HORNISH/OLSON	KTO	1/17/1991	0	RK	SA-3	F	3	KTO
0111W	COORS 14	HORNISH/OLSON	AL TAQADDUM	2/27/1991	254	RK	SA-3	F	1	BAG
0641W	MILLER 44	HORNISH/OLSON	KTO	1/18/1991	267	RU	M ACQ	F	2	KTO
0641W	MILLER 44	HORNISH/OLSON	KTO	1/18/1991	267	RU	M ACQ	F	1	KTO
0661W	COORS 64	HORNISH/OLSON	BAGHDAD	1/19/1991	281	RU	SA-2	F	3	BAG

MSN	CALLSIGN	CREW	TGTAREA	DATE	TAIL-NUMBER	TYPE-SHOT	TGT-TYPE	SUCCESS	QUALITY	THEATER
0661W	COORS 64	HORNISH/OLSON	BAGHDAD	1/19/1991	281	RU	SA-8	F	3	BAG
1755W	HAMMS 58	HORNISH/OLSON	BAGHDAD	1/28/1991	284	RK	SA-6	F	2	BAG
1755W	HAMMS 58	HORNISH/OLSON	BAGHDAD	1/28/1991	284	RK	SA-6	F	2	BAG
0761W	MILLER 64	HORNISH/OLSON	KTO	1/17/1991	7207	RU	SA-3	F	2	KTO
0741W	OLY 44	HORNISH/OLSON	WADI AL BATIN	1/18/1991	7231	RK	SA-3	U	1	KTO
6415W	OLY 16	HORNISH/OLSON	BAGHDAD	2/7/1991	7260	RU	SA-3	F	3	BAG
0415W	OLY 16	HORNISH/OLSON	BAGHDAD	2/7/1991	7260	RK	SA-8	T	3	BAG
1661W	LONESTAR61	JENNY/B+10	SCUD PARK WEST	1/20/1991	0	RK	SA-3	F	1	H2/3
2661W	BLATZ 61	JENNY/B+10	BAGHDAD	1/23/1991	0	RU	C	F	3	BAG
0741W	OLY 41	JENNY/B+10	KTO	1/17/1991	0	RK	SA-3	T	3	KTO
1661W	LONESTAR61	JENNY/B+10	SCUD PARK WEST	1/20/1991	0	RU	SA-3	T	1	H2/3
0665W	BLATZ 65	JENNY/B+10	BAGHDAD	1/21/1991	0	RU	SA-8	U	3	BAG
0665W	BLATZ 65	JENNY/B+10	BAGHDAD	1/21/1991	0	RU	SA-3	U	3	BAG
1065W	COORS 65	JENNY/B+10	TALLIL	1/22/1991	0	PET	ROLAN	U	3	KTO
2541W	LONESTAR41	JENNY/B+10		1/29/1991	0	RU	FW	U	3	KTO
5405W	MICHELOB05	JENNY/B+10	KTO	2/3/1991	243	RU	ROLAN	F	1	KTO
0761W	MILLER 61	JENNY/B+10	KTO	1/17/1991	246	RU	SA-6	F	1	KTO
0761W	MILLER 61	JENNY/B+10	KTO	1/17/1991	246	RK	SA-8	T	1	KTO
0741W	OLY 41	JENNY/B+10	KTO	1/18/1991	263	RK	SA-3	F	2	KTO
0661W	COORS 61	JENNY/B+10	BAGHDAD	1/19/1991	303	RU	W	F	1	BAG
0661W	COORS 61	JENNY/B+10	BAGHDAD	1/19/1991	303	RU	SA-8	F	1	BAG
0541W	MICHELOB41	JENNY/B+10	AL TAQADDUM	2/10/1991	304	PET	SA-2	U	2	BAG
2155W	FALSTAFF57	JENNY/B+10	KTO	2/2/1991	572	RU	D	F	2	KTO
2155W	FALSTAFF57	JENNY/B+10	KTO	2/2/1991	572	RU	X	F	2	KTO

0503W	BUD 03	JENNY/B+10	H-1	2/5/1991	7201	RU	SA-2	F	3	H2/3
0661W	MILLER 61	JENNY/B+10	BAGHDAD	2/15/1991	7207	PET	SA-3	F	2	KTO
0411W	COORS 11	JENNY/B+10	H-2	2/19/1991	7231	RU	FF	T	1	H2/3
0641W	MILLER 41	JENNY/B+10	KTO	1/18/1991	7260	RU	SA-2	T	2	KTO
0361W	MICHELOB61	JENNY/B+10	BAGHDAD	2/25/1991	9298	RK	SA-2	F	1	BAG
0221W	COORS 21	JENNY/B+10	AL TAQADDUM	2/26/1991	9298	RK	SA-3	T	1	BAG
0565W	MILLER 67	JERAKIS/BOWERS	BAGHDAD	2/5/1991	265	RK	SA-2	F	1	BAG
0565W	MILLER 67	JERAKIS/BOWERS	BAGHDAD	2/5/1991	265	RK	SA-2	F	1	BAG
2561W	OLY 61	JERAKIS/BOWERS	KTO	2/3/1991	284	RK	F	F	1	KTO
2561W	OLY 61	JERAKIS/BOWERS	KTO	2/3/1991	284	RK	F	F	1	KTO
2751W	STROHS 53	JERAKIS/BOWERS	KTO	1/18/1991	284	RU	D	T	2	KTO
5411W	MICHELOB13	JERAKIS/BOWERS	KTO	1/30/1991	304	RU	X	F	1	KTO
5411W	MICH 13	JERAKIS/BOWERS	KTO	1/30/1991	304	RU	M ACQ	T	1	KTO
0651W	FALSTAF 63	JERAKIS/BOWERS	AL JAHRA	1/23/1991	7257	RU	D	F	3	BAG
1431W	PABST 32	JOHNSON/KAD	LATIFAYA	1/26/1991	0	PET	SA-2	F	2	BAG
2145W	OLY 46	JOHNSON/KAD	BAGHDAD	2/17/1991	0	RU	SA-3	F	2	BAG
0451W	OLY 52	JOHNSON/KAD	BAGHDAD	1/21/1991	0	RU	SA-2	T	2	BAG
2061W	BUD 62	JOHNSON/KAD	H-2	1/22/1991	0	RU	EW	T	2	H2/3
1431W	PABST 32	JOHNSON/KAD	LATIFAYA	1/26/1991	0	RK	SA-3	T	2	BAG
0151W	COORS 52	JOHNSON/KAD	BAGHDAD	2/3/1991	0	RK	SA-8	T	3	BAG
2021W	HAMMS 24	JOHNSON/KAD	BAGHDAD	2/27/1991	0	RU	ROLAN	T	2	BAG
1341W	BLATZ 42	JOHNSON/KAD	LATIFIYA	1/18/1991	0	RK	SA-8	U	2	BAG
1341W	BLATZ 42	JOHNSON/KAD	LATIFIYA	1/18/1991	0	RK	SA-6	U	3	BAG
0171W	BUD 02	JOHNSON/KAD	BAGHDAD	2/6/1991	0	RK	SA-3	U	3	BAG
1765W	PABST 65	JOHNSON/KAD	H-2/H-3	1/19/1991	263	RU	D	F	2	H2/3
1765W	PABST 65	JOHNSON/KAD	H-2/H-3	1/19/1991	263	RU	SQEYE	F	2	H2/3

MSN	CALLSIGN	CREW	TGTAREA	DATE	TAIL-NUMBER	TYPE-SHOT	TGT-TYPE	SUCCESS	QUALITY	THEATER
2251W	PEARL 52	JOHNSON/KAD	AL TAQADDUM	1/17/1991	265	RU	SA-3	F	3	BAG
2251W	PEARL 52	JOHNSON/KAD	AL TAQADUMM	1/17/1991	265	RU	SA-3	F	3	BAG
1361W	WILLOW 62	JOHNSON/KAD	LATIFAYA	1/25/1991	296	RK	SA-2	T	1	BAG
1361W	WILLOW 62	JOHNSON/KAD	LATIFAYA	1/25/1991	296	RK	SA-3	U	1	BAG
0361W	BUD 62	JOHNSON/KAD	KTO	2/9/1991	572	RU	ROLAN	F	2	KTO
0313W	MICHELOB36	JOHNSON/VAN HAASTERT	BAGHDAD	2/24/1991	300	RU	ROLAN	T	1	BAG
5421W	STROHS 21	KAMMERER/LOHIDE	KTO	2/1/1991	267	RU	D	F	1	KTO
5424W	BUD 27	KAMMERER/SEABAUGH	KTO	1/29/1991	212	RK	X	T	1	KTO
5415W	MILLER 17	KAMMERER/SEABAUGH	KTO	2/6/1991	241	RK	FW	F	1	KTO
5435W	PABST 35	KAMMERER/SEABAUGH	KTO	2/4/1991	256	PET	SA-2	F	2	KTO
2631W	PEARL 33	KAMMERER/SEABAUGH	BASRAH	1/18/1991	286	PET	SA-3	U	3	KTO
2631W	PEARL 33	KAMMERER/SEABAUGH	BASRAH	1/18/1991	286	RU	SA-8	U	3	KTO
0261W	BLATZ 63	KAMMERER/SEABAUGH	TALLIL	1/19/1991	587	PET	ROLAN	F	2	KTO
0261W	BLATZ 63	KAMMERER/SEABAUGH	TALLIL	1/19/1991	587	RU	D	F	1	KTO
0261W	BLATZ 63	KAMMERER/SEABAUGH	TALLIL	1/19/1991	587	RU	D	F	1	KTO
0261W	BLATZ 63	KAMMERER/SEABAUGH	TALLIL	1/19/1991	587	RK	SA-6	F	1	KTO
2161W	LOWENBRA62	KARP/ELLICO	KTO	1/20/1991	0	RU	EW	U	3	KTO
5427W	BUD 28	KENNEDY/D+9	KTO	1/29/1991	0	RK	SA-2	F	3	KTO
5411W	OLY 16	KENNEDY/D+9	KTO	2/15/1991	0	RK	SA-6	F	3	KTO
5411W	OLY 16	KENNEDY/D+9	KTO	2/15/1991	0	RK	SA-6	T	3	KTO
0565W	COORS 62	KENNEDY/D+9	SHAIBAH	1/17/1991	0	PET	SA-3	U	3	KTO
0565W	COORS 62	KENNEDY/D+9	SHAIBAH	1/17/1991	0	RK	SA-2	U	3	KTO
1761W	BLATZ 61	KENNEDY/D+9	KTO	1/30/1991	253	PET	SA-3	F	2	KTO
1331W	BUD 33	KENNEDY/D+9	AL TAQADDUM	2/27/1991	286	RK	SA-8	F	3	BAG

0441W	LONESTAR44	KINWORTHY/KIMM	BAGHDAD	1/17/1991	0	RK	SA-8	F	2	BAG
0441W	LONESTAR44	KINWORTHY/KIMM	BAGHDAD	1/17/1991	0	RU	SA-8	F	2	BAG
1161W	PEARL	KINWORTHY/KIMM	BAGHDAD	1/18/1991	0	RU	SA-8	U	3	BAG
1161W	PEARL 64	KINWORTHY/KIMM	BAGHDAD	1/18/1991	0	RU	ROLAN	U	3	BAG
1531W	FALSTAFF34	KINWORTHY/KIMM	H-2	1/20/1991	0	RU	RASIT	U	2	H2/3
1531W	FALSTAFF34	KINWORTHY/KIMM	H-2	1/20/1991	0	RK	SA-3	U	2	H2/3
0161W	PEARL 64	KINWORTHY/KIMM	BAGHDAD	2/8/1991	0	RU	SA-3	U	3	BAG
0531W	MILLER 34	KINWORTHY/KIMM	BAGHDAD	1/26/1991	246	RK	SA-2	U	3	BAG
0531W	MILLER 34	KINWORTHY/KIMM	BAGHDAD	1/26/1991	246	RK	SA-3	U	2	BAG
1741W	LOWENBRA44	KINWORTHY/KIMM	AL TAQADDUM	2/26/1991	263	RU	ROLAN	F	2	BAG
0761W	MICHELOB64	KINWORTHY/KIMM	BAGHDAD	1/28/1991	281	RK	SA-3	T	2	BAG
0361W	MICH 61	KINWORTHY/KIMM	BAGHDAD	1/23/1991	300	RK	FW	U	2	BAG
0361W	MICH 61	KINWORTHY/KIMM	BAGHDAD	1/23/1991	300	PET	TROPO	U	2	BAG
5441W	HAMMS 42	KINWORTHY/KIMM	KTO	2/22/1991	7207	RK	E	F	1	KTO
2061W	COORS 64	KINWORTHY/KIMM	BAGHDAD	2/13/1991	7257	RK	SA-3	F	2	BAG
1261W	OLY 62	KNIGHT/SCOTTO	KTO	1/20/1991	248	RU	TPS43	U	1	KTO
1121W	BUD 24	KNIGHT/SCOTTO	SALMAN PAK	1/17/1991	267	RU	SA-6	F	1	BAG
1121W	BUD 24	KNIGHT/SCOTTO	SALMAN PAK	1/17/1991	267	RU	D	F	1	BAG
5431W	PABST 32	KNIGHT/WHITLER	KTO	2/13/1991	579	RK	SA-6	T	1	KTO
0451W	MICHELOB54	LASCH/BECKINGER	BAGHDAD	1/17/1991	0	RK	SA-8	F	3	BAG
0451W	MICHELOB54	LASCH/BECKINGER	BAGHDAD	1/17/1991	0	RK	SA-6	F	3	BAG
0561W	OLY 64	LASCH/BECKINGER	BAGHDAD	1/24/1991	0	RK	SA-8	U	3	BAG
0561W	OLY 64	LASCH/BECKINGER	BAGHDAD	1/24/1991	0	RU	D	U	3	BAG
5425W	MICH 28	LASCH/BECKINGER	KTO	1/26/1991	0	RK	SA-2	U	2	KTO
5425W	MICH 28	LASCH/BECKINGER	KTO	1/26/1991	0	RK	SA-2	U	2	KTO
2361W	BUD 64	LASCH/BECKINGER	KTO	2/3/1991	0	RK	FW	U	2	KTO

MAGNUM! THE WILD WEASELS IN DESERT STORM

MSN	CALLSIGN	CREW	TGTAREA	DATE	TAIL-NUMBER	TYPE-SHOT	TGT-TYPE	SUCCESS	QUALITY	THEATER
0651W	MILLER 54	LASCH/BECKINGER	AL TAQADDUM	2/25/1991	0	PET	SA-3	U	3	BAG
1331W	BUD 34	LASCH/BECKINGER	BAGHDAD	1/18/1991	253	RK	SA-8	U	2	BAG
1331W	BUD 34	LASCH/BECKINGER	BAGHDAD	1/18/1991	253	RK	SA-2	U	2	BAG
1331W	BUD 32	LONG/KUXHAUS	BAGHDAD	1/18/1991	0	RK	SA-6	T	1	BAG
1331W	BUD 32	LONG/KUXHAUS	BAGHDAD	1/18/1991	0	RK	SA-6	U	2	BAG
1731W	BUD 32	LONG/KUXHAUS	BAGHDAD	1/20/1991	0	PET	SA-6	U	2	BAG
1731W	BUD 32	LONG/KUXHAUS	BAGHDAD	1/20/1991	0	RU	SA-2	U	2	BAG
5411W	FALSTAFF12	LONG/KUXHAUS	KTO	2/1/1991	216	RU	D	F	1	KTO
0461W	OLY 62	LONG/KUXHAUS	AR RAMADI	2/8/1991	251	PET	SA-2	F	1	BAG
0451W	MICHELOB52	LONG/KUXHAUS	BAGHDAD	1/17/1991	281	RU	SA-3	F	1	BAG
0451W	MICHELOB52	LONG/KUXHAUS	BAGHDAD	1/17/1991	281	RU	SA-3	F	1	BAG
0561W	OLY 62	LONG/KUXHAUS	BAGHDAD	1/24/1991	304	RU	D	F	1	BAG
0561W	OLY 62	LONG/KUXHAUS	BAGHDAD	1/24/1991	304	RU	D	T	1	BAG
5471W	HAMMS 76	MALFER/PFLIEGER	AL TAQADDUM	2/19/1991	210	RK	FW	T	2	BAG
0165W	OLY 06	MALFER/PFLIEGER	BAGHDAD	2/8/1991	7268	RK	SA-2	F	1	BAG
0165W	OLY 06	MALFER/PFLIEGER	BAGHDAD	2/8/1991	7268	RK	SA-2	T	1	BAG
0363W	HAMMS 66	MALFER/SHERMAN	BAGHDAD	2/3/1991	232	RK	SA-2	T	2	BAG
1431W	COORS 34	MALFER/SHERMAN	BAGHDAD	2/5/1991	245	RK	SA-3	F	1	BAG
1431W	COORS 34	MALFER/SHERMAN	BAGHDAD	2/5/1991	245	RK	SA-6	T	1	BAG
0631W	STROHS 32	MANCUSO/PEARCY	BAGHDAD	1/26/1991	0	RU	FF	T	2	BAG
0621W	PEARL 22	MANCUSO/PEARCY	AL TAQADDUM	2/10/1991	0	RU	SA-3	T	2	BAG
5405W	COORS 06	MANCUSO/PEARCY	KTO	2/6/1991	202	RK	HF	F	1	KTO
0611W	MICHELOB12	MANCUSO/PEARCY	BAGHDAD	2/27/1991	202	RU	SA-2	U	1	BAG
0611W	MICHELOB12	MANCUSO/PEARCY	BAGHDAD	2/27/1991	202	RU	SA-3	U	1	BAG

							D			
2065W	PABST 66	MANCUSO/PEARCY	KTO	1/18/1991	242	RU	SA-6	F	1	KTO
2111W	MICHELOB12	MANCUSO/PEARCY	KTO	2/13/1991	248	RU	SA-6	T	1	KTO
0461W	PEARL 62	MANCUSO/PEARCY	KTO	1/23/1991	250	RK	SA-6	T	1	KTO
0461W	PEARL 62	MANCUSO/PEARCY	KTO	1/23/1991	250	RK	SA-2	T	1	KTO
5415W	LONESTAR16	MANCUSO/PEARCY	KTO RPG	1/24/1991	256	RK	SA-3	F	1	KTO
0461W	LONESTAR66	MANCUSO/PEARCY	BAGHDAD	2/14/1991	267	RK	SA-6	T	1	BAG
5411W	FALSTAFF12	MANCUSO/PEARCY	KTO	1/28/1991	287	RK	SA-8	F	2	KTO
1121W	BUD 22	MANCUSO/PEARCY	SALMAN PAK	1/17/1991	571	RU	SA-3	F	1	BAG
1121W	BUD 22	MANCUSO/PEARCY	SALMAN PAK	1/17/1991	571	RU	SA-2	F	1	BAG
1765W	PABST 61	MCNEESE/PIETRAS	H-2/H-3	1/19/1991	0	PET	FW	F	2	H2/3
0313W	MICHELOB35	MCNEESE/PIETRAS	BAGHDAD	2/24/1991	7201	RK	I	U	1	BAG
2163W	HAMMS 63	MCNEESE/PIETRAS	KTO	2/15/1991	7207	RK	SA-2	F	3	KTO
2251W	PEARL 51	MCNEESE/PIETRAS	AL TAQADDUM	1/17/1991	7233	RK	SA-2	F	2	BAG
0151W	COORS 51	MCNEESE/PIETRAS	BAGHDAD	2/3/1991	7257	RK	FW	T	3	BAG
1431W	PABST 31	MCNEESE/PIETRAS	BAGHDAD	1/26/1991	7260	RK	SA-3	T	2	BAG
1341W	BLATZ 41	MCNEESE/PIETRAS	LATIFIYA	1/18/1991	7550	RK	SA-8	T	1	BAG
1341W	BLATZ 41	MCNEESE/PIETRAS	LATIFIYA	1/18/1991	7550	RK	ROLAN	T	3	BAG
0451W	OLY 51	MCNEESE/PIETRAS	BAGHDAD	1/21/1991	7550	RU	SA-3	T	3	BAG
0451W	OLY 51	MCNEESE/PIETRAS	BAGHDAD	1/21/1991	7550	RK	SA-8	T	3	BAG
0171W	BUD 01	MCNEESE/PIETRAS	BAGHDAD	2/6/1991	7550	RK	RASIT	T	3	BAG
0621W	PEARL 25	MCNEESE/PIETRAS	BAGHDAD	2/10/1991	7550	RU	SA-3	T	2	BAG
1761W	SCHLITZ 61	MCNEESE/PIETRAS	KTO	1/24/1991	7550	RK	SA-2	U	1	KTO
1361W	WILLOW 61	MCNEESE/PIETRAS	LATIFAYA	1/25/1991	7550	RU	TROPO	U	1	BAG
0361W	BUD 61	MCNEESE/PIETRAS	KTO	2/9/1991	7550	RU	SA-6	U	1	KTO
2361W	LOWENBRA61	MCNEESE/PIETRAS	KTO	1/20/1991	9298	RU	SA-6	F	2	KTO
2361W	LOWENBRA61	MCNEESE/PIETRAS	KTO	1/20/1991	9298	RU	SA-6	U	3	KTO

Magnum! The Wild Weasels in Desert Storm

MSN	CALLSIGN	CREW	TGTAREA	DATE	TAIL-NUMBER	TYPE-SHOT	TGT-TYPE	SUCCESS	QUALITY	THEATER
2361W	LOWENBRA61	MCNEESE/PIETRAS	KTO	1/20/1991	9298	RK	CROTL	U	3	KTO
2361W	LOWENBRA61	MCNEESE/PIETRAS	KTO	1/20/1991	9298	RK	CROTL	U	3	KTO
2141W	OLY 41	MERRITT/ALEXANDER	BAGHDAD	2/17/1991	0	RK	SUPER	T	1	BAG
2561W	HAMMS 63	MERRITT/ALEXANDER	KTO	1/23/1991	0	PET	ROLAN	U	3	KTO
2561W	HAMMS 63	MERRITT/ALEXANDER	KTO	1/23/1991	0	PET	ROLAN	U	3	KTO
5401W	PEARL 03	MERRITT/ALEXANDER	AL QAIM	2/1/1991	0	RK	SA-3	U	3	H2/3
5401W	PEARL 03	MERRITT/ALEXANDER	AL QAIM	2/1/1991	0	RK	FW	U	3	H2/3
0111W	COORS 11	MERRITT/ALEXANDER	AL TAQADDUM	2/27/1991	303	RK	SA-3	U	2	BAG
1761W	BUD 61	MILLER/CARNAHAN	H-2/H-3	1/19/1991	0	PET	ROLAN	U	3	H2/3
0461W	SCHLITZ 61	MILLER/CARNAHAN	BAGHDAD	2/11/1991	0	RK	FW	U	2	BAG
0411W	PEARL 11	MILLER/CARNAHAN	AL TAQADDUM	2/7/1991	243	RK	SA-3	F	1	BAG
1261W	OLY 61	MILLER/CARNAHAN	BAGHDAD	2/2/1991	243	RK	FW	T	2	BAG
0411W	PEARL 11	MILLER/CARNAHAN	AL TAQADDUM	2/7/1991	243	RK	SA-2	T	1	BAG
2251W	PEARL 55	MILLER/CARNAHAN	AL TAQADDUM	1/17/1991	284	PET	SA-3	F	3	BAG
2251W	PEARL 55	MILLER/CARNAHAN	AL TAQADUMM	1/17/1991	284	RK	SA-3	T	3	BAG
1621W	MICHELOB11	MILLER/CARNAHAN	TALLIL	1/18/1991	284	RU	D	T	3	KTO
1621W	MICHELOB11	MILLER/CARNAHAN	TALLIL	1/18/1991	284	RU	ROLAN	T	3	KTO
1661W	BUD 61	MILLER/CARNAHAN	TALLIL	1/23/1991	7201	PET	SA-6	F	1	KTO
0731W	MILLER 31	MILLER/CARNAHAN	AL TAQADDUM	2/27/1991	7201	PET	SA-3	F	2	BAG
0455W	FALSTAFF55	MILLER/CARNAHAN	AL TAQADDUM	1/21/1991	7201	RK	SA-3	T	2	BAG
0455W	FALSTAFF55	MILLER/CARNAHAN	AL TAQADDUM	1/21/1991	7201	RK	SA-2	T	2	BAG
5441W	STROHS 41	MILLER/CARNAHAN	BAGHDAD	2/6/1991	7201	RK	SA-2	T	1	BAG
5441W	STROHS 41	MILLER/CARNAHAN	BAGHDAD	2/6/1991	7201	RK	SA-2	T	1	BAG
1365W	SPRUCE 65	MILLER/CARNAHAN	BAGHDAD	1/25/1991	7231	RK	SA-3	T	1	BAG

1755W	HAMMS 56	OSBORNE/SHARP	BAGHDAD	1/28/1991	281	RK	FF	T	2	BAG
1755W	HAMMS 56	OSBORNE/SHARP	BAGHDAD	1/28/1991	281	RK	SA-6	U	2	BAG
0441W	LONESTAR	PATTERSON/HALE	BAGHDAD	1/17/1991	0	RU	SA-6	F	1	BAG
0441W	LONESTAR	PATTERSON/HALE	BAGHDAD	1/17/1991	0	RU	SA-8	F	1	BAG
1161W	PEARL 63	PATTERSON/HALE	BAGHDAD	1/18/1991	0	RU	SA-2	F	3	BAG
0531W	MILLER 33	PATTERSON/HALE	BAGHDAD	1/26/1991	0	RK	SA-3	F	1	BAG
0531W	MILLER 33	PATTERSON/HALE	BAGHDAD	1/26/1991	0	RK	SA-2	F	1	BAG
1161W	PEARL 63	PATTERSON/HALE	BAGHDAD	1/18/1991	0	RK	SA-6	T	3	BAG
0561W	MICH 63	PATTERSON/HALE	BAGHDAD	1/23/1991	0	RK	FW	U	3	BAG
0561W	MICH 63	PATTERSON/HALE	BAGHDAD	1/23/1991	0	RU	SA-6	U	3	BAG
1531W	FALSTAFF33	PATTERSON/HALE	H-2	1/20/1991	273	RK	SA-3	T	1	H2/3
1531W	FALSTAFF33	PATTERSON/HALE	H-2	1/20/1991	273	RK	SA-2	T	1	H2/3
2321W	LOWENBRA21	PATTERSON/HALE	ALI AL SALEM	2/11/1991	300	RK	SA-6	F	1	KTO
5415W	PEARL 17	PATTERSON/HALE	JALIBAH	1/30/1991	7231	RU	EW	U	1	KTO
0763W	POPLAR 63	PATTERSON/HALE	BAGHDAD	1/25/1991	7257	RK	SA-3	F	1	BAG
0763W	POPLAR 63	PATTERSON/HALE	BAGHDAD	1/25/1991	7257	RK	SA-3	F	1	BAG
1675W	OLY 76	PATTON/COPELIN	AL TAQADDUM	2/4/1991	278	RK	SA-2	T	2	BAG
1675W	OLY 76	PATTON/COPELIN	AL TAQADDUM	2/4/1991	278	RK	SA-3	T	2	BAG
2631W	PEARL 34	PATTON/D+9	BASRAH	1/18/1991	212	RK	SA-3	F	3	KTO
2631W	PEARL 34	PATTON/D+9	BASRAH	1/18/1991	212	RK	SA-2	F	3	KTO
2631W	PEARL 34	PATTON/D+9	BASRAH	1/18/1991	212	RK	SA-3	T	3	KTO
5455W	PEARL 55	PATTON/HOPPER	KTO	2/9/1991	246	RU	T1098	F	1	KTO
5445W	HAMMS 45	PATTON/STROUD	KTO	2/22/1991	0	RK	SA-3	F	1	KTO
1125W	MILLER 28	PENCE/CUMMIN	SALMAN PAK	1/17/1991	0	RU	SA-8	F	2	BAG
1125W	MILLER 28	PENCE/CUMMIN	SALMAN PAK	1/17/1991	0	RK	SA-6	F	2	BAG
5401W	MICHELOB04	PENCE/CUMMIN	KTO	2/4/1991	0	RK	FW	F	1	KTO

MSN	CALLSIGN	CREW	TGTAREA	DATE	TAIL-NUMBER	TYPE-SHOT	TGT-TYPE	SUCCESS	QUALITY	THEATER
0245W	COORS 48	PENCE/CUMMIN	S. BAGHDAD	1/26/1991	232	RK	FW	F	2	BAG
2331W	LOWENBRA34	PENCE/CUMMIN	BAGHDAD	1/19/1991	245	RK	SA-2	U	3	BAG
2331W	LOWENBRA34	PENCE/CUMMIN	BAGHDAD	1/19/1991	245	RU	SA-6	U	3	BAG
5411W	SCHLITZ 14	PENCE/CUMMIN	KTO	1/20/1991	253	RK	SA-3	U	2	KTO
5411W	SCHLITZ 14	PENCE/CUMMIN	KTO	1/20/1991	253	RK	SA-2	U	2	KTO
5411W	SCHLITZ 14	PENCE/CUMMIN	KTO	1/20/1991	253	RK	SA-3	U	2	KTO
5411W	SCHLITZ 14	PENCE/CUMMIN	KTO	1/20/1991	253	RK	SA-2	U	2	KTO
0251W	COORS 54	PENCE/CUMMIN	AL TAQADDUM	2/25/1991	270	RU	FF	F	2	BAG
2361W	MICHELOB64	PFEIFIER/GREGORY	BAGHDAD	2/15/1991	0	RK	SUPER	F	1	BAG
2361W	HAMMS 61	QUINN/HANSEN	AL JARRAH	1/17/1991	0	RU	ROLAN	U	2	KTO
0621W	PEARL 21	QUINN/HANSON	AL TAQADDUM	2/10/1991	0	PET	SA-2	F	2	BAG
2361W	HAMMS 61	QUINN/HANSON	AL JARRAH	1/17/1991	0	RU	ROLAN	U	2	KTO
5437W	MICHELOB37	QUINN/HANSON	KTO	1/28/1991	0	RK		U	3	KTO
0461W	LONESTAR65	QUINN/HANSON	AL TAQADDUM	2/14/1991	0	RU	SA-3	U	1	KTO
5437W	MICH 37	QUINN/HANSON	KTO	1/27/1991	241	RU	SA-2	F	2	KTO
2111W	MICH 11	QUINN/HANSON	KTO	2/13/1991	253	RK	SA-6	T	1	KTO
0611W	MICHELOB11	QUINN/HANSON	SHAIK AMAZAR	2/27/1991	278	RU	ROLAN	U	3	BAG
0611W	MICHELOB11	QUINN/HANSON	SHAIK AMAZAR	2/27/1991	278	RU	ROLAN	U	3	BAG
2065W	PABST 65	QUINN/HANSON	KTO	1/18/1991	286	RU	D	T	1	KTO
1121W	BUD 21	QUINN/HANSON	SALMAN PAK	1/17/1991	556	RU	M ACQ	U	2	BAG
1121W	BUD 21	QUINN/HANSON	SALMAN PAK	1/17/1991	556	RU	SA-8	U	2	BAG
0631W	STROHS 31	QUINN/HANSON	BAGHDAD	1/26/1991	558	PET	SA-3	F	2	BAG
1241W	BLATZ 41	QUINN/SPAAR	BASRAH	1/17/1991	0	RU	SA-3	F	3	KTO
1241W	BLATZ 41	QUINN/SPAAR	BASRAH	1/17/1991	0	RU	SA-2	F	3	KTO

1241W	BLATZ 41	QUINN/SPAAR	BASRAH	1/17/1991	0	RU	SA-2	F	3	KTO
1661W	HAMMS 61	QUINN/SPAAR	AL TAQADDUM	1/18/1991	0	RU	SA-3	F	1	BAG
1661W	HAMMS 61	QUINN/SPAAR	AL TAQADDUM	1/18/1991	0	RU	ROLAN	F	1	BAG
1071W	LONESTAR71	QUINN/SPAAR	KTO	1/19/1991	0	RU	SA-3	F	1	KTO
1071W	LONESTAR71	QUINN/SPAAR	KTO	1/19/1991	0		D	F	1	KTO
1651W	MICHELOB51	QUINN/SPAAR	KTO	1/21/1991	0	RU	SA-2	F	3	KTO
5451W	FALSTAFF51	QUINN/SPAAR	TAJI	2/19/1991	0	RU	SA-3	F	1	BAG
5451W	FALSTAFF51	QUINN/SPAAR	TAJI	2/19/1991	0	RU	ROLAN	F	1	BAG
1241W	BLATZ 41	QUINN/SPAAR	BASRAH	1/17/1991	0	RU	SA-2	T	3	KTO
1071W	LONESTAR71	QUINN/SPAAR	KTO	1/19/1991	0	RU	SA-3	T	1	KTO
1071W	LONESTAR71	QUINN/SPAAR	KTO	1/19/1991	0	RU	D	T	1	KTO
1651W	MICHELOB51	QUINN/SPAAR	KTO	1/21/1991	0		SA-2	T	3	KTO
1651W	MICHELOB51	QUINN/SPAAR	KTO	1/21/1991	0		SA-2	T	3	KTO
0211W	LONE 11	QUINN/SPAAR	AL TAQADDUM	2/7/1991	0	RK	SA-3	T	2	BAG
0211W	LONE 11	QUINN/SPAAR	AL TAQADDUM	2/7/1991	0	RK	SA-2	T	2	BAG
5461W	COORS 61	QUINN/SPAAR	TAJI	2/22/1991	0	RU	SA-3	T	2	BAG
5461W	COORS 61	QUINN/SPAAR	TAJI	2/22/1991	0	RU	SA-3	T	2	BAG
1271W	PEARL 71	QUINN/SPAAR	SAMARRA	1/20/1991	241	RK	SA-3	T	2	BAG
1271W	PEARL71	QUINN/SPAAR	SAMARRA	1/20/1991	241	RK	SA-3	T	2	BAG
1561W	STROHS 61	QUINN/SPAAR	KTO	2/2/1991	248	RU	RASIT	U	3	KTO
5441W	PEARL 41	QUINN/SPAAR	KTO	1/26/1991	262	RU	SUPER	F	1	KTO
5441W	PEARL 41	QUINN/SPAAR	KTO	1/26/1991	262	RU	SUPER	F	1	KTO
2561W	CEDAR 61	QUINN/SPAAR	BAGHDAD	1/25/1991	270	RU	ROLAN	F	1	BAG
2561W	CEDAR 61	QUINN/SPAAR	BAGHDAD	1/25/1991	270	RU	I	F	1	BAG
1461W	LONESTAR61	QUINN/SPAAR	H-3	1/22/1991	270	RU	M ACQ	T	2	H2/3
1363W	PABST 63	QUINN/SPAAR	TALLIL	1/29/1991	587	RU	FF	F	1	KTO

Magnum! The Wild Weasels in Desert Storm

MSN	CALLSIGN	CREW	TGTAREA	DATE	TAIL-NUMBER	TYPE-SHOT	TGT-TYPE	SUCCESS	QUALITY	THEATER
1363W	PABST 63	QUINN/SPAAR	TALLIL	1/29/1991	587	RU	X	F	1	KTO
0565W	BUD 65	QUINN/SPAAR	AL TAQADDUM	2/4/1991	7257	RK	SA-3	F	1	BAG
0565W	BUD 65	QUINN/SPAAR	AL TAQADDUM	2/4/1991	7257	RK	SA-3	F	1	BAG
0431W	COORS 33	RUFFIN/AVRIT	BAGHDAD	1/17/1991	0	RK	SA-6	T	1	BAG
0431W	COORS 33	RUFFIN/AVRIT	BAGHDAD	1/17/1991	0	RK	SA-6	T	1	BAG
5441W	MILLER 43	RUFFIN/AVRIT	KTO	1/30/1991	0	RU	X	U	3	KTO
5441W	MILLER 43	RUFFIN/AVRIT	KTO	1/30/1991	0	RU	X	U	3	KTO
0561W	STROHS 63	RUFFIN/AVRIT	BAGHDAD	2/3/1991	238	RK	SA-2	F	1	BAG
0561W	STROHS 63	RUFFIN/AVRIT	BAGHDAD	2/3/1991	238	RK	SA-3	F	1	BAG
1165W	LONESTAR67	RUFFIN/AVRIT	BAGHDAD	1/18/1991	273	RK	SA-3	U	1	BAG
5417W	STROHS 17	RUFFIN/AVRIT	KTO	1/29/1991	284	RU	I	F	1	KTO
5417W	STROHS 17	RUFFIN/AVRIT	KTO	1/29/1991	284	RU	EW	F	1	KTO
0321W	LONESTAR23	RUFFIN/AVRIT	SHAIK AMAZAR	2/26/1991	284	PET	SA-3	F	2	BAG
5471W	MICHELOB71	RUFFIN/AVRIT	AL JARRAH	2/27/1991	284	RU	M	F	2	KTO
2761W	OAK 61	RUFFIN/AVRIT	KTO	1/25/1991	303	RU	X	U	2	KTO
1261W	OLY 63	RUFFIN/AVRIT	KTO	1/21/1991	7207	RU	D	F	3	KTO
0661W	COORS 62	SCHREINER/SHARP	BAGHDAD	1/19/1991	0	RK	SA-3	F	1	BAG
1065W	COORS 66	SCHREINER/SHARP	TALLIL	1/22/1991	0	RK	FF	U	3	KTO
2541W	LONESTAR42	SCHREINER/SHARP	KTO	1/29/1991	0	RU	EW	U	3	KTO
2155W	FALSTAFF56	SCHREINER/SHARP	KTO	2/2/1991	238	RK	1 EYE	T	2	KTO
2155W	FALSTAFF56	SCHREINER/SHARP	KTO	2/2/1991	238	RK	SUPER	T	2	KTO
5405W	MICHELOB06	SCHREINER/SHARP	KTO	2/3/1991	284	RU	ROLAN	F	2	KTO
0761W	MILLER 62	SCHREINER/SHARP	KTO	1/17/1991	300	RU	SA-8	F	1	KTO
0761W	MILLER 62	SCHREINER/SHARP	KTO	1/17/1991	300	RK	SA-8	T	1	KTO

Code	Aircraft	Crew	Location	Date	Number	Code2	Code3	Code4	Num	Area
0665W	BLATZ 66	SCHREINER/SHARP	BAGHDAD	1/21/1991	303	RU	SA-3	U	3	BAG
0665W	BLATZ 66	SCHREINER/SHARP	BAGHDAD	1/21/1991	303	RU	SA-2	U	3	BAG
0631W	COORS 62	SCHREINER/SHARP	BAGHDAD	2/1/1991	572	RU	1 EYE	T	2	BAG
0361W	MICHELOB62	SCHREINER/SHARP	BAGHDAD	2/25/1991	7207	RU	SA-2	F	2	BAG
0361W	MICHELOB62	SCHREINER/SHARP	BAGHDAD	2/25/1991	7207	PET	SA-3	F	2	BAG
0503W	BUD 04	SCHREINER/SHARP	H-1	2/5/1991	7260	PET	SA-2	T	1	H2/3
0661W	COORS 62	SCHRNER/SHARP	BAGHDAD	1/19/1991	0	RU	SA-2	T	2	BAG
5441W	MICHELOB42	SCHRIEEINER/SHARP	KTO	1/30/1991	246	RU	SUPER	F	3	KTO
0661W	MILLER 62	SCHRIEEINER/SHARP	BAGHDAD	2/15/1991	300	RU	SA-3	F	2	BAG
0455W	FALSTAF 52	SHAW/STAMPER	AL TAQADDUM	1/21/1991	216	RU	FW	T	2	BAG
2261W	PABST 62	SHAW/STAMPER	H-2	1/22/1991	251	RU	FW	F	2	H2/3
2221W	SCHLITZ 22	SHAW/STAMPER	LATIFAYA	2/19/1991	254	RK	HF	T	1	BAG
5441W	STROHS 42	SHAW/STAMPER	BAGHDAD	2/6/1991	265	RK	SA-2	F	1	BAG
5441W	STROHS 42	SHAW/STAMPER	BAGHDAD	2/6/1991	265	RK	SA-8	F	1	BAG
2251W	PEARL 52	SHAW/STAMPER	AL TAQADDUM	1/17/1991	267	PET	SA-6	F	2	BAG
2251W	PEARL 52	SHAW/STAMPER	AL TAQADDUM	1/17/1991	267	RU	SA-3	T	2	BAG
1761W	BUD 62	SHAW/STAMPER	H-2/H-3	1/19/1991	273	RU	FF	F	2	H2/3
1365W	SPRUCE 66	SHAW/STAMPER	BAGHDAD	1/25/1991	7207	RK	SA-2	F	1	BAG
1365W	SPRUCE 66	SHAW/STAMPER	BAGHDAD	1/25/1991	7207	RK	SA-3	T	1	BAG
0411W	PEARL 12	SHAW/STAMPER	AL TAQADDUM	2/7/1991	7257	RK	SA-8	T	1	BAG
0565W	BLATZ 51	SHELOR/LOHIDE	KTO	1/17/1991	0	RK	SA-2	F	2	KTO
0565W	BLATZ 51	SHELOR/LOHIDE	KTO	1/17/1991	0	RU	SA-6	F	2	KTO
0305W	FALSTAFF05	SHELOR/LOHIDE	KTO	2/20/1991	0	PET	SA-3	U	3	KTO
1371W	HAMMS 72	SHELOR/LOHIDE	BAGHDAD	1/27/1991	212	RK	SA-2	F	3	BAG
1331W	BUD 31	SHELOR/LOHIDE	AL TAQADDUM	2/27/1991	212	RK	SA-8	F	3	BAG
0261W	BLATZ 61	SHELOR/LOHIDE	TALLIL	1/19/1991	234	RU	D	F	2	KTO

MSN	CALLSIGN	CREW	TGTAREA	DATE	TAIL-NUMBER	TYPE-SHOT	TGT-TYPE	SUCCESS	QUALITY	THEATER
0261W	BLATZ 61	SHELOR/LOHIDE	TALLIL	1/19/1991	234	PET	ROLAN	F	2	KTO
0751W	BLATZ 51	SHELCR/LOHIDE	KTO	1/18/1991	556	RK	SA-2	F	1	KTO
0751W	BLATZ 51	SHELOR/LOHIDE	KTO	1/18/1991	556	RK	SA-2	T	1	KTO
1431W	LOWENBRA31	SHOGRY/COPELIN	BAGHDAD	2/19/1991	212	RK	SA-2	T	1	BAG
0651W	STROHS 53	SHOGRY/COPELIN	KTO	1/17/1991	241	PET	SA-2	F	2	KTO
5445W	COORS 45	SHOGRY/COPELIN	KTO	2/21/1991	253	RK	RASIT	T	3	KTO
5453W	MICHELOB53	SHOGRY/COPELIN	KTO	2/9/1991	267	RK	RASIT	F	1	KTO
1761W	BLATZ 63	SHOGRY/COPELIN	H-2	2/20/1991	267	RU	FF	F	2	H2/3
0561W	COORS 63	SHOGRY/COPELIN	KTO	1/19/1991	278	RK	W	F	2	KTO
0561W	COORS 63	SHOGRY/COPELIN	KTO	1/19/1991	278	RK	SA-2	T	2	KTO
1461W	LONESTA 63	SHOGRY/COPELIN	BAGHDAD	1/21/1991	278	RK	A	T	2	BAG
1161W	MICHELOB61	SHOGRY/COPELIN	KTO	1/19/1991	558	RK	SA-6	F	2	KTO
1161W	MICHELOB61	SHOGRY/COPELIN	KTO	1/19/1991	558	RK	SA-6	U	3	KTO
5441W	MILLER 42	SINCLAIR/MEYER	KTO	1/23/1991	0	RK	I	U	3	KTO
5411W	MILLER 12	SINCLAIR/MEYER	KTO	2/14/1991	210	RK	X	F	1	KTO
0751W	BLATZ 52	SINCLAIR/MEYER	KTO	1/18/1991	267	RU	SA-2	T	1	KTO
0405W	PEARL 05	STEFANIAK/BECKINGER	KTO	2/14/1991	0	RU	D	F	2	BAG
0321W	COORS 25	STEFANIAK/BEDGOOD	LATIFAYA	2/12/1991	265	PET	SA-6	F	1	BAG
2361W	HAMMS 63	STEFANIAK/BOWERS	KTO	1/20/1991	263	PET	SA-6	F	1	KTO
2761W	COORS 61	STEFANIAK/ELLICO	KTO	1/22/1991	288	RU	EW	T	2	KTO
5431W	LOWENBRA34	STEFANIAK/PHILLIPS	TAJI	2/27/1991	254	RK	SA-8	F	2	BAG
0361W	FALSTAFF62	STEFANIAK/SMITH	SCUD SEARCH	1/27/1991	281	RU	SA-3	F	1	H2/3
0361W	FALSTAFF62	STEFANIAK/SMITH	SCUD SEARCH	1/27/1991	281	RU	FF	F	1	H2/3
0511W	STROHS 13	STEPHANIAK/STROUD	KTO	1/31/1991	0	RK	X	U	3	KTO

							M ACQ	U		
0511W	STROHS 13	STEPHANIAK/STROUD	KTO	1/31/1991	0	RU		U	3	KTO
0345W	FALSTAFF46	STIPO/CURLEY	BAGHDAD	2/9/1991	0	RU	SA-3	F	1	BAG
0345W	FALSTAFF46	STIPO/CURLEY	BAGHDAD	2/9/1991	0	RK	FW	T	1	BAG
5401W	PEARL 06	STIPO/CURLEY	KTO	2/13/1991	263	RK	SA-6	F	1	KTO
5421W	COORS 21	STIPO/CURLEY	KTO	2/20/1991	281	RK	SKYGD	F	1	KTO
0131W	PEARL 32	STIPO/CURLEY	KTO	1/29/1991	7257	PET	TROPO	F	1	KTO
5425W	FALSTAFF28	STIPO/CURLEY	KTO	1/30/1991	7260	RK	I	F	2	KTO
5401W	MICHELOB04	STIPO/CURLEY	KTO	2/2/1991	7260	RU	ROLAN	F	1	KTO
2561W	BLATZ61	STIPO/CURLY	KTO	2/5/1991	216	RU	EW	T	3	KTO
1163W	LOWEN 63	STIPO/CURLY	KTO	2/6/1991	7260	RU	ROLAN	F	1	KTO
0531W	MILLER 31	SULLY/ESPEJO	BAGHDAD	1/26/1991	0	RU	SA-3	F	2	BAG
0531W	MILLER 31	SULLY/ESPEJO	BAGHDAD	1/26/1991	0	RU	SA-3	F	2	BAG
0441W	LONESTAR42	SULLY/ESPEJO	BAGHDAD	1/17/1991	0	RK	M	T	3	BAG
0441W	LONESTAR42	SULLY/ESPEJO	BAGHDAD	1/17/1991	0	RK	SA-8	T	3	BAG
1161W	PEARL 62	SULLY/ESPEJO	BAGHDAD	1/18/1991	0	RU	SA-8	T	3	BAG
1161W	PEARL 62	SULLY/ESPEJO	BAGHDAD	1/18/1991	0	RK	SA-3	T	3	BAG
0361W	MICH 62	SULLY/ESPEJO	BAGHDAD	1/23/1991	0	RK	SA-3	U	3	BAG
0361W	MICH 62	SULLY/ESPEJO	BAGHDAD	1/23/1991	0	RK	SA-3	U	3	BAG
1311W	COORS 12	SULLY/ESPEJO	BAGHDAD	2/1/1991	0		SA-2	U	3	BAG
0761W	POPLAR 62	SULLY/ESPEJO	BAGHDAD	1/25/1991	281	RU	M	F	2	BAG
0761W	POPLAR 62	SULLY/ESPEJO	BAGHDAD	1/25/1991	281	RU	D	T	2	BAG
1531W	FALSTAFF32	SULLY/ESPEJO	H-2	1/20/1991	7201	RK	SA-3	F	2	H2/3
1531W	FALSTAFF32	SULLY/ESPEJO	H-2	1/20/1991	7201	RK	SA-3	F	2	H2/3
0761W	MICHELOB62	SULLY/ESPEJO	BAGHDAD	1/28/1991	7207	RK	SA-3	F	2	BAG
0761W	MICHELOB62	SULLY/ESPEJO	BAGHDAD	1/28/1991	7207	RK	SA-3	F	2	BAG
0161W	PEARL 62	SULLY/SCHLIEPER	BAGHDAD	2/8/1991	263	RK	SA-8	T	2	BAG

MSN	CALLSIGN	CREW	TGTAREA	DATE	TAIL-NUMBER	TYPE-SHOT	TGT-TYPE	SUCCESS	QUALITY	THEATER
0161W	PEARL 62	SULLY/SCHLIEPER	BAGHDAD	2/8/1991	263	RK	SA-8	U	2	BAG
5441W	HAMMS 45	SWANSON/JOHNS	TAJI	2/25/1991	0	RK	SA-8	T	3	BAG
1231W	COORS 33	SWANSON/JOHNS	S. KUWAIT	1/17/1991	212	RK	SA-3	F	1	KTO
1231W	COORS 33	SWANSON/JOHNS	S. KUWAIT	1/17/1991	212	RK	SA-6	F	1	KTO
1231W	COORS 33	SWANSON/JOHNS	S. KUWAIT	1/17/1991	212	RK	SA-2	F	1	KTO
1231W	COORS 53	SWANSON/JOHNS	S. KUWAIT	1/17/1991	212	RK	SA-2	T	1	KTO
2661W	BLATZ 63	SWANSON/JOHNS	BAGHDAD	1/20/1991	248	RK	SA-3	T	1	BAG
0661W	HAMMS 63	SWANSON/JOHNS	BAGHDAD	1/21/1991	248	RK	SA-3	U	3	BAG
0661W	HAMMS 63	SWANSON/JOHNS	BAGHDAD	1/21/1991	248	RK	SA-2	U	3	BAG
5471W	LOWENBRA71	SWANSON/JOHNS	AL QAIM	2/22/1991	256	RU	FF	F	2	BAG
2661W	HAMMS 63	SWANSON/JOHNS	BAGHDAD	1/19/1991	262	PET	SA-3	F	2	BAG
2031W	MICHELOB31	SWANSON/JOHNS	KTO	2/8/1991	262	RK	TS	F	2	KTO
2065W	PABST 65	SWANSON/JOHNS	AL JAHRA	1/31/1991	286	RK	SA-3	F	1	BAG
1521W	BLATZ 23	SWANSON/JOHNS	AL TAQADDUM	2/26/1991	286	RK	SA-3	F	2	BAG
1521W	BLATZ 23	SWANSON/JOHNS	AL TAQADDUM	2/26/1991	286	RK	SA-3	T	2	BAG
0111W	SCHLITZ 11	SWANSON/JOHNS	BAGHDAD	2/2/1991	579	RK	SA-6	F	1	BAG
0565W	BUD 68	TABER/PETERSON	AL TAQADDUM	2/4/1991	268	RK	SA-3	T	1	BAG
0565W	BUD 68	TABER/PETERSON	AL TAQADDUM	2/4/1991	268	RK	SA-3	T	1	BAG
0451W	MICHELOB51	TAIT/FINKE	BAGHDAD	1/17/1991	0	RU	SA-8	F	1	BAG
0451W	MICHELOB51	TAIT/FINKE	BAGHDAD	1/17/1991	0	RK	SA-6	T	1	BAG
1061W	PEARL 61	TAIT/FINKE	KTO	1/22/1991	0	RK	SA-2	T	3	KTO
1331W	BUD 31	TAIT/FINKE	BAGHDAD	1/18/1991	0	RK	SA-2	U	3	BAG
1331W	BUD 31	TAIT/FINKE	BAGHDAD	1/18/1991	0	RU	SA-2	U	3	BAG
1731W	BUD 31	TAIT/FINKE	BAGHDAD	1/20/1991	0	RK	SA-6	U	3	BAG

Code	Beer	Crew	Location	Date	Num	Svc	SA	Cls	Wt	Area
1731W	BUD 31	TAIT/FINKE	BAGHDAD	1/20/1991	0	RK	SA-2	U	3	BAG
5425W	MICHELOB25	TAIT/FINKE	KTO	1/26/1991	0	RK	SA-2	U	3	KTO
0651W	MILLER 51	TAIT/FINKE	AL TAQADDUM	2/25/1991	216	PET	SA-3	F	1	BAG
2251W	STROHS 51	TAIT/FINKE	KTO	2/2/1991	216	RU	ROLAN	U	1	KTO
5411	PEARL 11	TAIT/FINKE	KTO	2/5/1991	263	RU	SA-6	F	1	KTO
0561W	OLY 61	TAIT/FINKE	BAGHDAD	1/24/1991	7260	RU	SA-2	F	1	BAG
0561W	OLY 61	TAIT/FINKE	BAGHDAD	1/24/1991	7260	RK	SA-2	F	1	BAG
0761W	PEARL 62	TAYLOR/ROBINSON	BASRAH	2/3/1991	243	RK	A	F	1	KTO
0761W	PEARL 62	TAYLOR/ROBINSON	BASRAH	2/3/1991	243	RU	B	F	1	KTO
5461W	BLATZ62	TAYLOR/ROBINSON	KTO	2/13/1991	273	RK	RASIT	T	2	KTO
0661W	FALSTAF 62	TAYLOR/ROBINSON	AL JAHRA	1/23/1991	281	RK	FW	F	3	BAG
2335W	SCHLITS 36	TAYLOR/ROBINSON	BAGHDAD	1/19/1991	300	RK	SA-3	F	2	BAG
2335W	SCHLITZ 36	TAYLOR/ROBINSON	BAGHDAD	1/19/1991	300	RK	SA-2	F	2	BAG
2145W	BUD 46	TAYLOR/ROBINSON	TALLIL	1/17/1991	304	RK	SA-2	F	2	KTO
2145W	BUD 46	TAYLOR/ROBINSON	TALLIL	1/17/1991	304	PET	FW	F	2	KTO
2145W	BUD 46	TAYLOR/ROBINSON	TALLIL	1/17/1991	304	PET	FW	F	2	KTO
2145W	BUD 46	TAYLOR/ROBINSON	TALLIL	1/17/1991	304	RU	ROLAN	F	2	KTO
5403W	COORS 04	TAYLOR/ROBINSON	KTO	2/8/1991	572	RU	J	F	2	KTO
0435W	MICHELOB03	TAYLOR/ROBINSON	TALLIL	2/2/1991	7207	RK	FW	T	2	KTO
5441W	HAMMS 44	TAYLOR/ROBINSON	TAJI	2/25/1991	9298	RK	SA-3	F	2	BAG
5441W	HAMMS 44	TAYLOR/ROBINSON	TAJI	2/25/1991	9298	RK	SA-3	U	2	BAG
1231W	COORS 35	TURBERVILLE/GARLAND	S. KUWAIT	1/17/1991	2786	RK	SA-2	F	1	KTO
1231W	COORS 35	TURBERVILLE/GARLAND	S. KUWAIT	1/17/1991	7286	RK	SA-2	F	1	KTO
1231W	COORS 35	TURBERVILLE/GARLAND	S. KUWAIT	1/17/1991	7286	RU	SA-2	T	1	KTO
1231W	COORS 35	TURBERVILLE/GARLAND	S. KUWAIT	1/17/1991	7286	RK	SA-2	T	1	KTO
1461W	LONESTAR62	USTICK/SOKOLY	BAGHDAD	1/21/1991	0	RK	FW	U	3	BAG

Magnum! The Wild Weasels in Desert Storm

MSN	CALLSIGN	CREW	TGTAREA	DATE	TAIL-NUMBER	TYPE-SHOT	TGT-TYPE	SUCCESS	QUALITY	THEATER
1565W	MICHELOB65	USTICK/SOKOLY	BAGHDAD	1/20/1991	212	RK	SA-2	F	1	BAG
1565W	MICHELOB65	USTICK/SOKOLY	BAGHDAD	1/20/1991	212	RK	SA-3	T	1	BAG
5435W	MICHELOB35	USTICK/SOKOLY	KTO	1/28/1991	234	RU	X	F	1	KTO
2223W	LONESTAR23	USTICK/SOKOLY	KTO	1/30/1991	234	RK	I	T	3	KTO
0561W	COORS 61	USTICK/SOKOLY	KTO	1/19/1991	250	RK	SA-2	F	2	KTO
0561W	COORS 61	USTICK/SOKOLY	KTO	1/19/1991	250	RK	W	T	2	KTO
5451W	MICHELOB51	USTICK/SOKOLY	KTO	2/10/1991	253	RU	D	F	1	KTO
1651W	OLY 51	USTICK/SOKOLY	KTO	1/18/1991	270	RU	FF	F	1	KTO
1431W	LOWENBRA33	USTICK/SOKOLY	TAJI	2/19/1991	270	RK	SA-2	F	1	BAG
1651W	OLY 51	USTICK/SOKOLY	KTO	1/18/1991	270	RU	ROLAN	T	1	KTO
1431W	LOWENBRA33	USTICK/SOKOLY	TAJI	2/19/1991	270	RK	SA-3	T	1	BAG
1675W	OLY 75	USTICK/SOKOLY	AL TAQADDUM	2/4/1991	7286	RK	SA-8	F	1	BAG
1675W	OLY 75	USTICK/SOKOLY	AL TAQADDUM	2/4/1991	7286	RK	SA-2	T	1	BAG
0345W	FALSTAFF45	VOLLMER/EUKER	BAGHDAD	2/9/1991	263	RU	SA-3	T	1	BAG
0345W	FALSTAFF45	VOLLMER/EUKER	BAGHDAD	2/9/1991	263	RU	X	T	1	BAG
0521W	PEARL 23	VOLLMER/PATTILLO	H-2/H-3	2/15/1991	265	RU	FF	T	2	H2/3
5401W	PEARL 05	VOLLMER/PATTILLO	KTO	2/13/1991	273	RK	SA-6	T	2	KTO
5401W	PEARL 05	VOLLMER/PATTILLO	KTO	2/13/1991	273	RU	D	U	2	KTO
5401W	MICHELOB03	VOLLMER/PATTILLO	KTO	2/2/1991	284	RU	ROLAN	U	3	KTO
5417W	PEARL 18	VOLLMER/PATTILLO	JALIBAH	1/30/1991	288	RU	D	U	3	KTO
5417W	PEARL 18	VOLLMER/PATTILLO	JALIBAH	1/30/1991	288	RK	FW	U	3	KTO
0221W	COORS 23	VOLLMER/PATTILLO	AL TAQADDUM	2/26/1991	7201	RK	SA-3	F	2	BAG
0221W	COORS 23	VOLLMER/PATTILLO	AL TAQADDUM	2/26/1991	7201	RK	SA-3	F	2	BAG
5421W	STROHS 22	VOLLMER/PATTILLO	KTO	1/28/1991	7231	PET	D	F	2	KTO

5425W	PABST 26	VOLLMER/PATTILLO	KTO	2/21/1991	7260	RU	D	U	2	KTO
5411W	MILLER 12	WALDEN/WEST	KTO	2/10/1991	265	RU	FF	T	2	KTO
0561W	PEARL 62	WALDEN/WEST	ALI AL SALEM	1/17/1991	286	RU	SA-2	F	1	KTO
0561W	PEARL 62	WALDEN/WEST	ALI AL SALEM	1/17/1991	286	RK	SA-6	T	1	KTO
0561W	PEARL 62	WALDEN/WEST	ALI AL SALEM	1/17/1991	286	RK	SA-2	T	1	KTO
0561W	PEARL 62	WALDEN/WEST	ALI AL SALEM	1/17/1991	286	RK	SA-6	T	1	KTO
0321W	LONESTAR21	WALTON/REDMOND	SHAIK AMAZAR	2/26/1991	0	PET	SA-3	F	2	BAG
1261W	OLY 61	WALTON/REDMOND	KTO	1/21/1991	0	RU	M	U	3	KTO
1261W	OLY 61	WALTON/REDMOND	KTO	1/21/1991	0	RU	SA-6	U	3	KTO
0165W	LONESTAR	WALTON/REDMOND	BAGHDAD	1/18/1991	263	RU	SA-8	F	1	BAG
0165W	LONESTAR	WALTON/REDMOND	BAGHDAD	1/18/1991	263	RK	SA-2	T	1	BAG
5411W	MILLER 15	WALTON/REDMOND	SHAIBAH	2/10/1991	265	RU	FF	T	2	KTO
5441W	MILLER41	WALTON/REDMOND	KTO	1/30/1991	281	RU	D	T	2	KTO
5401W	FALSTAFF01	WALTON/REDMOND	KTO	2/12/1991	284	RU	SA-6	F	2	KTO
1361W	OLY 61	WALTON/REDMOND	KTO	1/20/1991	288	PET	SA-6	F	1	KTO
5415W	MILLER 15	WALTON/REDMOND	SHAIBAH	1/28/1991	288	RU	D	F	2	KTO
5415W	STROHS 15	WALTON/REDMOND	KTO	1/29/1991	288	RU	D	F	2	KTO
5421W	HAMMS 21	WALTON/REDMOND	KTO	2/9/1991	288	RU	D	F	2	KTO
5421W	HAMMS 21	WALTON/REDMOND	KTO	2/9/1991	288	RU	EW	F	2	KTO
0431W	COORS 31	WALTON/REDMOND	BAGHDAD	1/17/1991	288	RU	SA-3	T	1	BAG
0431W	COORS 31	WALTON/REDMOND	BAGHDAD	1/17/1991	288	RK	SA-2	T	1	BAG
1361W	OLY 61	WALTON/REDMOND	KTO	1/20/1991	288	RU	D	T	1	KTO
2661W	ASH 61	WALTON/REDMOND	TALLIL	1/25/1991	288	RK	SA-2	T	1	KTO
5415W	MILLER 15	WALTON/REDMOND	SHAIBAH	1/28/1991	288	RU	ROLAN	T	2	KTO
5401W	FALSTAFF01	WALTON/REDMOND	KTO	2/12/1991	288	RU	SA-6	T	2	KTO
0561W	STROHS 61	WALTON/REDMOND	BAGHDAD	2/3/1991	7231	RK	SA-2	F	1	BAG

MSN	CALLSIGN	CREW	TGTAREA	DATE	TAIL-NUMBER	TYPE-SHOT	TGT-TYPE	SUCCESS	QUALITY	THEATER
0561W	STROHS 61	WALTON/REDMOND	BAGHDAD	2/3/1991	7231	RK	SA-8	T	1	BAG
0311W	MICHOLOB33	WILSON/BURTON	BAGHDAD	2/24/1991	0	RK	SA-3	F	2	BAG
0741W	OLY 43	WILSON/BURTON	KTO	1/17/1991	0	RK	SA-3	T	3	KTO
0641W	MILLER 41	WILSON/BURTON	KTO	1/18/1991	238	RU	D	F	2	KTO
0641W	MILLER 41	WILSON/BURTON	KTO	1/18/1991	238	RU	SA-2	U	2	KTO
0661W	COORS 63	WILSON/BURTON	BAGHDAD	1/19/1991	243	RK	SA-2	U	2	BAG
0661W	COORS 63	WILSON/BURTON	BAGHDAD	1/19/1991	243	RK	SA-8	U	2	BAG
0741W	OLY 43	WILSON/BURTON	KTO	1/18/1991	246	RK	SA-3	T	2	KTO
0665W	BLATZ 67	WILSON/BURTON	BAGHDAD	1/21/1991	251	RK	SA-6	F	2	BAG
0655W	BLATZ 67	WILSON/BURTON	BAGHDAD	1/21/1991	251	RK	SA-2	F	2	BAG
0361W	MICHELOB63	WILSON/BURTON	BAGHDAD	2/25/1991	281	RK	SA-2	F	2	BAG
0361W	MICHELOB63	WILSON/BURTON	BAGHDAD	2/25/1991	281	RK	SA-2	F	2	BAG
0415W	OLY 15	WILSON/BURTON	BAGHDAD	2/7/1991	303	RK	SA-3	T	2	BAG
0415W	OLY 15	WILSON/BURTON	BAGHDAD	2/7/1991	303	RK	SA-8	U	2	BAG
1755W	HAMMS 57	WILSON/BURTON	BAGHDAD	1/28/1991	304	RK	SA-6	F	1	BAG
5405W	MICHELOB07	WILSON/BURTON	KTO	2/3/1991	7201	RU	ROLAN	F	2	KTO
0661W	MILLER 63	WILSON/BURTON	BAGHDAD	2/15/1991	7231	RK		U	3	BAG
5411W	PEARL 13	WILSON/PHILLIPS	KTO	2/4/1991	304	RK	SA-3	T	1	KTO
5403W	PEARL 04	WRIGHT/PULSIFER	KTO	2/13/1991	300	RK	SA-6	U	2	KTO
5403W	PEARL 04	WRIGHT/PULSIFER	KTO	2/13/1991	300	RK	SA-6	U	2	KTO
0311W	MILLER 12	ZEECK/BISHOP	JALIBAH	1/18/1991	238	PET	ROLAN	F	2	KTO
5415W	FALSTAFF61	ZEECK/BISHOP	KTO	1/20/1991	238	RU	D	F	2	KTO
5415W	FALSTAFF61	ZEECK/BISHOP	KTO	1/20/1991	238	PET	SA-2	F	2	KTO
5415W	FALSTAFF61	ZEECK/BISHOP	KTO	1/20/1991	238	RU	X	F	2	KTO

5415W	FALSTAFF61	ZEECK/BISHOP	KTO	1/20/1991	238	RU	D	F	2	KTO
2661W	HAMMS 62	ZEECK/BISHOP	AL ASAD	1/22/1991	238	PET	SA-2	F	2	BAG
2755W	HAMMS 56	ZEECK/BISHOP	BAGHDAD	2/14/1991	238	RU	SA-3	T	1	KTO
1363W	SCHLITZ64	ZEECK/BISHOP	KTO	2/6/1991	251	PET	SA-3	F	1	KTO
5441W	MILLER 42	ZEECK/BISHOP	ALI AL SALEM	2/4/1991	7233	RU	ROLAN	F	2	KTO
5401W	PEARL 02	ZEECK/BISHOP	AL QAIM	2/1/1991	7257	RK	SA-3	T	1	H2/3
1671W	SCHLITZ 72	ZEECK/BISHOP	BAGHDAD	2/12/1991	7257	RK	FW	T	1	BAG

Bibliography

BOOKS

Allen, Charles, *Thunder and Lightning – the RAF in the Gulf: Personal Experiences of War*, HMSO, UK, 1991

Beschloss, Michael R., *Mayday: Eisenhower, Khrushchev and the U-2 Affair*, Harper & Row Publishers, New York, 1986

Chadwick, Frank and Matt Caffrey, *Gulf War Fact Book*, GDW, Inc., Bloomington, IN, 1991

Cohen, Eliot A., *Gulf War Air Power Survey*, Vol II, 'Operations, and Effects and Effectiveness', Government Printing Office, Washington, DC, 1993

Cohen, Eliot A., *Gulf War Air Power Survey*, Vol V, 'A Statistical Compendium and Chronology', Government Printing Office, Washington, DC, 1993

Coyne, James P., *Airpower in the Gulf*, Aerospace Education Foundation, VA, 1992

Davis Richard G.,*On Target: Organizing and Executing the Strategic Air Campaign Against Iraq*, USAF History and Museums Program, Washington, DC, 2002

Halberstadt, Hal, *The Wild Weasels: History of USAF SAM Killers, 1965 to Today*, Motorbooks International Publishers, Osceola, WI, 1992

Hewitt, William A., *Planting the Seeds of SEAD: The Wild Weasel In Vietnam*, Thesis Presentation to the School of Advanced Airpower Studies, Air University, Maxwell AFB, 1992

Houlahan, Thomas, *Gulf War: The Complete History*, Schrenker Military History Publishing, New London, NH, 1999

Jamieson Perry D., *Lucrative Targets: The US Air Force in the Kuwaiti Theater of Operations*, USAF History and Museums Program, Washington, DC, 2001

Lambeth, Benjamin S., *The Winning of Air Supremacy in Operation Desert Storm (P-7837)* , RAND, Santa Monica, CA, 1993

Putney, Diane T., *Airpower Advantage: Planning the Gulf War Campaign 1989–1991*, USAF History and Museums Program, Washington, DC, 2004

Rock, Edward T., Col USAF (ret), editor, *First In, Last Out: Stories of the Wild Weasels*, Authorhouse, Bloomington, IN, 2005

Stiles, Gerald J., *The Wild Weasel Development Programs: One Run, One Hit, One Error (P-771-RGS)*, RAND, Santa Monica, CA, 1990

Thornborough, Anthony M. & Peter E. Davies, *The Phantom Story*, Arms & Armour Press, London, 1994

Thornborough, Anthony M. & Frank B. Mormillo, *Iron Hand: Smashing the Enemy's Air Defences*, Patrick Stephens Ltd/Haynes Publishing, Sparkford, Somerset, UK, 2002

Toomey, Charles L., *XVIII Airborne Corps in Desert Storm*, Hellgate Press, Central Point, OR, 2004

Werrell, Kenneth P., *Archie, Flak, AAA, and SAM: A Short Operational History of Ground-based Air Defense*, Air University Press, Maxwell Air Force Base, AL, 1988

Wiley, Richard G., *Electronic Intelligence: The Interception of Radar Signals*, Artech House, Dedham, MA, 1985

Winnefeld, James B., Preston Niblack, and Dana J. Johnson, *A League of Airmen: US Airpower in the Gulf War*, RAND, Santa Monica, CA, 1994

Technical Order 1F-4G-34-1-1, Aircrew Weapons Delivery Manual (Nonnuclear), USAF, 1990

PERIODICALS/ON-LINE

Canan, James W., 'Airpower Opens the Fight', *Air Force Magazine*, March 1991

Canan, James W., 'The Electronic Storm', *Air Force Magazine*, June 1991

Eisel, Braxton R., 'Do I Feel Lucky?' *Flight Journal*, June 2005

Kopp, Carlo, 'F-4G: Anatomy of a Wild Weasel', *Australian Aviation*, July 1986

Kopp, Carlo, 'Desert Storm – The Electronic Battle', *Australian Aviation*, June, July, August 1993

Pepperell, Kim, 'History of the Wild Weasel', http: www.wild weasels.org/history.htm, accessed 21 April 2004

US Air Force Fact Sheet: 'AGM-88 High Speed Anti-Radiation Missile (HARM)', dated February 2006, http://www.af.mil/factsheet, accessed 9 February 2007

PERSONAL INTERVIEWS/CORRESPONDENCE

Ballanco, Edward, Lt Col (ret), USAF, F-4G pilot

Baxley, Brian, Lt Col (ret), USAF, F-4G pilot

Brown, Craig, Maj, USAFR, F-111F pilot

Buccigrossi, Mark, Col, USAF, F-4G EWO

Fisher, Edward, Lt Col (ret), USAF, F-4G EWO
Gregory, Paul, Lt Col (ret), USAF, F-4G EWO
Gummo, Thomas, Maj (ret), USAF, F-4G pilot
Hale, Kevin, Maj (ret), USAF, F-4G EWO
Hanson, Ken Maj (ret), USAF, F-4G EWO
Healy, Joe, Maj (ret) USAF, F-4G EWO
Horner, Charles, Gen (ret), USAF, CENTAF Commander/CENTCOM
    Deputy Commander
Johns, Steve, Lt Col (ret), USAF, F-4G EWO
Keck, James, Lt Col (ret), USAF, F-4G EWO
Lucia, David, Col, USAF, F-4G pilot
Malfer, Dennis, Col, USAF, F-4G pilot
Mayeux, Sid, Col, USAF, F-4G EWO
Quinn, Bart, Lt Col (ret), USAF, F-4G pilot
Quinn, Vinnie, Lt Col (ret), USAF, F-4G pilot
Rattray, Gary, Lt Col (ret), F-4G EWO
Redmond, William, Col (ret), USAF, F-4G EWO
Spaar, Ken, Lt Col (ret), USAF, F-4G EWO
Uken, James, Col (ret), USAF, F-4G EWO
Vaughn, Brian, Col, USAF, E-3B/C AWACS weapons controller

Index

Abler, Colonel, 34, 35
Aircraft
   A-10, Fairchild, 24, 25, 49, 79, 204
   A-6/EA-6, Grumman, 50,62,66, 76,
      91,204
   AH-64, McDonnell-Douglas, 96
   AV-8B, McDonnell-Douglas, 64, 66, 76,
      91
   B-52 (BUFF), Boeing, 125, 129, 130, 144,
      147, 148, 167, 169, 170, 179,
      181–184, 192, 197, 198
   BQM-74C, Northrup, 97
   Buccaneer, Blackburn, 186, 205
   C-130/EC-130/MC-130, Lockheed, 62,
      68, 73, 76, 156, 184
   C-141, Lockheed, 46
   C-21, Lear, 63, 74
   C-5, Lockheed, 38, 46
   E-3 (AWACS), Boeing, 63, 79, 91, 102,
      109, 117, 132, 135, 136, 139, 145,
      150, 154, 157, 162, 163, 196
   F/A-18, McDonnell-Douglas, 49, 62, 66,
      69, 76, 82, 100, 121, 139, 229
   F1, Dassault, 85, 96, 102, 132
   F-100, North American, 14, 15, 212, 213
   F-105, Republic, 15, 16, 22, 213, 214
   F-111/EF-111, General Dynamics, 62,
      73, 79, 97, 102, 103, 105, 111, 113,
      136, 137, 143, 144, 156, 161, 167,
      185
   F-117, Lockheed, 77, 97, 102, 105, 106,
      109
   F-14, Grumman, 136, 168
   F-15C/E, McDonnell-Douglas, 25, 33,
      36, 58, 77, 79, 83, 102, 107, 117, 139,
      142, 143, 156, 162, 163

F-16, General Dynamics, 22, 25–27, 36,
      49, 70–72, 79, 85, 93, 113, 121, 131,
      135, 156, 159, 162, 163, 165, 217,
      229
F-4, McDonnell-Douglas, 72-76, 79, 82,
      86, 97, 100, 123,135, 144, 146, 150,
      156, 157, 159-163, 165, 166, 176,
      186, 211, 214-216
F-5, Northrop, 49, 192
Hunter, Hawker, 8
KC-135, Boeing, 38, 131, 144, 156, 162
MH-53J, Sikorsky, 96
MiG-19, 226
MiG-21, 106
MiG-23, 108, 227
MiG-25, 139, 228
MiG-29, 229
OV-10, North American, 26
RC-135 (Rivet Joint), Boeing, 79
Tornado, Panavia, 62, 131, 132, 135, 167,
      171, 173, 174, 179, 186, 188, 203-205
U-2, Lockheed, 1, 91
Airfield/Air Base/Air Force Base
   Ahmed Al Jabar, 100, 131
   Al Taqqadum, 143, 204
   As Salmon, 200, 203
   Baghdad International, 134, 196
   Basrah, 100
   Basrah West, 100
   Bentwaters, RAF, 24
   Bitburg, 158
   Clark, 21, 22, 175,176
   Columbus, 49
   Davis-Monthan, 25
   George, 21, 25, 26, 29, 34, 44, 60, 62, 70,
      74, 86, 96, 123

H2/H3, 135, 143, 204
Incirlik, 156, 159, 161
King Abdul Aziz, 64
King Khalid Military City (KKMC), 104,
    145, 146, 152
Kuwait International, 100
Lajes, 44, 45
Mt. Home, 30
Nellis, 62
Seymour-Johnson, 36, 37, 44
Shaibah, 100, 121
Shayka Mazhar, 108
Sheikh Isa, 45, 47, 49, 50, 67, 73, 75, 93,
    125, 129, 130, 135, 137, 146, 148,
    154, 157, 166, 177, 196
Sigonella, 159, 160
Spangdahlem, 21, 21, 70, 74, 75, 122, 158
Taji, 196
Tallil, 121, 203
Tobuk, 136
Arnett, Peter, 198, 205
Air Tasking Order (ATO), 56, 61, 63, 74,
    93–95, 99, 101, 120, 142–144, 157, 166

Baghdad, ix, 9, 64,96, 97, 99, 101, 102, 119,
    130, 134, 137, 139, 150, 154, 157, 171,
    184, 186, 189, 190, 192, 196–198, 202,
    204
Bahrain, 37, 40, 41, 47, 49, 65, 67, 75, 80,
    111, 134, 135, 175, 178, 192
Ballanco, Ed, 72, 73, 93, 103, 165
Baxley, Brian, 157
Baxley, Rhonda, 157, 158
Beckinger, Bill, 46
BLU-82, 183, 184
Brown, Craig, 105, 106
Buccigrossi, Mark, 125, 127, 128, 130
Burke, Tim, 143–146
Bush, George H.W., President, 29, 61, 77,
    83, 85, 91, 191, 192, 208

Cheney, Dick, Secretary of Defense, 31, 85
Conner, 'MikeBob,' 31
Cooper, Vince, 122, 169
Copelin, Shaun, 169

Deas, Mike, 111, 113–115
DESERT SHIELD, Operation, 26, 38, 66,
    72, 75, 93, 142, 158
DESERT STORM, Operation, ix, 4, 12, 71,

93, 123, 125, 147, 156, 157, 176,
    220–229
Diego Garcia, 147, 183
Donovan, Jack, 14
Dubai, 32

Electronics
    AN/ALQ-184, 154
    AN/ALQ-72, 13
    AN/APQ-120, 22, 75, 116, 130
    AN/APR-23, 12
    AN/APR-25, 13, 14
    AN/APR-38–20, 22, 216
    AN/APR-47, 28, 71, 75, 104, 110, 112,
        119, 120, 123, 128–130, 132, 154,
        164, 169, 185, 186, 204, 216
    IR-133, 14
Ellico, Brad, 74

Farrell, Vinnie, 179
Feinstein, Jeff, 143
Fisher, Ed, 177–179, 184, 193, 204

Galindez, Juan, 143–146
Glosson, 'Buster,' 56
Gregory, Paul, 122, 169
Gummo, Tom, 44, 45, 125, 146, 147, 177

Hale, Kevin, 101, 154, 183
Hanson, Ken, 103, 111, 130, 135, 136
HARM, AGM-88, ix, 22, 33, 62, 71–73, 75,
    87, 99, 100, 105, 107, 115–117,
    119–123, 128, 130, 132, 134, 139, 143,
    144, 150, 157, 161, 164, 168–170, 173,
    185, 186, 188, 196, 202, 203, 216–218,
    230
Hartle, Jim, 111, 205
Healy, Joe, 115, 132, 187, 193, 203, 205
Henry, Larry, 61, 70, 97
Horner, Charles 'Chuck,' 77, 86, 165
Hussein, Saddam, ix, 28, 29, 36, 62, 64, 68,
    78, 79, 87, 89, 123, 125, 134, 142, 143,
    147, 167 - 169, 184, 189, 191, 192, 198,
    199, 201, 202

Iran–168–170
Iraq, ix, 4, 5, 7–10, 28, 36, 37, 58, 61, 62, 64,
    65, 70, 78, 79, 81, 83, 85, 91, 93, 96, 97,
    99, 100, 102, 104, 106–109, 111,
    115–117, 121, 123, 131, 132, 134, 135,

139, 142–144, 146–150, 156, 158, 160,
162, 163, 165–173, 178, 179, 181, 184,
188–192, 196, 204, 209, 219–230
Israel–148, 169, 191

Jenny, Steve, - 125, 130, 137, 139, 141
Johns, Steve, 74, 75, 79, 120, 195
J-79, 73, 146, 147

KARI air defense system–4, 91, 97
Keck, Jim, 62, 63, 70, 142, 143
Kirkuk, 161
Kissel, TR, 159
Knight, Derek, 105
Kruschev, Nikita, 1
Kuwait, ix, 4, 5, 9, 28, 29, 37, 58, 62, 64, 78,
79, 87, 89, 93, 96, 99, 100, 103,
119–123, 131, 156, 167, 168, 170,
179–181, 183, 184, 188, 189, 191,
198–204, 224, 230

Lake Van, 163
Lamb, Allen, 14
LFE, Large Force Employment, 79, 80, 85
Lucia, Dave, 26- 28, 41

Malfer, Dennis, 193
Manama, 49
Mayeux, Sid, 71, 203
Miller, Bill, 160
Monroe, Lee, 108
Moore, Chip, 31
Mosel, 161

NATO, North Atlantic Treaty
Organization, 1, 40, 72, 156, 219, 226
North Vietnam, 1–3, 12, 16, 226, 227

Patriot Missile, 65, 149, 193, 195
Patterson, Jack, 101, 154
Poe, Ted, 109
Powell, Colin, Chairman, Joint Chiefs of
Staff, 31
Powers, Francis Gary, 1
Proffitt, Glenn, 99

Qatar, 85, 93
Quinn, Bart, 91, 102, 103, 110, 111, 115,
130–132, 134, 135, 137

Quinn, Vinnie, 74, 103, 121, 122, 133, 134,
143–145, 147, 185

Radars
Bar Lock, 5
Fan Song, 2, 6, 13–15, 72, 122, 219
Flat Face, 5, 220
One Eye, 172–174
Spoon Rest, 5, 219
Squat Eye, 5, 220
Rattray, gary, 111, 188
Rice, Donald, Secretary of the Air Force, 81
Riyadh, 56, 61, 62, 70, 73, 74, 93, 94, 120,
136, 142, 166, 172
ROE, Rules of Engagement, 94, 176

SAM, surface to air missile
SA-7 'Grail,'–2 221, 222
SA-10 'Grumble,' 2
SA-14 'Gremlin,' 2, 222, 223
HAWK/I-HAWK–28, 76, 83, 103, 107,
110, 202, 223, 224
SA-8, ix, 6, 8, 103, 105, 115, 119, 185, 188,
222
Roland, 6, 8, 185, 223
SA-3 'Goa,' 6, 7, 9, 10, 71, 103, 122, 134,
139, 150, 169 174, 185, 186, 190,
196, 197, 204, 205, 207, 220
SA-6, 2, 7, 17, 72, 100, 105, 107, 108, 135,
185–188, 220, 221
SA-2 'Gainful,' 1–3, 7, 9, 10, 12, 13, 72,
100, 120–122, 125, 127–130, 135,
150, 164, 183, 185, 186, 188, 189,
207, 212, 219, 220
SA-9, 9
Saudi Arabia, 36, 56, 62, 64, 75, 78, 79, 114,
129, 136, 144, 148, 184, 199
Schwarzkopf, Norman, 4, 76, 199
Scott, Larry, 123
SCUD missile, 65, 148, 192, 193, 195, 196
Sharp, Dan, 85, 124, 127, 129, 152, 153
Shelor, Dan, 74
Shogry, Lou, 169
Shrike, AGM-45, 12, 13, 15, 22, 33, 71–73,
203, 213, 214, 217
Sidewinder, AIM-9, 20, 58, 164, 214, 215,
217, 218
Spaar, Ken, 74, 121, 133, 134, 143, 145, 147,
185

274 MAGNUM! THE WILD WEASELS IN DESERT STORM

Sparrow, AIM-7, 20, 22, 33, 117, 164, 215, 217
SPINS, Special Instructions, 94
Swanson, Scott, 120

Tate, Steve, 102
Turkey, 156, 159, 161, 163

Units, military
   21st Tactical Flying Training Squadron (TFTS), 26
   23d Tactical Fighter Squadron (TFS), 22, 70, 156–158
   2d Marine Division, 200
   35th Tactical Fighter Wing (TFW), 21, 91, 157
   3d Marine Air Wing (MAW), 49
   480th TFS, 21, 70, 91
   52d TFW, 70, 72, 73, 91
   561st TFS, 21, 37, 44, 45, 48, 70, 74, 91, 99, 101
   562d TFTS, 21, 28, 99, 101
   563d TFS, 21
   7440th Composite Wing, 156
   81st TFS, 21, 22, 70, 73–75, 79, 91, 99, 102, 122
   90th TFS, 21, 175
   British 1st Armoured Division, 201
   Central Command (CENTCOM), 142
   Central Command Air Force (CENTAF), 56, 62, 63, 70
   Egyptian II Corps, 200
   French Daguet Division, 200
   Joint Forces Command–East, 199
   Joint Forces Command–North–200
   Joint Task Force (JTF) Proven Force, 156, 157
   Military Airlift Command (MAC), 47
   Republican Guard, 100, 125, 147, 170, 179, 183, 199, 201, 204, 209
   Royal Air Force (RAF) 62, 79, 131, 171, 203
   United States Air Forces Europe (USAFE), 72, 156, 160
   US 101st Airborne Division, 200
   US 1st Armored Calvary Division, 199
   US 1st Armored Division, 201
   US 1st Infantry Division, 201
   US 1st Marine Division, 199
   US 24th Mechanized Infantry Division, 201
   US 3d Armored Division, 201
   US 82d Airborne Division, 36, 200
   US Tiger Brigade, 200
   US VII Corps, 201
   US XVIII Airborne Corps, 200, 201
Uken, Jim, 99, 165

Walton, George, 37, 45, 74, 80, 85, 143
Washington, D.C., 61, 80, 85
Wong, Ronald, 169